Learning Swift 2 Programming

Second Edition

Addison-Wesley Learning Series

Visit **informit.com/learningseries** for a complete list of available publications.

The Addison-Wesley Learning Series is a collection of hands-on programming guides that help you quickly learn a new technology or language so you can apply what you've learned right away.

Each title comes with sample code for the application or applications built in the text. This code is fully annotated and can be reused in your own projects with no strings attached. Many chapters end with a series of exercises to encourage you to reexamine what you have just learned, and to tweak or adjust the code as a way of learning.

Titles in this series take a simple approach: they get you going right away and leave you with the ability to walk off and build your own application and apply the language or technology to whatever you are working on.

✦Addison-Wesley   **informIT** | **Safari** Books Online

PEARSON

Learning Swift 2 Programming

Second Edition

Jacob Schatz

✦Addison-Wesley

Boston • Columbus • Indianapolis • New York • San Francisco • Amsterdam • Cape Town • Dubai
• London • Madrid • Milan • Munich • Paris • Montreal • Toronto • Delhi • Mexico City •
São Paulo • Sydney • Hong Kong • Seoul • Singapore • Taipei • Tokyo

Learning Swift 2 Programming
Second Edition
Copyright © 2016 by Pearson Education, Inc.

ISBN-13: 978-0-13-443159-8

ISBN-10: 0-13-443159-6

Library of Congress Control Number: 2015957570

Printed in the United States of America

First Printing: December 2015

Trademarks

All terms mentioned in this book that are known to be trademarks or service marks have been appropriately capitalized. The publisher cannot attest to the accuracy of this information. Use of a term in this book should not be regarded as affecting the validity of any trademark or service mark.

Warning and Disclaimer

Every effort has been made to make this book as complete and as accurate as possible, but no warranty or fitness is implied. The information provided is on an "as is" basis. The author and the publisher shall have neither liability nor responsibility to any person or entity with respect to any loss or damages arising from the information contained in this book.

Special Sales

For information about buying this title in bulk quantities, or for special sales opportunities (which may include electronic versions; custom cover designs; and content particular to your business, training goals, marketing focus, or branding interests), please contact our corporate sales department at corpsales@pearsoned.com or (800) 382-3419.

For government sales inquiries, please contact governmentsales@pearsoned.com.

For questions about sales outside the U.S., please contact international@pearsoned.com.

Acquisitions Editor
Mark Taber

Managing Editor
Sandra Schroeder

Project Editor
Seth Kerney

Copy Editor
Cheri Clark

Indexer
Cheryl Lenser

Proofreader
Megan
Wade-Taxter

Technical Editor
Mike Keen

Editorial Assistant
Vanessa Evans

Designer
Chuti Prasertsith

Compositor
codeMantra

Contents at a Glance

Table of Contents

About the Author

Jacob Schatz is a senior software engineer with more than eight years of experience writing code for the masses. His code is often used by millions of people, and his advice is often sought. Jacob also goes by the name Skip Wilson and has a popular YouTube channel currently covering Swift and Python. Jacob is always selectively consuming the latest programming trends. He has a passion for making a difference and is constantly solving problems. Lately he has been deep into Swift, but he also writes tons of JavaScript, Python, Objective-C, and other languages. He is always learning more languages and thoroughly enjoys making new things. He is, at heart, a pedagogue, and he enjoys teaching and finding new ways to explain advanced concepts.

Dedication

For Tiffany and Noa

Acknowledgments

I could not have written this book without the help of many people. Thank you to the following:

Logan Wright, who wrote tons of YouTube tutorials with me and helped me with this book.

Cody Romano, who graciously helped me write and proofread, and whose endless knowledge has helped me debug more than a few bugs.

Mike Keen, who tirelessly proofread chapters and tried all my examples to make sure they were legit. He also provided an endless source of inspiration.

Mom and Dad, who, even though they had no idea what they were reading, sat there and read this book thoroughly, providing sage advice.

My wife, who put up with me spending countless hours in front of my computer, and through the process of this book has become an advanced programmer.

We Want to Hear from You!

As the reader of this book, *you* are our most important critic and commentator. We value your opinion and want to know what we're doing right, what we could do better, what areas you'd like to see us publish in, and any other words of wisdom you're willing to pass our way.

We welcome your comments. You can email or write directly to let us know what you did or didn't like about this book—as well as what we can do to make our books better.

Please note that we cannot help you with technical problems related to the topic of this book, and that due to the high volume of mail we receive, we might not be able to reply to every message.

When you write, please be sure to include this book's title and author, as well as your name and phone or email address.

Email: errata@informit.com

Mail: Addison-Wesley/Prentice Hall Publishing
         ATTN: Reader Feedback
         330 Hudson Street
         7th Floor
         New York, New York, 10013

Reader Services

Register your copy of *Learning Swift 2 Programming* (ISBN 978-0-13-443159-8) at informit.com/register for convenient access to downloads, updates, and corrections as they become available.

Introduction

WELCOME TO *LEARNING SWIFT 2 PROGRAMMING*, SECOND EDITION. This book will launch you into the world of iOS programming using the exciting new Swift programming language. This book covers Swift from start to finish, in a quick but complete way.

This Introduction covers the following:

- Who should read this book
- Why you should read this book
- What you will be able to achieve using this book
- What Swift is and why it is awesome
- How this book is organized
- Where to find the code examples

Ready?

Who Should Read This Book

This book is for those who already have one or many programming languages under their belt. You may be able to get through this book with Swift as your first language, but you'll find it easier if you can relate it to other languages. If you have experience with iOS programming with Objective-C, you should really be able to take to Swift quickly. This book often relates Swift concepts to those of other popular programming languages, including JavaScript, Python, Ruby, C, and Objective-C.

Why You Should Read This Book

This book will teach you all aspects of Swift programming so you can start writing high-quality apps as quickly as possible. However, it is not an exhaustive reference; it is a complete yet easy-to-digest initiation into Swift. This book will make you a better developer; because Swift is a mixture of many languages, you are bound to learn new concepts here. Swift is very robust on its own, and at the same time it allows you to mix in Objective-C.

If you are reading this book, you've probably heard people talking about Swift's amazing features. You've heard about its advanced design, how fast it runs, and how much easier your development will be. This book shows you all those features of the Swift language, as well as some very exciting discoveries I've made with it. Now is the perfect time to jump right in. This book will get you fully immersed and provide everything you need in order to get up and running as quickly as possible.

What You Will Learn from This Book

Reading this book will make you an official Swift programmer and allow you to write real-world, production-quality apps. You'll write apps that take advantage of the most advanced features of Swift, so you'll be writing refined, clean code. After reading this book, you'll be able to create any app you want in Swift. Here are just a few things you will learn while reading this book:

- How to combine existing Objective-C code into new Swift applications

- How to use advanced features like generics to write less code

- How to create optionals as a quicker way to make sure your code doesn't crash at runtime due to nonexistent values

- How to write closures to pass around little blocks of functionality, which can be written in as little as four characters

- How to create a 2D side-scrolling game using SpriteKit

- How to create a 3D game using SceneKit

- How to read bits and bytes so you can do things like read a PDF

What Is Swift?

Swift is a new programming language from Apple that replaces and also works alongside languages like C and Objective-C. The idea with Swift is to make it easier to write apps for iOS with a language that is fresh and new. The Swift language relates to many other languages. It is also so customizable that you can write Swift in many ways. For example, Swift allows you to define what square brackets do; instead of always using them for array and dictionary access, you can technically make them do whatever you want. Swift allows you to define your own operators and override existing ones. If you want to make a new triple incrementor (such as +++) that increments twice instead of once, then you can do that. Plus, you can create custom operators to work with your custom classes, which means you'll write less code and therefore make your life easier. For example, if you were to write a program about automobiles, you could define what would happen if you were to add two cars instances to each other. Normally you can only add numbers to each other, but in Swift you can override the + operator to do whatever you want.

Swift is well structured and completely compatible with Objective-C. All the libraries available in Objective-C are also available in Swift. Swift allows you to create bridges that connect languages.

How This Book Is Organized

This book is divided into 12 chapters, which cover the language itself and walk you through creating a few apps:

- Chapters 1–4 cover basic language syntax, including variables, constants, arrays, dictionaries, functions, classes, enums, and structs. These are the basic building blocks of the Swift language.

- Chapter 5 takes a break from the language syntax and helps you create a basic game of tic-tac-toe.

- Chapters 6–9 cover more advanced language features, including closures, subscripts, advanced operators, protocols and extensions, generics, and programming on the bit and byte levels.

- Chapters 10–12 show you how to create real-world apps using the knowledge you've gained from previous chapters.

Enjoy the Ride

My goal was to make this book fun to read, and I had a lot of fun writing it. I want to show you how exciting learning a new language can be.

When a new language comes out, often not a whole lot of knowledge is out there about it. This book aims to give you direct access to knowledge that is hard to find, and it is an easy-to-read version of a lot of knowledge that is hard to read. Searching online for answers can be difficult because Swift evolves and we all are still figuring out Swift together. There are, of course, bugs in the language, and I'm sure there will continue to be bugs. I wrote this book while Swift was still in beta (and constantly changing) and finished it up as Swift became version 2.0. Swift will continue to change and improve as more people use it and report bugs as time goes on. This book has been tested against the latest version of Swift (as of this writing), but that doesn't mean that Swift won't change. I hope you enjoy learning to use Swift.

1

Getting Your Feet Wet: Variables, Constants, and Loops

Swift is a new programming language created by Apple, with the intention of making development of software for Apple products significantly easier. If you have experience in C and Objective-C, you should find Swift to be a walk in the park. All the classes and types that are available to you in C and Objective-C are ported over and available in their exact incarnations in Swift.

If, however, you come from a Ruby or Python background, you will find Swift's syntax to be right up your alley. Swift borrows and iterates on many ideas from Python and Ruby.

If you come from the JavaScript world, you will be pleased to know that Swift also doesn't ask you to declare types, as old strict Java does. You will also be pleased to know that Swift has its own version of `indexOf` and many other familiar JavaScript functions. If they aren't the exact replicas of said functions, they will at least be familiar.

If you come from the Java world, you will be happy to know that even though Swift does not force you to declare types, you still can and Swift most certainly enforces those types, very strictly.

These are all just basic syntax comparisons; the real magic evolves from Swift's chameleon-like capability to be written in any way that makes you the programmer comfortable. If you want to write the tersest one-liner that does everything you ever needed in one fell swoop, Swift has you covered. If you want to write Haskell-like functional programming, Swift can do that, too. If you want to write beautiful object-oriented programming with classic design patterns, Swift will do that as well.

In the future (or now, depending on when you are reading this), Swift will be open source so that you can officially (theoretically) write Swift on Linux or Windows. Someone may even create a web framework like Ruby on Rails in Swift.

This chapter covers the basic building blocks of Swift. It starts with variables and constants. With this knowledge, you will be able to store whatever you'd like in memory. Swift has a special feature called *optionals,* which allows you to check for `nil` values in a smoother way than in other programming languages. As I briefly mentioned before, Swift has strong type inference; this allows you to have strict typing without needing to declare a type. This chapter also goes over how Swift handles loops and `if/else` statements.

Building Blocks of Swift

Swift allows you to use variables and constants by associating a name with a value of some type. For example, if you want to store the string `"Hi"` in a variable named `greeting`, you can use a variable or a constant. You create a variable by using the `var` keyword. This establishes an associated value that can be changed during the execution of the program. In other words, it creates a mutable storage. If you do not want mutable storage, you can use a constant. For example, you might record the number of login retries a user is allowed to have before being refused access to the site. In such a case, you would want to use a constant, as shown in this example:

```
var hiThere = "Hi there"
hiThere = "Hi there again"

let permanentGreeting = "Hello fine sir"
permanentGreeting = "Good morning sir"
```

Notice that you don't use a semicolon as you would in many other languages. Semicolons are not mandatory, unless you want to combine many statements together on the same line. In Swift you would not put a semicolon on the end of the line, even though Swift will not complain. Here is an example that shows you when you would use the semicolon in Swift when multiple lines are combined into one:

```
let numberOfRetries = 5; var currentRetries = 0
```

Also unique to Swift, you can use almost any Unicode character to name your variables and constants. Developers can name resources using Hebrew, Simplified Chinese, and even special Unicode characters, such as full-color koala emoji.

When declaring multiple variables, you can omit the `var` keyword. Here is an example:

```
var yes = 0, no = 0
```

Computed Properties (Getters and Setters)

In Swift you can also declare variables as computed properties. You would use this when you want to figure out the value of the variable at runtime. Here is an example of a getter, where the value of the score is determined by how much time is left. In this example we are creating a read-only computed property.

```
var timeLeft = 30
var score:Int {
get{
    return timeLeft * 25
}
}
print(score)
```

In this example we can reference (or read) `score` anywhere because it is in the global scope. What is really interesting is that if we try to set the score, it will give us an error because we have created a read-only property. If we want to be able to set this property, we need to create a setter. You cannot create a setter without a getter. Aside from the fact that it would not make sense, it also just will not work. Let's create a setter to go along with our getter. It does not make sense for a setter to set the computed property directly because the value of the property is computed at runtime. Therefore, you use a setter when you want to set other values as a result of the setter being set. Also, setters work well in some sort of organizational unit, which we haven't covered yet, but it's worth diving into briefly. Here is a full Swift example, which includes many elements we have not covered yet.

```
import UIKit
struct Book {
    var size = CGSize()
    var numberOfPages = 100;
    var price:Float {
    get{
        return Float(CGFloat(numberOfPages) * (size.width * size.height))
    }
    set(newPrice){
        numberOfPages = Int(price / Float(size.width * size.height))
    }
    }
}

var book = Book(size: CGSize(width: 0.5, height: 0.5), numberOfPages: 400)
print(book.price)
book.price = 400
print(book.numberOfPages)
```

In this example we create a book `struct`, which is a way to organize code so that it is reusable. I would not expect you to understand all of this example, but if you have ever coded in any other languages, you will notice that there is a lot of type casting going on here. Type casting is a something you do all the time in Objective-C and most other languages. We will cover all aspects of this code in this book, but you should know that we created a setter, which sets the number of pages in the book relative to the new price.

Using Comments

You indicate comments in Swift by using a double forward slash, exactly as in Objective-C. Here's an example:

```
// This is a comment about the number of retries
let numberOfRetries = 5 // We can also put a comment on the end of a line.
```

If you want to create comments that span multiple lines, you can use this /* */ style of comments, which also works well for documentation.

```
/* Comments can span
multiple lines */
```

Inference

Swift uses inference to figure out what *types* you are trying to use. Because of this, you do not need to declare a type when creating variables and constants. However, if you want to declare a type you may do so, and in certain situations, it is absolutely necessary. When declaring a variable, the rule of thumb is that Swift needs to know what type it is. If Swift cannot figure out the type, you need to be more explicit. The following is a valid statement:

```
var currentRetries = 0
```

Notice that Swift has to figure out what type of number this is. `currentRetries` may be one of the many types of numbers that Swift offers (Swift will infer this as an `Int` in case you are wondering, but more on that later). You could also use this:

```
var currentRetries:Int = 0
```

In this case, you explicitly set the type to `Int` by using the colon after the variable name to declare a type. Although this is legit, it is unnecessary because Swift already knows that 0 is an `Int`. Swift can and will infer a type on a variable that has an initial value.

When do you need to declare the type of a variable or constant? You need to declare the type of a variable or constant if you do not know what the initial value will be. For example:

```
var currentRetries:Int
```

In this case, you must declare `Int` because without it, Swift cannot tell what type this variable will be. This is called *type safety*. If Swift expects a string, you must pass Swift a string. You cannot pass an `Int` when a `String` is expected. This style of coding is a great time-saver. You will do a lot less typing with your fingers and a lot more thinking with your brain. Every default value you give a variable without a type will be given a type. Let's talk about numbers first.

For number types, Swift gives us the following:

- `Int` is available in 8, 16, 32, and 64 bits, but you will most likely stay with just `Int`. It's probably large enough for your needs. Here's what you need to know about `Int`:

  `Int` on 32-bit platforms is `Int32`.

  `Int` on 64-bit platforms is `Int64`.

That is, when you declare a variable as `Int`, Swift will do the work of changing that to `Int32` or `Int64`. You don't need to do anything on your end.

`Int` can be both positive and negative in value.

`Int` will be the default `type` when you declare a variable with a number and no decimals:

```
var someInt = 3 // this will be an Int
```

`UInt` is provided as an *unsigned* integer. An unsigned number must be positive, whereas a *signed* number (an `Int`) can be negative. For consistency, Apple recommends that you generally use `Int` even when you know that a value will never be negative.

- `Double` denotes 64-bit floating-point numbers. `Double` has a higher precision than `float`, with at least 15 decimal digits. `Double` will be the chosen type when you declare a variable that has decimals in it:

```
var someDouble = 3.14 // this will be a double
```

Combining any integer with any floating-point number results in a `Double`:

```
3 + 3.14 // 6.14 works and will be a double

var three = 3

var threePointOne = 3.1

three + threePointOne //Error because you can't mix types
```

- `Float` denotes 32-bit floating-point numbers. `Float` can have a precision as small as 6. Whether you choose `Float` or `Double` is completely up to you and your situation. Swift will choose `Double` when no type is declared.

Along with `Decimal` numbers, you can use `Binary`, `Octal`, and `Hexadecimal` numbers:

- `Decimal` is the default for all numbers, so no prefix is needed.

- Create a `Binary` number by adding a `0b` prefix.

- `Octal` uses a `0o` prefix.

- `Hexadecimal` uses a `0x` prefix.

You can check the type of the object by using the `is` keyword. The `is` keyword will return a Boolean. In this example we use the `Any` class to denote that `pi` can be anything at all until we type it as a `Float`:

```
var pi:Any?
pi = 3.141
pi is Double //true
pi is Float  //false
```

Notice that you declare this type as `Any?` in the preceding example. The question mark denotes an optional, which allows us to not set an initial value without causing an error. The `Any` type can be any type (exactly what it says). Objective-C is not as strict as Swift, and you need to be able to intermingle the two languages. For this purpose, `Any` and `AnyObject` were created, which allows you to put any type in an object. Think about arrays in Objective-C, which can mix different types together; for that purpose you need to give Swift the ability to have arrays of different types. You'll learn more about this later in the chapter.

Swift is the only programming language (that I know of) that lets you put underscores in numbers to make them more legible. Xcode ignores the underscores when it evaluates your code. You might find using underscores especially useful with big numbers when you want to denote a thousand-comma separator, as in this case:

```
var twoMil = 2_000_000
```

Before you can add two numbers together, they must be made into the same type. For example, the following will not work:

```
var someNumA:UInt8 = 8
var someNumB:Int8 = 9
someNumA + someNumB
//Int8 is not convertible to UInt8
```

The reason this does not work is that `someNumA` is a `UInt8` and `someNumB` is an `Int8`. Swift is very strict about the combination of things.

To make this work, you must convert one of the types so that the two types are the same. To do this, use the *initializer* of the type. For example, you can use the initializer `UInt8`, which can convert `someNumB` to a `UInt8` for you:

```
someNumA + UInt8(someNumB)
```

Swift is strict and makes sure that you convert types before you can combine them.

We had to do a lot of conversions of types in a previous example.

Merging Variables into a `String`

When you want to combine a variable in a string there is a special syntax for that. Take an example in which you have a variable `message` and you want to mix it into a string. In Objective-C you would do something like this:

```
[NSString stringWithFormat:@"Message was legit: %@", message];
```

In JavaScript you would do something like this:

```
"Message was legit:" + message;
```

In Python you would do something like this:

```
"Message was legit: %s" % message
```

In Ruby you would do something like this:

```
"Message was legit: #{message}"
```

In Swift you do something like this:

```
"Message was legit: \(message)"
```

You use this syntax of \() to add a variable into a string. Of course, this will interpret most things you put in between those parentheses. This means you can add full expressions in there like math. For example:

```
"2 + 2 is \(2 + 2)"
```

This makes it very simple to add variables into a string. Of course, you could go the old-school way and concatenate strings together with the plus operator. In most situations you don't need to do this because the \() makes things so much easier. One thing to remember is that Swift has strict type inference, so if you try to combine a String with an Int, Swift will complain. The error it gives is not the easiest to decipher. For example:

```
"2 + 2 is " + (2 + 2)
```

This returns the following error (depending on your version of Swift and how you are running it):

```
<stdin>:3:19: error: binary operator '+' cannot be
applied to operands of type 'String' and 'Int'
print("2 + 2 is " + (2 + 2))
~~~~~~~~~~~ ^ ~~~~~~~
<stdin>:3:19: note: overloads for '+' exist with these
partially matching parameter lists: (Int, Int),
(String, String), (UnsafeMutablePointer<Memory>,
Int), (UnsafePointer<Memory>, Int)
print("2 + 2 is " + (2 + 2))
```

What this means is that you can't mix Strings and Ints. So you have to convert the Int to a String.

```
"2 + 2 is " + String(2 + 2)
```

This works because you are now combining a String and an Int. One of the most important things to keep in mind when writing Swift is that you'll often do a lot of type conversion to deal with the strict typing.

Optionals: A Gift to Unwrap

In our tour through the basic building blocks of Swift, we come to optionals. Optionals are a unique feature of Swift, and they are used quite extensively. Optionals allow you to safely run code where a value may missing, which would normally cause errors. Optionals take some getting used to. Optionals help you achieve clean-looking code with fewer lines while also being stricter.

In many languages, you need to check objects to see whether they are `nil` or `null`. Usually, you write some pseudo-code that looks like the following. In this example we check for not null in JavaScript:

```
if(something != null) {...
```

In Swift, an optional either contains a value or it doesn't. In other languages, we often have to deal with missing values, such as a variable that once contained a value but no longer does. Or when a variable is initialized without a value. To mark something as optional, you just include a ? next to the type of the object. For example, here's how you create a `String` optional:

```
var someString:String? = "Hey there!"
```

You can now say that `someString` is of type `String?` (a "String optional") and no longer just of type `String`. Try printing that variable as an optional string and then as a regular string. Notice the difference in their returned values.

```
var greetingOptional:String? = "hi there"
var greeting:String = "Hi"
print(greetingOptional) //Optional("hi there")
print(greeting) //"Hi"
```

If you choose to use an optional and it does contain a value, you must do something special to get raw value out. Optionals must be "unwrapped" in order to get their value back. There are a couple ways to get the value out of an optional. When you see a variable of type `String?`, you can say that this variable may or may not contain a value. You will test this `String` optional to find out whether it does in fact have a value. How do you test an optional? There are a couple of ways. First try to use *value binding*.

Value binding allows you to do two things. First, it allows you to test the optional to see whether it is `nil` (whether it contains a value). Second, if that variable is not `nil`, value binding allows you to grab the value out of the optional and have it passed into a constant as a locally scoped variable. To see this in action, take a look at an example, but before you can try it out, you first need to open a new playground:

1. Open Xcode.

2. Click Get started with a playground.

3. Save a new playground file by giving it a filename.

Now you can try out value binding with optionals:

```
var hasSomething:String? = "Hey there!"
if let message = hasSomething {
    "Message was legit: \(message)"
} else {
    "There was no message!"
}
```

A couple of new things are going on here. Let's go through this example one step at a time:

1. On the first line, you create a variable as usual, but you add the ? to say that this is a String optional. This means that this String may contain a value or nil. In this case, it contains a value. That value is the string "Hey there!".

2. Next, you write an if statement. You are testing whether the variable hasSomething is nil. At the same time, you are assigning that value of the optional to a constant message. If the variable contains a value, you get a new constant (available only in the local scope, so we call it a locally scoped constant), which is populated with the raw value of the optional. You will then enter into the if statement body.

3. If you do enter into that if statement, you now have a message to use. This constant will be available only in that if statement.

However, sometimes you are absolutely sure that your optional contains a value and is not empty. You can think of optionals as a gift that needs to be unwrapped. If an optional is nil inside, it will not throw an error when you use it. In other languages, trying to access something of nil (or null) value throws an error.

You can unwrap an optional by using an exclamation point. That is, you can get the value inside the optional by using an exclamation point. Let's look again at our earlier example:

```
var hasSomething:String? = "Hey there!"
print(hasSomething) // Optional("Hey there!")\n
// Now unwrap the optional with the "!"
print(hasSomething!) // "Hey there!\n"
```

If you were sure that the string contained a value, you could unwrap the optional with the "!." Now you can get the value out of the optional with one extra character. Remember how we said optionals are like wrapped-up presents? Well, it's sometimes good to think of them more like bombs in Minesweeper. If you are too young for Minesweeper, think of them as presents that could contain bombs. You want to unwrap an optional with the "!" only if you are absolutely sure it contains a value. You want to unwrap optional with the "!" only if you are absolutely sure it does not contain nil. If you unwrap an optional that's nil, using "!," then you will throw a fatal error, and your program will crash:

```
var hasSomething:String? //declare the optional string with no initial
    value
// Now try and force it open
hasSomething! // fatal error:
Execution was interrupted, reason: EXC_BAD_INSTRUCTION...
```

When you get an EXC_BAD_INSTRUCTION somewhere, it means that your app is trying to access something that does not exist, which could be an error with an empty optional trying to unwrap with the "!."

Printing Your Results

When you use the playground to test your code, you have two options for printing data. You can simply just write it, like this:

```
var someString = "hi there"
someString //prints "hi there" in the output area
```

You can also use `print()`, which prints to the console output area. When you are making a full-fledged app, compiling code outside a playground, you'll want to use `print()`, like this, because just writing the variable will not do anything:

```
var someString = "hi there"
print(someString) //prints "hi there" in the console output
```

Implicitly Unwrapped Optionals

Sometimes you want to create an optional that gets unwrapped automatically. To do this, you assign the type with an exclamation point instead of a question mark:

```
var hasSomething:String! = "Hey there"// implicitly unwrapped optional string
hasSomething // print the implicitly unwrapped optional and get the
    unwrapped value.
```

You can think of implicitly unwrapped optionals as a present that unwraps itself. You should not use an implicitly unwrapped optional if a chance exists that it may contain `nil` at any point. You can still use implicitly unwrapped optionals in value binding to check their values.

So why should you create implicitly unwrapped optionals in the first place if they can be automatically unwrapped? How does that make them any better than regular variables? Why even use them in the first place? These are fantastic questions, and we will answer them later, after we talk about classes and structures in Chapter 4, "Structuring Code: Enums, Structs, and Classes." One quick answer is that sometimes we want to say that something has no value initially but we promise that it will have a value later. Properties of classes must be given a value by the time initialization is complete. We can declare a property with the exclamation point to say, in effect, "Right now it does not have a value, but we promise we will give this property a value at some point."

Also, sometimes you will have a constant that cannot be defined during initialization, and sometimes you will want to use an Objective-C API. For both of these reasons and more, you will find yourself using implicitly unwrapped optionals. The following example has two examples (with some concepts not covered yet) in which you would commonly use implicitly unwrapped optionals.

```
class SomeUIView:UIView {
    @IBOutlet var someButton:UIButton!
    var buttonWidth:CGFloat!
```

```
    override func awakeFromNib() {
        self.buttonOriginalWidth = self.button.frame.size.width
    }
}
```

In this example you have a button, which you cannot initialize yourself because the button will be initialized by Interface Builder. Also, the width of the button is unknown at the time of the creation of the class property, so you must make it an implicitly unwrapped optional. You will know the width of the button after `awakeFromNib` runs, so you promise to update it then.

Tuples

Using *tuples* (pronounced "TWO-pulls" or "TUH-pulls") is a way to group multiple values into one value. Think of associated values. Here is an example with URL settings:

```
let purchaseEndpoint = ("buy","POST","/buy/")
```

This tuple has a `String`, a `String`, and a `String`. This tuple is considered to be of type (`String`, `String`, `String`). You can put as many values as you want in a tuple, but you should use them for what they are meant for and not use them like an array or a dictionary. You can mix types in tuples as well, like this:

```
let purchaseEndpoint = ("buy","POST","/buy/",true)
```

This tuple has a `String`, a `String`, a `String`, and a `Bool`. You are mixing types here, and this tuple is considered to be of type (`String`, `String`, `String`, `Bool`). You can access this tuple by using its indexes:

```
purchaseEndpoint.1 // "POST"
purchaseEndpoint.2 // "/buy/"
```

This works well but there are some inconveniences here. You can guess what `POST` and `/buy/` are, but what does `true` stand for? Also, using indexes to access the tuple is not very pretty or descriptive. You need to be able to be more expressive with the tuple.

You can take advantage of Swift's capability to name individual elements to make your intentions clearer:

```
let purchaseEndpoint = (name: "buy", httpMethod: "POST",URL: "/buy/",useAuth: true)
```

This tuple has `String`, `String`, `String`, and `Bool` (true or false) values, so it is the same type as the previous tuple. However, now you can access the elements in a much more convenient and descriptive way:

```
purchaseEndpoint.httpMethod = "POST"
```

This is much better. It makes much more sense and reads like English.

You can *decompose* this tuple into multiple variables at once. Meaning you can take the tuple and make multiple constants or variables out of it in one fell swoop. So if you want to get the name, the `httpMethod`, and the `URL` into individual variables or constants, you can do so like this:

```
let (purchaseName, purchaseMethod, purchaseURL, _) = purchaseEndpoint
```

Here, you are able to take three variables and grab the meat out of the tuple and assign it right to those variables. You use an underscore to say that you don't need the fourth element out of the tuple. Only three out of the four properties of the tuple will be assigned to constants.

In Chapter 3, "Making Things Happen: Functions," you will use tuples to give functions multiple return values. Imagine having a function that returned a tuple instead of a string. You could then return all the data at once and do something like this:

```
func getEndpoint(endpoint:String) ->
    (description: String, method: String, URL: String) {
    return (description: endpoint, method: "POST", URL: "/\(endpoint)/")
}
let purchaseEndpoint = getEndpoint("buy")
print("You can access the
    \(purchaseEndpoint.description) endpoint at the URL \(purchaseEndpoint.URL)")
```

Number Types

Swift is interoperable with Objective-C, so you can use C, Objective-C, and Swift types and code all within Swift. As discussed earlier in the chapter, when you write a variable using an integer, Swift automatically declares it with a type `Int`, without your having to tell Swift you want an `Int`. In this example, you don't tell Swift to make this variable an `Int`:

```
let theAnswerToLifeTheUniverseAndEverything = 42
```

Rather, Swift infers that it is an `Int`. Remember that on 32-bit systems this `Int` will be an `Int32`, and on 64-bit systems it will be an `Int64`. If you don't remember that it won't matter because Swift will convert this for you automatically anyway. Even though you have many different `Int` types available to you, unless you need an `Int` of a specific size, you should stick with Swift's `Int`. When we say `Int32`, what we mean is a 32-bit integer. (This is similar to C.) You can also use `UInt` for unsigned (non-negative) integers, but Apple recommends that you stick with `Int` even if you know that your variable is going to be unsigned.

Again, when you write any type of floating-point number (a number with a decimal), and you don't assign a type, Swift automatically declares it with the type `Double`. Swift also gives you `Double` and `Float` types. The difference between them is that `Double` has a higher precision of around 15 decimal digits, whereas `Float` has around 6. Here is an example of a `Double` in Swift:

```
let gamma = 0.5772156649015328606065120900824024310421593359399232
```

Swift is strict about its types and they get combined together. If something is meant to be a `String`, and you give it an `Int`, then you will get an error. Swift needs you to be explicit with types. For example, this will not work:

```
var someInt = 5 // Inferred to be an Int
someInt + 3.141 // throws an error
```

This throws an error because you can't combine an `Int` and a `Double`. If you want to combine an `Int` and a `Double`, you must first convert the `Int` to a `Double` or vice versa, depending on your preference. Here we combine an `Int` and a `Double` by converting the `Int` to a `Double`:

```
var someInt = 5 // Inferred to be an Int
Double(someInt) + 3.141 // 8.141
```

```
var someInt = 5 // Inferred to be an Int
Float(someInt) + 3.141 // In this case 3.141 will be inferred to be a Float so
// it can combine with a Float
```

```
var someInt = 5 // Inferred to be an Int
Float(someInt) + Double(3.141) //This will throw an error and will not work
```

You can use the initializer (`Float(someInt)` or `Double(someInt)`, etc.) of the number type to convert between types. For example, you can use `Float()` to convert any number type into a `Float`.

So again, when you want to perform any operations on two or more number types, all sides of the operation must be of the same type. You'll see this pattern often in Swift, and not just with numbers. For example, you cannot directly add a `UInt8` and a `UInt16` unless you first convert the `UInt8` to a `UInt16` or vice versa.

From Objective-C to Swift

If you are coming from the world of Objective-C and C, you know that you have many number types at your disposal. Number types like `CGFloat` and `CFloat` are necessary to construct certain objects. For example, SpriteKit has the `SKSpriteNode` as a position property, which uses a `CGPoint` with two `CGFloat`s.

What is the different between `CGFloat` and `Float`? In this specific case we found that `CGFloat` is just a `typealias` for `Double`. This is what the code actually says:

```
typealias CGFloat = Double
```

What is a `typealias`? Great question. A `typealias` is just a shortcut to get to an already existing type by giving it a substitute name. You could give `String` an alternative name type of `Text`, like this:

```
typealias Text = String
var hello:Text = "Hi there"
```

Now `hello` is of type `Text`, which never existed before this point. So if `CGFloat` is a `typealias` for a `Double`, this just means that when you make `CGFloat`s, you are really just making `Double`s. It's worth it to Command+click around and see what is mapping to what. For example, a `CFloat` is a `typealias` for `Float`, and a `CDouble` is a `typealias` for `Double`.

That does not mean that you can suddenly add them together. You still need to convert them to combine them. For example, this will not work:

```
var d = 3.141
var g = CGFloat(3.141)
print(d + g)
```

To fix this example we would need to do something like this:

```
var d = 3.141
var g = CGFloat(3.141)
print(CGFloat(d) + g)
```

Control Flow: Making Choices

Controlling the order in which your code executes is obviously a crucial aspect of any programming language. By building on the traditions of C and C-like languages, Swift's control flow constructs allow for powerful functionality while still maintaining a familiar syntax.

`for` Loops

At its most basic, a `for` loop allows you to execute code over and over again. This is also called "looping." How many times the code gets executed is up to you (maybe infinitely). In the Swift language, there are two distinct types of `for` loops to consider. There is the traditional `for-condition-increment` loop, and there is the `for-in` loop. `for-in` is often associated with a process known as *fast enumeration*—a simplified syntax that makes it easier to run specific code for every item. `for-in` loops give you far less code to write and maintain than your typical C `for` loops.

`for-condition-increment` Loops

You use a `for-condition-increment` loop to run code repeatedly until a condition is met. On each loop, you typically increment a counter until the counter reaches the desired value. You can also decrement the counter until it drops to a certain value, but that is less common. The basic syntax of this type of loop in Swift looks something like this:

```
for initialization; conditional expression; increment {
    statement
}
```

As in Objective-C and C, in Swift you use semicolons to separate the different components of the `for` loop. However, Swift doesn't group these components into parentheses. Aside from this slight syntactic difference, `for` loops in Swift function as they would in any C language.

Here's a simple example of a `for-condition-increment` loop that simply prints `Hello` a few times:

```
for var i = 0; i < 5; ++i {
    print("Hello there number \(i)")
}
// Hello there number 0
// Hello there number 1
// Hello there number 2
// Hello there number 3
// Hello there number 4
```

This is fairly straightforward, but notice the following:

- Variables or constants declared in the *initialization expression* only exist within the scope of the loop. If you need to access these values outside the scope of the `for` loop, then the variable must be declared prior to entering the loop, like this:

  ```
  var i = 0
  for i; i < 5; ++i {...
  ```

- If you're coming from another language, particularly Objective-C, you will notice that the last example uses `++i` instead of `i++`. Using `++i` increments `i` before returning its value, whereas using `i++` increments `i` after returning its value. Although this won't make much of a difference in the earlier example, Apple specifically suggests that you use the `++i` implementation unless the behavior of `i++` is explicitly necessary.

`for-in` Loops and Ranges

In addition to giving you the traditional `for-condition-increment` loop, Swift builds on the enumeration concepts of Objective-C and provides an extremely powerful `for-in` statement. You will most likely want to use `for-in` for most of your looping needs because the syntax is the most concise and also makes for less code to maintain.

With `for-in`, you can iterate numbers in a range. For example, you could use a `for-in` loop to calculate values over time. Here you can loop through 1 to 4 with less typing:

```
class Tire{}
var tires = [Tire]()
for i in 1...4 {
    tires.append(Tire())
}
print("We have \(tires.count) tires")
```

We haven't covered the class and array syntax yet, but maybe you can take a guess at what they do. This example uses a `...` range operator for a closed range. The range begins at the first number and includes all the numbers up to and including the second number.

Swift also provides you with the half-open range operator, which is written like this:

```
1..<4
```

This range operator includes all numbers from the first number up to but not including the last number. The previous example, rewritten to use the non-inclusive range operator, would look like this:

```
class Tire{}
var tires = [Tire]()
for i in 1..<5 {
    tires.append(Tire())
}
print("We have \(tires.count) tires")
```

As you can see, the results are almost identical and both examples provide concise and readable code. When you don't need access to i, you can disregard the variable altogether by replacing it with an underscore (_). The code now might look something like this:

```
class Tire { }
var tires = [Tire]()
// 1,2,3, and including 4

class Tire {}
var tires = [Tire]()
for _ in 1...4 {
    tires.append(Tire())
}
print("We have \(tires.count) tires")
```

Let's pretend that a bunch of tires have gone flat, and you need to refill each tire with air. We could use the for in loop to loop through all of our tires in the tire array. We can add on to our earlier example by giving the tires air. You could do something like this:

```
class Tire { var air = 0 }
var tires = [Tire]()
for _ in 1...4 {
    tires.append(Tire())
}
print("We have \(tires.count) tires")

for tire in tires {
    tire.air = 100
    print("This tire is filled \(tire.air)%")
}
print("All tires have been filled to 100%")
```

With this type of declaration, Swift uses *type inference* to assume that each object in an array of type [Tire] will be a Tire. This means it is unnecessary to declare the type Tire explicitly. In a situation in which the array's type is unknown, the implementation would look like this:

```
class Tire { var air = 0 }
var tires = [Tire]()
for _ in 1...4 {
    tires.append(Tire())
}
print("We have \(tires.count) tires")

for tire: Tire in tires {
    tire.air = 100
    print("This tire has been filled to \(tire.air)%")
}
```

In this example we told the loop that each tire in the array of tires is going to be specifically of type Tire. In this specific example there is not a good reason to do this, but you may come upon a situation in which the type is not set explicitly. Since Swift must know what types it is dealing with, you should make sure that you communicate that information to Swift.

Looping Through Other Types

In Swift, a String is really a collection of Character values in a specific order. You can iterate values in a String by using a for-in statement, like so:

```
for char in "abcdefghijklmnopqrstuvwxyz".characters {
    print(char)
}
// a
// b
// c
// etc....
```

As long as something conforms to the SequenceType, you can loop through it. You cannot loop through the string directly; you need to access its character property.

When looping, there will be situations in which you will need access to the index as well as the object. One option is to iterate through a range of indexes and then get the object at the index. You would write that like this:

```
let numbers  = ["zero", "one", "two", "three", "four"]
for idx in 0..<numbers.count {
    let numberString = array[idx]
    print("Number at index \(idx) is \(numberString)")
}
// Number at index 0 is zero
// Number at index 1 is one
// etc....
```

This works just fine, but Swift provides a much swifter way to do this. Swift gives you an enumerate method as part of the array, which makes this type of statement much more concise. Let's use the for-in statement in with the enumerate method:

```
let numbers = ["zero", "one", "two", "three", "four"]
for (i, numberString) in numbers.enumerate() {
    print("Number at index \(i) is \(numberString)")
}
// Number at index 0 is zero
// Number at index 1 is one
// etc....
```

This is much clearer, and you would use it when you require an array element and its accompanying index. You can grab the index of the loop and the item being iterated over!

Up to this point, all the loops we've covered know beforehand how many times they will iterate. For situations in which the number of required iterations is unknown, you'll want to use a while loop or a do while loop. The syntax to use these while loops is very similar to that in other languages. Here's an example:

```
var i = 0
while i < 10 {
    i++
}
```

This says that this loop should increment the value of i while it is less than 10. In this situation, i starts out at 0, and on each run of the loop, i gets incremented by 1. Watch out, though, because you can create an infinite loop this way. There will be times when you really need an infinite loop.

One way to create an infinite while loop is to use while true:

```
while true {
}
```

In this example you use a while loop that always evaluates to true, and this loop will run forever, or until you end the program or it crashes itself.

This next example uses some of the looping capabilities plus if/else statements to find the prime numbers. Here's how you could find the 200th prime number:

```
var primeList = [2.0]
var num = 3.0
var isPrime = 1
while primeList.count < 200 {
    var sqrtNum = sqrt(num)
    // test by dividing only with prime numbers
    for primeNumber in primeList {
        // skip testing with prime numbers greater
        // than square root of number
        if num % primeNumber == 0 {
```

```
            isPrime = 0
            break
        }
        if primeNumber > sqrtNum {
            break
        }
    }
    if isPrime == 1 {
        primeList.append(num)
    } else {
        isPrime = 1
    }
    //skip even numbers
    num += 2
}
print(primeList)
```

Grabbing `primeList[199]` will grab the 200th prime number because arrays start at 0. You can combine `while` loops with `for-in` loops to calculate prime numbers.

To `if` or to `else` (if/else)

It's important to be able to make decisions in code. It's okay for you to be indecisive but you wouldn't want that for your code. Let's look at a quick example of how to make decisions in Swift:

```
let carInFrontSpeed = 54
if carInFrontSpeed < 55 {
    print("I am passing on the left")
} else {
    print("I will stay in this lane")
}
```

You use Swift's `if` and `else` statements to make a decision based on whether a constant is less than 55. Since the integer 54 is less than the integer 55, you print the statement in the `if` section.

One caveat to `if` statements is that in some languages you can use things that are "truthy," like 1 or a non-empty array. That won't work in Swift. You must conform to the protocol `BooleanType`. To make this simple, you must use `true` or `false`. For example, here are some examples that will not work:

```
if 1 { // 1 in an Int and can't be converted to a boolean
    //Do something
}
var a = [1,2,3]
if a.count{ // a.count is an Int and can't be converted to a boolean
    print("YES")
}
```

If you want to make these examples work, you would have to convert those numbers to a `Bool`. For example, check out what happens when we convert some simple integers to Booleans.

```
print(Bool(1)) // true
print(Bool(2)) // true
print(Bool(3)) // true
print(Bool(0)) // false
```

If `Int`s can be converted into `Bool`s, you can check for `if` with a truthy value if you first convert it to a `Bool`. Let's rewrite our previous failing examples and make them work.

```
if Bool(1) { // 1 in an Int and can't be converted to a boolean
    print("Duh it works!")
}
var a = [1,2,3]
if Bool(a.count){ // a.count is an Int and can't be converted to a boolean
    print("YES")
}
```

We were able to check for 1 and an array `count` in the `if` statement because we first converted them to `Bool`s.

You may also want to check multiple statements to see whether they're `true` or `false`. You want to check whether the car in front of you slows down below 55 mph, whether there is a car coming, and whether there is a police car nearby. You can check all three in one statement with the `&&` operator. This operator states that both the statement to its left and the one to its right must be `true`. Here's what it looks like:

```
var policeNearBy = false
var carInLane3 = false
var carInFrontSpeed = 45
if !policeNearBy && !carInLane3 && carInFrontSpeed < 55 {
    print("We are going to pass the car.")
} else {
    print("We will stay right where we are for now.")
}
```

Your code will make sure that all three situations are `false` before you move into the next lane (the `else`).

Aside from the and operator, you also have the or operator. You can check to see whether any of the statements is `true` by using the or operator, which is written as two pipes: `||`. You could rewrite the preceding statement by using the or operator. This example just checks for the opposite of what the preceding example checks for:

```
var policeNearBy = false
var carInLane3 = false
var carInFrontSpeed = 45
if policeNearBy || carInLane3 || carInFrontSpeed > 55 {
    print("We will stay right where we are for now.")
```

```
} else {
    print("We are going to pass the car.")
}
```

If any of the preceding variables is true, you will stay where you are; you will not pass the car.

Aside from just if and else, you may need to check for other conditions. You might want to check multiple conditions, one after the other, instead of just going straight to an else. You can use else if for this purpose, as shown in this example:

```
var policeNearBy = false
var carInLane3 = false
var carInFrontSpeed = 45
var backSeatDriverIsComplaining = true
if policeNearBy || carInLane3 || carInFrontSpeed > 55 {
    print("We will stay right where we are for now.")
} else if backSeatDriverIsComplaining {
    print("We will try to pass in a few minutes")
}else {
    print("We are going to pass the car.")
}
```

You can group as many of these else ifs together as you need. However, when you start grouping a bunch of else if statements together, it might be time to use the switch statement.

Switching It Up: `switch` Statements

You can get much more control and more readable code if you use a switch statement. Using tons of if else statements might not be as readable. Swift's switch statements are very similar to those in other languages with extra power added in. The first major difference with switch statements in Swift is that you do not use the break keyword to stop a condition from running through each case statement. Swift automatically breaks on its own when the condition is met.

Another caveat about switch statements is that they must be absolutely exhaustive. That is, if you are using a switch statement on an int, you need to provide a case for every int *ever*. This is not possible, so you can use the default statement to provide a match when nothing else matches. Here is a basic switch statement:

```
var num = 5
switch num {
case 2:print("It's two")
case 3:print("It's three")
default:print("It's something else")
}
```

This tests the variable num to see whether it is 2, 3, or something else. Notice that you must add a default statement. As mentioned earlier, if you try removing it, you will get an error because the switch statement must exhaust every possibility. Also note that case 3 will not run if case 2 is matched because Swift automatically breaks for you.

You can also check multiple values at once. This is similar to using the or operator (||) in if else statements. Here's how you do it:

```
var num = 5
switch num {
case 2,3,4:print("It's two") // is it 2 or 3 or 4?
case 5,6:print("It's five") // is it 5 or 6?
default:print("It's something else")
}
```

In addition, you can check within ranges. The following example determines whether a number is something between 2 and 6:

```
var num = 5
switch num {
// including 2,3,4,5,6
case 2...6:print("num is between 2 and 6")
default:print("None of the above")
}
```

You can use tuples in switch statements. You can use the underscore character (_) to tell Swift to "match everything." You can also check for ranges in tuples. Here's how you could match a geographic location:

```
var geo = (2,4)
switch geo {
//(anything, 5)
case (_,5):print("It's (Something,5)")
case (5,_):print("It's (5,Something)")
case (1...3,_):print("It's (1 or 2 or 3, Something)")
case (1...3,3...6):print("This would have matched but Swift already found a match")
default:print("It's something else")
}
```

In the first case, you are first trying to find a tuple whose first number is anything and whose second number is 5. The underscore means "anything," and the second number must be 5. Our tuple is 2,4 so that won't work because the second number in our tuple is 4.

In the second case, you are looking for the opposite of the first case. In this instance the first number must be 5 and the second number can be anything.

In the third case, you are looking for any number in the range 1 to 3, including 3, and the second number can be anything. Matching this case causes the switch to exit. We can use ranges to check numbers in switch statements, which makes them even more powerful.

The next case would also match, but because Swift has already found a match, it never executes. In this case we are checking two ranges.

Switch statements in Swift break on their own. If you've ever programmed in any other common language, you know you have to write break so that the case will stop. If you want that typical Objective-C, JavaScript functionality that will not use break by default (where the third case and fourth case will match), you can add the keyword fallthrough to the case, and the case will not break:

```
var geo = (2,4)
switch geo {
//(anything, 5)
case (_,5):print("It's (Something,5)")
case (5,_):print("It's (5,Something)")
case (1...3,_):
    print("It's (1 or 2 or 3, Something)")
    fallthrough
case (1...3,3...6):
    print("We will match here too!")
default:print("It's something else")
}
```

Now the third case and fourth case match, and you get both print statements:

```
It's (1 or 2 or 3, Something)
We will match here too!
```

Remember the value binding example from earlier? You can use this same idea in switch statements. Sometimes it's necessary to grab values from the tuple. You can even add in a where statement to make sure you get exactly what you want. Here is the kitchen-sink example of switch statements:

```
var geo = (2,4)
switch geo {
case (_,5):print("It's (Something,5)")
case (5,_):print("It's (5,Something)")
case (1...3,let x):
    print("It's (1 or 2 or 3, \(x))")
case let (x,y):
    print("No match here for \(x) \(y)")
case let (x,y) where y == 4:
    print("Not gonna make it down here either for \(x) \(y)")
default:print("It's something else")
}
```

You might get a warning here telling you that a case will never be executed, and that is okay. This is the mother of all switch statements. Notice that the last two cases will never run. You can comment out the third and fourth switch statements to see each run. We talked about the first case and second case. The third case sets the variable x (to 4) to be passed into the `print` if there is a match. The only problem is that this works like the underscore by accepting everything. You can solve this with the `where` keyword. In the fourth `case`, you can declare both x and y at the same time by placing the `let` outside the tuple. Finally, in the last `case`, you want to make sure that you pass the variables into the statement, and you want y to be equal to 4. You control this with the `where` keyword.

Stop...Hammer Time

It's important to have some control over your `switch` statements and loops. You can use `break`, `continue`, and labels to provide more control.

Using `break`

Using `break` stops any kind of loop (`for`, `for in`, or `while`) from carrying on. Say that you've found what you were looking for, and you no longer need to waste time or resources looping through whatever items remain. Here's what you can do:

```
var mystery = 5
for i in 1...8 {
    if i == mystery {
        break
    }
    print(i) // Will be 1, 2, 3, 4
}
```

The loop will never print 5 and will never loop through 6, 7, or 8.

Using `continue`

Much like `break`, `continue` will skip to the next loop and not execute any code below the `continue`. If you start with the preceding example and switch out `break` with `continue`, you will get a result of 1, 2, 3, 4, 6, 7, and 8:

```
var mystery = 5
for i in 1...8 {
    if i == mystery {
        continue
    }
    print(i) // Will be 1, 2, 3, 4, 6, 7, 8
}
```

Using Labeled Statements

`break` and `continue` are fantastic for controlling flow, but what if you had a `switch` statement inside a `for in` loop? You want to `break` the `for` loop from inside the `switch` statement, but you can't because the `break` you write applies to the `switch` statement and not the loop.

In this case, you can label the `for` loop so that you can tell the `for` loop to break and make sure that the `switch` statement does not break:

```
var mystery = 5
rangeLoop: for i in 1...8 {
    switch i {
    case mystery:
        print("The mystery number was \(i)")
        break rangeLoop
    case 3:
        print("was three. You have not hit the mystery number yet.")
    default:
        print("was some other number \(i)")
    }
}
```

Here, you can refer to the right loop or `switch` to break. You could also break `for` loops within `for` loops without returning a whole function. The possibilities are endless.

Summary

This chapter has covered a lot of ground. You can see that Swift isn't another version of Objective-C. Swift is a mixture of principles from a lot of languages, and it really is the best of many languages. It has ranges, which pull syntax straight out of Ruby. It has `for in` loops with `enumerate` and tuples, which both are straight out of Python. It has regular `for` loops with `i++` or `++i`, which come from C and many other languages. It also has optionals, which are Swift's own invention.

You'll see shortly that Swift has a lot of cool features that make it easy to use along with your Objective-C and C code. You have already gotten a small taste of arrays. Chapter 2, "Collecting Your Data: Arrays and Dictionaries," covers arrays and dictionaries in detail. You'll see how Swift's strong typing and optionals come into play.

2

Collecting Your Data: Arrays and Dictionaries

This chapter talks about the types of collections that Swift has available. Objective-C has `NSArray` and `NSDictionary` through Cocoa. Swift is compatible and is used alongside Objective-C, so you have all those `NS` tools available to you. In addition, you'll have Swift's native arrays and dictionaries available.

This chapter describes arrays and dictionaries and the different tools available in each. You will learn how to add and remove elements from collections. You will also learn how Swift's strong type inference allows for quickly written and strongly typed arrays and dictionaries. You will learn when to use `NSArrays` and when to use Swift's own arrays.

Using Arrays

Arrays allow you to store stuff in a list for later use. These lists of stuff can be in order (arrays) or in no particular order (dictionaries). In Swift all these objects must be the same type. In Swift you can't have a list of `Ints` and `Doubles` or a list of `Strings` and `Cars` (assuming you had a `Car` object available to you). In Swift your array must be made up of all `Ints`, or all `Doubles`, or all `Strings`. However, since Swift works well with Objective-C and Objective-C can store different types of objects in one array (an array of `Ints`, `Doubles`, and `Strings` in one `NSArray`, for example), Swift must be able to do it, too. Swift can store different types in one array by making up an array of `Any`, or `AnyObject`. `AnyObject` is used to represent any object so that you can represent an `Int` and a `Double` at the same time. We will learn more about that through this chapter.

Your First Array the Long Way

You can create an array by declaring a variable to hold the array and then telling Swift exactly what is going to be in that array. Here's how you do that:

```
var myFirstArray:Array<Int> = Array<Int>()
print(myFirstArray) // prints []
```

This code declares the variable `myFirstArray`, which is a horribly boring name for an array, and you declare the variable to be of type `Array<Int>`. This says that the array is made up of only integers. You then set `myFirstArray` equal to a new array of integers by adding an empty set of parentheses at the end.

> **Note**
>
> Of course you can write this verbose array syntax, but you will most likely use the shorthand syntax.

A Quicker Array

You know from Chapter 1, "Getting Your Feet Wet: Variables, Constants, and Loops," that Swift has powerful type inference. You don't need to declare an array as verbosely as you did earlier. Here is a quicker way:

```
var quickerArray = [Int]()
```

Use `Int` surrounded by square brackets to mean "an array of `Int`s."

You can also instantiate an array with items directly in it. When you do this, Swift can infer the type of the array so you don't even have to declare a type. Here's how it works:

```
var arrayOfInts = [1,2,3,4]
```

This gives you an array of `Int`s, and if you try to add a `String` to it, Swift complains because Swift is strictly typed. You can add items to an array using `append`, but more on that topic later in this chapter:

```
arrayOfInts.append("hi")
// Type 'Int' does not conform to protocol 'StringLiteralConvertible'
```

We haven't talked about `append` yet, but you can guess that it adds an item to the array.

Working with arrays in Swift gets even more awesome because you can add any old thing into an array without Swift complaining. Believe it or not, the array will still be strictly typed:

```
var mixedArray:NSArray = [1,"hi",3.0,Float(4)]
```

Here you have made an array with an `Int`, a `String`, a `Double`, and a `Float`. Notice that Swift does not complain.

Using `AnyObject`

With Swift you can make an array of `AnyObject`s. You will see this done frequently where something has a return value of `[AnyObject]`. This is a nonspecific type to represent any type of class. Objective-C does not have strictly typed arrays, so in order to interface with Cocoa APIs properly, you need some flexibility to return arrays so that they can contain a mixed bag. You will often see Cocoa APIs return `[AnyObject]`. You can use this as in the preceding example.

```
var mixedArray:[AnyObject] = [1,1.2,1,"b"]
```

When you use `AnyObject`, you are using a protocol, which can represent an instance of literally any type at all. Therefore, `AnyObject` can represent a `String`, an `Int`, a `Double`, literally anything.

Differences Between `NSArray`s and Swift Arrays

In Objective-C you'll have mutable arrays that are represented by `NSMutableArray` and immutable arrays that are represented by `NSArray`. Did you notice that we didn't mention anything about mutable and immutable versions of the Swift array? *Mutable* means that something can be changed, and *immutable* means it cannot be changed. An immutable array cannot change after it is created. Swift does have mutable and immutable version of arrays as well as all other classes, but you don't need two different classes for each. To make an immutable array in Swift, you just assign it to a constant with `let`. If you want to make a mutable array in Swift, you just assign it to a variable using the keyword `var`:

```
var mutableArray = [1,2,3,4,5]
let immutableArray = [1,2,3,4,5]
```

The following is a comparison of Swift arrays and Objective-C `NSArray` and `NSMutableArray`:

Language	Type	Mutability
Swift	`let a:Array<Int>`	Immutable
Swift	`var a:Array<Int>`	Mutable
Objective-C	`NSArray`	Immutable
Objective-C	`NSMutableArray`	Mutable

Modifying Arrays

Creating arrays is easy, but what can you do with them? You can append, insert, remove, and iterate over them. You can change them as long as they are mutable.

Accessing Array Elements

You can access elements from an array by using what Swift calls *subscripts*. You will learn much more about subscripting later, but for now, you just need to know that you can use the square-brackets notation that you see in many other languages to access elements of an array. Here's an example:

```
var myArray = [1,2,3,4]
myArray[0] // 1
```

Arrays start from an index of 0. Grabbing the 0th element will give you back the first element. You can also use the `startIndex` property of the array to find this out. You can also grab the total number of items in an array by using the `count` method:

```
myArray.count  // 4
```

Adding Elements to an Array

If you have an array of prime numbers and want to add a new prime number to the list, you can use Swift's `append` method, like this:

```
var primes = [2,3,5,7,11,13,17,19,23,29]
primes.append(31) // [2,3,5,7,11,13,17,19,23,29,31]
```

> **Note**
>
> If you have appended to an array in Python before, you know that Python also uses `append` to add to arrays. You will see some things in Swift from other languages from time to time.

You can also use `+=` to easily concatenate two arrays:

```
raining += ["dogs","pigs","wolves"] // ["cats","dogs","pigs","wolves"]
```

When you append to an array, you are adding an element to the end of an array. The element you append will always become the last element.

If you want to add an element at the beginning of the array, you can use `insert`. Maybe it's raining dogs and cats instead of cats and dogs:

```
var raining = ["cats"]
raining.insert("dogs",atIndex: 0)
raining // ["dogs","cats"]
```

Removing Elements from Arrays

If you want to remove items from an array, you can use a number of methods in Swift. For example, you can remove the last item with `removeLast()`:

```
raining.removeLast()
```

And you can remove an element at a specific index by using `removeAtIndex(:atIndex)`:

```
var raining = ["cats","octopuses"] // cats, octopuses
raining.insert("dogs", atIndex: 1)
raining // cats, dogs, octopuses
raining.removeAtIndex(1) // this returns the element it removed: "dogs"
raining // cats, octopuses
```

Here's what's going on here:

1. You start with an array of two elements.

2. You insert an element at index 1.

3. Then you just remove the same item you added at index 1.

When you are removing elements from an array, it is important to remember that it works like a deck of cards. If you remove the third card from a deck, the fourth card becomes the third card, and so on with every card below the fourth card. The second card does stay in the second position.

You can also do the following:

- Create arrays with any type
- Create arrays of mixed types
- Add and remove items at the end of the array

Iterating Over Arrays

When you iterate over an array, you start at the beginning of the array and access each element of the array until you get to the end. Often you are looking for an element that meets a certain condition. Sometimes you will successfully find that element and will not need to iterate any further, so you will break the loop. The `for-in` loop is well suited for iterating over arrays. Here's what it looks like:

```
for animal in raining {
    print(animal)
}
// cats
// octopuses
```

Sometimes you need to access the current index for tracking purposes. For this purpose, Swift provides a global `enumerate` function, which gives you access to the current index and current element. Here's how it works:

```
for (i,animal) in raining.enumerate {
    print("Animal number \(i) is the \(animal)")
}
// Animal number 0 is the cats
// Animal number 1 is the octopuses
```

Extra Bits of Arrays

You can create arrays that are empty or with prepopulated contents. You can create and prepopulate an array by using the extra parameters `extra:` and `repeatedValue:`. Here's an example:

```
var mapRow1 = [Int](count:10,repeatedValue:0) // [0,0,0,0,0,0,0,0,0,0,0]
```

Here we created a map for a game. If you were using this map for a game, you could place arrays within arrays to create a multidimensional array. You can use one array for each row and place that in one big array, like this:

```
var mapRow1 = [Int](count:10,repeatedValue:0)
var cols = 10
var rows = 10
var map = [[Int]]()
for row in 0..<rows {
    var newRow = [Int](count:cols, repeatedValue:0)
    map.append(newRow)
}
print(map)
```

In this example, you create an array within an array. So the type of map is `[[Int]]`, which means an array of arrays of `Int`s. Because `[Int]` is an array of `Int`s, wrapping that in square brackets will give you an array of `Int`s. This type of multidimensional array can be used in games to create a sort of tile map. Maybe for this map 0 is ground, 1 is road, and 2 is tree. The preceding example makes a whole map of ground. Notice that it does so without making a nested `for` loop.

Emptying an Array

You can completely empty an array by setting it equal to `[]`. This technique is used in other languages as well.

```
map = []
print(map.count) // 0
```

Using Dictionaries

Dictionaries are similar to arrays in that they are both containers that store multiple values of the same type. Dictionaries are different from arrays in that each value is stored with a key. You use that key to access the value. In arrays, you access elements by index. Arrays are stored in a specific order, and dictionaries are not. Just like arrays, though, dictionaries want to know what type you will be storing for their values. They also want to know what type you will use for their keys. You can write a dictionary in verbose form or shorthand. First the verbose:

```
var people:Dictionary<Int,String> = [186574663:"John Smith",
                                     198364775:"Francis Green",
                                     176354888:"Trevor Kalan"]
people[176354888] // "Trevor Kalan"
```

This dictionary is of type `[Int : String]`. Again, you can three-finger-click or tap the variable name to find the type of the dictionary. The keys are of type `Int`, and the values are of type `String`. There are a couple of things to note here. For one thing, you can access the dictionary by using the same syntax that you use to access arrays. Note that by accessing the dictionary,

Swift returns an optional (see Chapter 1). Why does Swift return an optional? It is possible that you are trying to access something that is not there. If you were sure that there is a value at the key you were accessing, you could force the value out with an exclamation point, like this:

```
people[176354888]! // "Trevor Kalan"
```

Of course, there is a shorthand way to write dictionaries since Swift can automatically infer the types of dictionaries. You can rewrite a dictionary without an explicit type, like this:

```
var people = [186574663:"John Smith",
              198364775:"Francis Green",
              176354888:"Trevor Kalan"]
```

It's still the same dictionary as before.

Adding, Removing, and Inserting with Dictionaries

Previously, you used the subscript syntax (the square-brackets syntax) to access elements of a dictionary. You can use that syntax to also set values by key. In the preceding example, you can set a person with a Social Security number of 384958338:

```
people[384958338] = "Skip Wilson"
```

If the key exists, you will replace that Social Security value with Skip Wilson. If not, you will have a new key/value pair. Try to assign a key using a string, and you get an error.

You can also use the method updateValue(forKey:) to update your dictionary. This method also updates a value for a key if it exists, or it creates a new key value if it does not exist. updateValue returns an optional, which is the old value it replaced, or nil if it did not replace anything.

To remove items from a dictionary, you can just assign it to nil:

```
people[384958338] = nil
```

Now the person with Social Security number 384958338 is removed from the dictionary. You can also use removeValueForKey to do the same thing. It returns the old value it removed if the key exists. If not, it returns nil. It is otherwise known as an optional, and it looks like this:

```
people.removeValueForKey(176354888) // {Some "3343"}
people.removeValueForKey(24601) // nil
```

Iterating Over Dictionaries

You can iterate over a dictionary much the same way that you iterate over an array—by using a for-in loop. The only difference between an array for-in loop and a dictionary for-in loop is that with the dictionary loop, you are able to get both keys and values while looping, like this:

```
for (ssn,name) in people {
    print("SSN: \(ssn) Name: \(name)")
}
```

```
// SSN: 198364775 Name: Francis Green
// SSN: 176354888 Name: Trevor Kalan
// SSN: 186574663 Name: John Smith
```

You can also loop through just the keys of a dictionary, with `.keys`. In addition, you can loop through just the values with `.values`:

```
for ssn in people.keys {
    print("SSN: \(ssn)")
}
for name in people.values {
    print("Name: \(name)")
}
```

Extra Bits of Dictionaries

You can create a new dictionary like this:

```
var vehicles = Dictionary<String,String>()
```

It is worth noting that once again, if you Command+click on the dictionary, you will see that it is made up of a `struct` and subscripts. The `<>` characters tell you that the dictionary is made with generics, and it will accept any type at all for its keys and values. (Generics are a powerful feature of Swift that you will learn much more about in Chapter 9, "Becoming More Flexible: Generics.")

If you want to count the number of key/value pairs in a dictionary, you can use `.count`:

```
people.count // 3
```

Emptying a Dictionary

You can empty a dictionary just by calling `[:]`, like this:

```
people = [:] // 0 key/value pairs
```

Testing Dictionaries for the Presence of Values

Dictionaries return optionals when you try to access items. Therefore, you might want to place them into value bindings. If you don't need the value of the key you are testing, you can instead use a regular `if` statement, like this:

```
if people[198364775] != nil {
    print("Got him")
} else {
    print("No one with that Social Security number")
}
```

If you do, in fact, want the unwrapped value from the optional (if it does succeed), you can use full value binding, like this:

```
if let person = people[198364775] {
    print("Got \(person)")
} else {
    print("No one with that Social Security number")
}
```

Now you will have the unwrapped value of the optional available to you if there is a value to be had.

Putting It All Together

Next, you will create a little program from the massive amounts of knowledge you have acquired thus far. Enter the code in Listing 2.1.

Listing 2.1 **A Complete Example**

```
import Foundation

let city = "Boston"
let trainName = "the Red Line"

var subwayStops = [
    // Stop name and busyness on a scale of 1-10
    ("Harvard Square", 6),
    ("Kendall / MIT", 5),
    ("Central Square", 7),
    ("Charles MGH", 4),
    ("Park Street", 10)
]

var passengers = 0

for i in 0..<subwayStops.count {
    var (stopName, busyness) = subwayStops[i]
    // New passengers boarding the train
    var board:Int

    switch (busyness) {
    case 1...4: board = 15
    case 5...7: board = 30
    case 7..<9: board = 45
    case 10: board = 50
    default: board = 0
    }
```

```
    // Some passengers may leave the train at each stop
    let randomNumber = Int(arc4random_uniform(UInt32(passengers)))

    //Ensure that passengers never becomes negative
    if randomNumber < passengers {
        passengers -= randomNumber
        print("\(randomNumber) leave the train")
    }

    passengers += board
    print("\(board) new passengers board at \(stopName)")
    print("\(passengers) current on board")
}
print("A total of \(passengers) passengers were left on \(trainName) in \(city)")
```

You can paste this code directly into the playground so you can step through it:

- Line 3: You create a city constant (Boston, in this case).

- Line 4: You create a train name constant.

- Lines 6–13: You create the subway stops array. This is of type [(String, Int)], which means an array of tuples in which the tuples are of types String and Int.

Note

For bonus points, make the array into an array of named tuples or reimplement it as a dictionary.

- Line 15: You specify the current number of passengers.

- Line 17: This is the main game loop, which loops from 0 to the number of subway stops.

- Line 18: You grab values out of the tuples smoothly and simultaneously.

- Line 22: You specify a switch with ranges, based on the busyness of the current stop.

- Lines 23–26: If the busyness level is between x and y, you board z number of people.

- Line 27: You need a default because the switch is not exhaustive. Your passengers might be exhausted, though.

- Line 31: You choose a random number of passengers between 0 and the number of passengers currently on the train to leave the train at each stop.

- Line 34: You have to make sure randomNumber is less than the current number of passengers. You make those people leave the train.

- Line 39: You choose the number of passengers to board from the switch statement.

- Line 40: You print the number of new passengers.
- Line 41: You print the number on board.
- Line 44: You finish the game with the total number of passengers left on board.

Summary

With arrays and dictionaries you are able to store data in many different ways. They are like the tools in a carpenter's kit. Arrays and dictionaries are an essential asset to successful Swift programming. Swift has given us multiple ways of accessing, adding, and removing items from these collections. The ways in which you can use collections is up to you, and you will find there are many different uses for them.

3

Making Things Happen: Functions

This chapter discusses functions. You will find that Swift functions are based on a similar implementations of functions in other languages like. Swift functions provide you with lots of flexibility to create parameters that are both "internal" and "external," which jibes well with Objective-C. Internal and external parameters allow you to have functions that are easy to read. You'll be able to quickly read the name of a function and know exactly what it does. This is one excellent feature of Objective-C that has made its way into Swift.

A function itself can also be passed as a parameter of another function, also known as anonymous functions. This makes it easy to pass parameters around to different contexts. Functions can contain other functions; these are called *closures* and are discussed in Chapter 6, "Reusable Code: Closures." Closures and functions go hand in hand.

A function groups commonly used code together so that it can be reused as many times as is needed. Say that you have a game in which a character jumps in the air, which is a supercommon functionality in a game. You would need to write the code to make the character jump. Jumping in games gets rather complicated, and you wouldn't want to rewrite that code every time you wanted the character to jump; handling the jumping character that way would be messy and error prone. Instead, you could create a function to wrap all that jumping code into a nice little package of goodness. Then, instead of writing all that code again, you could just use your `jump()` function. This is like using a real-life button press to make something work. That button connects to all the functionality contained within the component you're activating. You don't necessarily have to know how it works; you just know that pressing the button will make it work.

When you think about writing Swift code, you have to realize that there is a lot of functionality that just *works*. You may never know how it was written or how many lines of code it took to write it. You just know that when you call it, it will work.

For example, calling `countElements` on the string `"Hi"` returns 2, which is the number of characters in the string. You didn't have to write that function. It came with Swift. With Swift, you can write your own functions and then forget how you made them work. After you've written `jump()`, you can call it to have your character jump.

Defining Functions

In Swift, a function is made up of three components: a name, parameters, and a return type. The syntax for this type of declaration is as follows:

```
func functionName(parameterName: parameterType) -> returnType {
  //code
}
```

This syntax is very different from Objective-C method declarations. However, if you have ever used JavaScript, Python, C, or many other languages, then this syntax will be pretty familiar. You will find that although the structure of functions is different, there are parts that make it compatible with Objective-C.

Let's look at some examples, starting with a function that takes no arguments and has no return values:

```
func sayHello() {
    print("Hello!")
}
```

Here you write the keyword `func` and then name the function `sayHello`. You use `()` to house parameters when you need them; for now, you can leave these parentheses empty. You use curly brackets to contain the code that needs to run when the function is called. To call this function, you simply use its name followed by parentheses. You would call `sayHello` like this:

```
sayHello()
```

This is about as basic a function as you can create. You can go a step further and add an argument that allows the function to "say hello" to a specific person. To do that, you need to allow the function to take a single argument of type `String` that represents a name. That type of declaration might look like this:

```
func sayHello(name: String) {
  print("Hello, \(name)!")
}
```

Now you've added a parameter to the function. That parameter is of type `String` and is called name.

> **Note**
>
> If you're following along in your own playground, it isn't necessary to overwrite your old implementation of `sayHello`. The type inference in Swift allows you to differentiate between your different declarations of `sayHello` based on the arguments. This means that if you call this, Swift will infer that you are looking for `sayHello` with no arguments:
>
> ```
> sayHello()
> // Hello!
> ```

If, however, you add an argument of type `String` to the function call, like this, Swift will now infer that you're looking for the implementation of `sayHello` that takes one argument of type `String`:

```
sayHello("Skip")
// Hello, Skip!
```

As long as the argument types, the return types, or both are different, declaring functions with the same name will not cause issues with the compiler. You can actually have multiple functions with the same name sitting in the same file, so you shouldn't erase your other functions.

Next, you'll create another implementation of your `sayHello` function that says "hello" to someone a certain number of times. This will give you a chance to look at how to declare a function with multiple parameters:

```
func sayHello(name: String, numberOfTimes: Int) {
  for _ in 1...numberOfTimes {
    sayHello(name)
  }
}
```

This function declaration can be read as "a function named `sayHello` that takes two arguments of type `String` and type `Int` with no return value." The syntax is almost identical to that of the single argument function, just with an extra comma added to separate the arguments. You are even using the same name for the function. In fact, you are calling the first implementation of `sayHello` within the new declaration. Now, if you wanted to use this function, here's how it would look:

```
sayHello("Skip", numberOfTimes:5)
//Hello Skip!
//Hello Skip!
//Hello Skip!
//Hello Skip!
//Hello Skip!
```

We'll elaborate a bit more on how Swift differentiates between these declarations when we discuss function types later in the chapter in "Functions as Types," but for now, we're going to move on to adding a return type to the function implementations.

To add a return argument in the function declaration, you simply include the pointer arrow, `->`, followed by the return type.

Return Types

Next you'll create a function that returns its sum, which will also be of return type `Int`:

```
func sum(a: Int, b: Int) -> Int {
  return a + b
}
```

This declaration can be read as "a function, sum, that takes two arguments of type Int and has a return value of type Int." If you wanted to call the new function, it could look something like this:

```
let total = sum(14, b: 52)
// total = 66
```

Returning a single value is just fine, but sometimes you want to return multiple values. In Objective-C, this problem is usually solved by creating an object class or by returning some sort of collection. These solutions would work in Swift as well, but there is a better way: You can return multiple arguments in Swift by using tuples, as described in the next section.

Multiple Return Values

Like Objective-C functions, Swift functions can return only one value. Unlike Objective-C, though, Swift lets you use tuples as values, which can be useful for packaging together multiple return values so that you can pass around multiple values as one value. Consider a situation in which a function is required to return the sum of two numbers as well as the higher of the two. This means that you need the function to returns two values, both of type Int encapsulated in a tuple. Here's what it looks like:

```
func sumAndCeiling(a: Int, b: Int) -> (Int, Int) {
    let ceiling = a > b ? a : b
    let sum = a + b
    return (sum, ceiling)
}
```

You can declare multiple return values by encapsulating them in parentheses, separated by a comma. This is the syntax for a tuple. The preceding function can be read "a function named sumAndCeiling that takes two arguments of type Int and returns a tuple of type (Int, Int)." You can grab values from the returned tuple, from its indexes, like so:

```
let result = sumAndCeiling(4, b: 52)
let sum = result.0
let ceiling = result.1
```

This is a good way to return multiple values within one function, but using indexes to access values can be confusing. It's also not very pretty, and it's hard to remember which is which. Imagine if someone decided to change the order of the tuples without reading how they were used. It wouldn't be very smart or very nice, and it would severely mess things up. It's more helpful to name the values within a tuple.

Here's how you can modify the sumAndCeiling function with named values within the tuple:

```
func sumAndCeiling(a: Int, b: Int) -> (sum: Int, ceiling: Int) {
    let ceiling = a > b ? a : b
    let sum = a + b
    return (sum, ceiling)
}
```

The syntax for a named tuple is almost identical to the syntax of a parameter. Adding named tuples is an easy way to create more readable code while dealing with fewer errors. Here's a new implementation:

```
let result = sumAndCeiling(16, b: 103)
let sum = result.sum
// sum = 119
// result.sum == result.0
let ceiling = result.ceiling
// ceiling = 103
// result.ceiling == result.1
```

> **Note**
>
> In general, I prefer accessing tuples by name rather than by index because it is easier to read. This way you always know exactly what the function is returning.

More on Parameters

You already know how to use parameters in functions. As discussed in the following sections, Swift also provides the following:

- External parameter names
- Default parameter values
- Variadic parameters
- In-out parameters
- Functions as parameters

External Parameter Names

Usually you create a function with parameters and just pass them. However, external parameters must be written. Part of what makes Objective-C such a powerful language is its descriptiveness. Swift engineers wanted to also include that descriptiveness, and this is why the language includes external parameter names. External parameters allow for extra clarity. The syntax for including external parameter names in a function looks like this:

```
func someFunction(externalName internalName: parameterType) -> returnType {
  // Code goes here
}
```

The keyword `func` is followed by the name of the function. In the parameters of the function, there's an extra name for the parameters. The whole parameter is an external name followed by an internal parameter followed by the parameter type. The return type of the function follows the function parameters, as usual.

Here's a function that takes the names of two people and introduces them to each other:

```
func introduce(nameOfPersonOne nameOne: String, nameOfPersonTwo nameTwo: String) {
    print("Hi \(nameOne), I'd like you to meet \(nameTwo).")
}
```

Writing this function with external parameters makes it more readable. If someone saw a function called `introduce`, it might not provide enough detail for the person to implement it. With a function called `introduce(nameOfPersonOne:,nameOfPersonTwo:)`, you know for sure that you have a function that introduces two people to each other. You know that you are introducing person one to person two. When you add two external parameters to the function declaration and then you call the `introduce` function, the `nameOfPersonOne` and `nameOfPersonTwo` parameters will appear in the call itself. This is what it looks like:

```
introduce(nameOfPersonOne: "John", nameOfPersonTwo: "Joe")
// Hi John, I'd like you to meet Joe.
```

By including external parameters in functions, you remove the ambiguity from arguments, which helps a lot when sharing code.

External parameters aren't required, but they do make for much greater readability.

Default Parameter Values

Swift supports default parameters, unlike in Objective-C, in which there is no concept of default parameter values. The following is an example of a function that adds punctuation to a sentence, in which you declare a period to be the default punctuation:

```
func addPunctuation(sentence sentence: String, punctuation: String = ".") -> String {
    return sentence + punctuation
}
```

If a parameter is declared with a default value, it will be made into an external parameter. If you'd like to override this functionality and not include an external parameter, you can insert an underscore (_) as your external variable. If you wanted a version of `addPunctuation` that had no external parameters, its declaration would look like this:

```
func addPunctuation(sentence sentence: String, _ punctuation: String =
".") -> String {
    return sentence + punctuation
}
```

Now you can remove the underscore from the parameters. Then you can call the function with or without the punctuation parameter, like this:

```
let completeSentence = addPunctuation(sentence: "Hello World")
// completeSentence = Hello World.
```

You don't declare any value for `punctuation`. The default parameter will be used, and you can omit any mention of it in the function call.

What if you want to use an exclamation point? Just add it in the parameters, like so:

```
let excitedSentence = addPunctuation(sentence: "Hello World", punctuation: "!")
// excitedSentence = Hello World!
```

Next you're going to learn about another language feature that allows an unlimited number of arguments to be implemented. Let's talk about variadic parameters.

Variadic Parameters

Variadic parameters allow you to pass as many parameters into a function as your heart desires. If you have worked in Objective-C, you know that doing this in Objective-C requires a `nil` terminator so that things don't break. Swift does not require such strict rules. Swift makes it easy to implement unlimited parameters by using an ellipsis, which is three individual periods (`...`). You tell Swift what type you want to use, add an ellipsis, and you're done.

The following function finds the average of a bunch of `int`s:

```
func average(numbers numbers: Int...) -> Int {
    var total = 0
    for n in numbers {
        total += n
    }
    return total / numbers.count
}
```

It would be nice if you could pass in any number of `int`s. The parameter is passed into the function as an array of `int`s in this case. That would be `[Int]`. Now you can use this array as needed. You can call the `average` function with any number of variables:

```
let averageOne = average(numbers: 15, 23)
// averageOne = 19
let averageTwo = average(numbers: 13, 14, 235, 52, 6)
// averageTwo = 64
let averageThree = average(numbers: 123, 643, 8)
// averageThree = 258
```

One small thing to note with variadic parameters: You may already have your array of `int`s ready to pass to the function, but you cannot do this. You must pass multiple comma-separated parameters. If you want to pass an array of `int`s to a function, you can write the function a little differently. For example, the following function will accept one parameter of type `[Int]`. You can have multiple functions with the same name in Swift, so you can rewrite the function to have a second implementation that takes the array of `int`s:

```
func average(numbers: [Int]) -> Int {
    var total = 0
    for n in numbers {
        total += n
    }
```

```
    return total / numbers.count
}
```

Now you have a function that takes an array of ints. You might have this function written exactly the same way twice in a row. That works, but we are repeating ourselves. You could rewrite the first function to call the second function:

```
func average(numbers numbers: Int...) -> Int {
    return average(numbers: numbers)
}
```

Now you have a beautiful function that can take either an array of ints or an unlimited comma-separated list of ints. By using this method, you can provide multiple options to the user of whatever API you decide to make:

```
let arrayOfNumbers: [Int] = [3, 15, 4, 18]
let averageOfArray = average(numbers: arrayOfNumbers)
// averageOfArray = 10
let averageOfVariadic = average(numbers: 3, 15, 4, 18)
// averageOfVariadic = 10
```

In-Out Parameters

In-out parameters allow you to pass a variable from outside the scope of a function and modify it directly inside the scope of the function. You can take a reference *into* the function's scope and send it back *out* again—hence the keyword inout. The only syntactic difference between a normal function and a function with inout parameters is the addition of the inout keyword attached to any arguments you want to be inout. Here's an example:

```
func someFunction(inout inoutParameterName: InOutParameterType) -> ReturnType {
  // Your code goes here
}
```

Here's a function that increments a given variable by a certain amount:

```
func incrementNumber(inout number number: Int, increment: Int = 1) {
    number += increment
}
```

Now, when you call this function, you pass a reference instead of a value. You prefix the thing you want to pass in with an ampersand (&):

```
var totalPoints = 0
incrementNumber(number: &totalPoints)
// totalPoints = 1
```

In the preceding code, a totalPoints variable represents something like a player's score. By declaring the parameter increment with a default value of 1, you make it easy to quickly increment the score by 1, and you still have the option to increase by more points when necessary. By declaring the `number` parameter as `inout`, you modify the specific reference without having to assign the result of the expression to the `totalPoints` variable.

Say that the user just did something worth 5 points. The function call might now look like this:

```
var totalPoints = 0
incrementNumber(number: &totalPoints, increment: 5)
// totalPoints = 5
incrementNumber(number: &totalPoints)
// totalPoints = 6
```

Functions as Types

In Swift, a function is a type. This means that it can be passed as arguments, stored in variables, and used in various ways. Every function has an inherent type that is defined by its arguments and its return type. The basic syntax for expressing a function type looks like this:

```
(parameterTypes) -> ReturnType
```

This is a funky little syntax, but you can use it as you would use any other type in Swift, which makes passing around self-contained blocks of functionality easy.

Let's next look at a basic function and then break down its type. This function is named `double` and takes an `int` named `num`:

```
func double(num: Int) -> Int {
    return num * 2
}
```

It also returns an `int`. To express this function as its own type, you use the preceding syntax, like this:

```
(Int) -> Int
```

Here you add the parameter types in parentheses, and you add the return type after the arrow.

You can use this type to assign a type to a variable:

```
var myFunc:(Int) -> Int = double
```

This is similar to declaring a regular variable of type `string`, for example:

```
var myString:String = "Hey there buddy!"
```

All we are doing is assigning a variable. The only difference is that the type of the variable is a function and not a `String`. You could easily make another function of the same type that has different functionality. Just as `double`'s functionality is to double a number, you can make a function called `triple` that will triple a number:

```
func triple(num:Int) -> Int {
    return num * 3
}
```

The double and triple functions do different things, but their type is exactly the same. You can interchange these functions anywhere that accepts their type. Anyplace that accepts (Int) -> Int would accept both the double and triple functions. Here is a function that modifies an int based on the function you send it:

```
func modifyInt(number number: Int, modifier:(Int) -> Int) -> Int {
    return modifier(number)
}
```

Although some languages just accept any old parameter, Swift is very specific about the functions it accepts as parameters.

Putting It All Together

Now it's time to combine all the things you've learned so far about functions. You've learned that the pound sign means that the function has an external parameter named the same as its internal parameter. The parameter modifier takes a function as a type. That function must have a parameter that is an int and a return value of an int. You have two functions that meet those criteria perfectly: double and triple. If you are an Objective-C person, you are probably thinking about blocks right about now. In Objective-C, blocks allow you to pass around code similar to what you are doing here. (Hold that thought until you get to Chapter 6.) For now, you can pass in the double or triple function:

```
let doubledValue = modifyInt(number: 15, modifier: double)
// doubledValue == 30
let tripledValue = modifyInt(number: 15, modifier: triple)
// tripledValue == 45
```

> **Note**
>
> This example is obviously completely hard coded, and your examples will be completely dynamic. For example, you would probably replace the number 30 with the current speed of the character when he hits the sonic speed button. For now, you can just settle for 30 and 45.

Listing 3.1 is an example of creating functions in Swift.

Listing 3.1 **A Tiny Little Game**

```
var map = [ [0,0,0,0,2,0,0,0,0,0],
            [0,1,0,0,0,0,0,0,1,0],
            [0,1,0,0,0,0,0,0,1,0],
            [0,1,0,1,1,1,1,0,1,0],
            [3,0,0,0,0,0,0,0,0,0]]

var currentPoint = (0,4)
func setCurrentPoint(){
    for (i,row) in map.enumerate(){
```

```
            for (j,tile) in row.enumerate(){
                if tile == 3 {
                    currentPoint = (i,j)
                    return
                }
            }
        }
    }
}

setCurrentPoint()

func moveForward() -> Bool {
    if currentPoint.1 - 1 < 0 {
        print("Off Stage")
        return false
    }
    if isWall((currentPoint.0,currentPoint.1 - 1)) {
        print("Hit Wall")
        return false
    }
    currentPoint.1 -= 1
    if isWin((currentPoint.0,currentPoint.1)){
        print("You Won!")
    }
    return true
}

func moveBack() -> Bool {
    if currentPoint.1 + 1 > map.count - 1 {
        print("Off Stage")
        return false
    }
    if isWall((currentPoint.0,currentPoint.1 + 1)) {
        print("Hit Wall")
        return false
    }
    currentPoint.1 += 1
    if isWin((currentPoint.0,currentPoint.1)){
        print("You Won!")
    }
    return true
}

func moveLeft() -> Bool {
    if currentPoint.0 - 1 < 0 {
        return false
    }
```

```
        if isWall((currentPoint.0 - 1,currentPoint.1)) {
            print("Hit Wall")
            return false
        }
        currentPoint.0 -= 1
        if isWin((currentPoint.0,currentPoint.1)){
            print("You Won!")
        }
        return true
    }

func moveRight() -> Bool {
    if currentPoint.0 + 1 > map.count - 1 {
        print("Off Stage")
        return false
    }
    if isWall((currentPoint.0 + 1,currentPoint.1)) {
        print("Hit Wall")
        return false
    }
    currentPoint.0 += 1
    if isWin((currentPoint.0,currentPoint.1)){
        print("You Won!")
    }
    return true
}

func isWall(spot:(Int,Int)) -> Bool {
    if map[spot.0][spot.1] == 1 {
        return true
    }
    return false
}

func isWin(spot:(Int,Int)) -> Bool {
    print(spot)
    print(map[spot.0][spot.1])
    if map[spot.0][spot.1] == 2 {
        return true
    }
    return false
}

moveLeft()
moveLeft()
moveLeft()
moveLeft()
```

```
moveBack()
moveBack()
moveBack()
moveBack()
```

This is a map game. This game allows the user to navigate through the map by using function calls. The goal is to find the secret present (the number 2). If the player combines the right moves in the move function, he or she can find the secret present. Your current status will read out in the console log.

Let's step through this code:

- You have a multidimensional array map, which is an array within an array.

- The function setCurrentPoint finds the 3, which is the starting point, and sets it as the current point.

- You have four directional functions that move the current point's x or y position.

- In each of those functions, you check whether you hit a wall using the isWall function.

- In each of those functions, you also move the player's actual position.

- After the position is moved, you check whether you won the game by seeing whether you landed on a 2.

- You can call each function one by one and the console will trace out whether you won. It will not move if you are going to hit a wall. It also will not move if you are going to go offstage.

Summary

This chapter just scratches the surface of using functions in Swift. You learned most of what there is to learn syntactically, but there is more to come with the possibilities of implementation. Now that you know all the different ways to use functions in Swift, it is time to start experimenting and implementing. Functions are one of the puzzle pieces of object-oriented programming, but you need more pieces to complete the picture. Next you will learn how to turn functions into methods of a class, struct, and enum. You will learn the basic building blocks of structuring code. When combined with classes, structs, and enums, functions become a part of that bigger object-oriented programming picture.

4

Structuring Code: Enums, Structs, and Classes

This chapter covers the basic structural methods of Swift: enums, structs, and classes. With these tools, you can more easily organize your code for reuse. You will find yourself typing less code when using these tools properly. Structs, enums, and classes are similar to functions in that they allow you to group some code together for reuse. They are different from functions because they can *contain* functions.

If you are familiar with Objective-C, C, C++, or Java and other languages, you should know about enums because they are a part of many languages. You write `typedef` because in Objective-C and C (but not C++), you have to always precede an enum with the word `enum`. You create a `typedef` to make a shortcut to the enum to reduce the typing. In Swift, you use enum types anytime you need to represent a fixed set of constants, including things like the planets in our solar system. You use it in situations in which you know all the possible values—for example, menu options or command-line options.

Structures and classes have a lot of similarities in their intended functionalities. Structs, enums, and classes can have methods, which are functions within the enum, struct, or class. These methods provide that specific object with something it can *do*. Methods are doers. Methods (which you can think of as functions within classes, structs, or enums) give you some information about the object.

Structs and classes are very similar in that they contain a design for representing objects. The big difference is that structs are always created new or copied when passed around, and classes are passed around by reference. If your friend wanted to borrow something from you, you would definitely lend it to him because you two are best buds. If that to-be-borrowed something was a struct, you would have to pull out the 3D printer and print your friend a brand-new one and hand it over. If that something was a class, you would give your friend a card that told exactly where to find that something anytime he looked for it.

Enums

Enums, structs, classes, and protocols are all written in a very similar way. Here is how you create an enum for the suits in a deck of cards:

```
enum Suit {
    //... enum implementation goes here
}
```

You should choose a singular name (not plural) for the enum—like Suit in this case. You write the word enum and then give the enum a name and write a pair of curly brackets. The enum implementation goes inside the curly brackets. Here is a simple enum that declares all possible suits in a deck of cards:

```
enum Suit {
    case Hearts
    case Clubs
    case Diamonds
    case Spades
}
```

Now you can declare Suit.Clubs:

```
var thisCardSuit = Suit.Clubs
```

Now thisCardSuit is of type Suit. Each of the choices is called a "member" of the enum. Each member is a constant and cannot be changed. You want to name your enums so they are easily read. When you read the preceding declaration, you can think of it as saying, "This card suit is a suit which is clubs" (or, simplified, "This card suit is clubs"), which reads like a sentence.

If the variable you declare is already declared as a type Suit, you do not have to write the full name of the enum. You can use this instead:

```
var thisCardSuit:Suit // declaring the type suit.
thisCardSuit = .Clubs // Because suit is declared, we don't need to write
    Suit.Clubs          // Just .Clubs
```

Notice how you can write just .Clubs. A good example of this is UIImagePickerControllerSourceType, which you use when allowing the user to choose an image from the camera (to take a picture right now), saved photo albums, or the photo library. If you were to create a function that took a UIImagePickerControllerSourceType as a parameter, you could pass it just .Camera, like this:

```
func showImagePickerForSourceType(imageView:UIImageView,
sourceType:UIImagePickerControllerSourceType) {...
...
}
showImagePickerForSourceType(imageView, .Camera)
```

In this example, you can pass the function .Camera because it knows that sourceType must be of type UIImagePickerControllerSourceType.

Which Member Was Set?

After the `sourceType` for `UIImagePickerControllerSourceType` is set, how do you figure out which enum value was set? You use a `switch` statement. Let's go back to the suits in the deck of cards example. You will reuse the `thisCardSuit` variable like so:

```
switch thisCardSuit {
case .Hearts:
    print("was hearts")
case .Clubs:
    print("was clubs")
case .Diamonds:
    print("was diamonds")
case .Spades:
    print("was spades")
}
// was clubs
```

Of course, this `switch` statement must be exhaustive (see Chapter 1, "Getting Your Feet Wet: Variables, Constants, and Loops"). This example prints out `was clubs`.

Associated Values

You will often want to associate a value with a member of an enum. Having the member itself is helpful, but sometimes you need more information. Here's how you could create a `Computer` enum to get an idea of what I mean:

```
enum Computer {
    //ram and processor
    case Desktop(Int,String)
    //screen size, model
    case Laptop(Int, String)
    //screen size, model, weight
    case Phone(Int, String, Double)
    //screen size, model, weight
    case Tablet(Int, String, Double)
}
var tech:Computer = .Desktop(8, "i5")
```

Here you have made a computer that is of type `Computer`, with a value of `Desktop`, and with 8GB of RAM and an i5 processor. Notice how you can give each member value different required associated values. `Desktop` has `Int` and `String`, and `Phone` has `Int`, `String`, and `Double`. To use this `Computer` enum in a theoretical app, you would make the user choose a technology. You could have her choose a desktop, laptop, phone, or tablet. After she chooses, you could specify the RAM and processor. If she chose a desktop, she would provide the screen size and model. If she chose a laptop, phone, or tablet, she would provide the size, model, and weight.

Now you can check the selected `tech` value by using a `switch` statement and simultaneously grabbing the associated values:

```
switch tech {
case .Desktop(let ram, let processor):
    print("We chose a desktop with \(ram) and a \(processor) processor")
case .Laptop(let screensize):
    print ("We chose a laptop which has a \(screensize) in screen")
default:
    print ("We chose some other unimportant computer.")
}
```

You see here that you can grab the associated values out of the chosen `Computer` member by assigning a constant using `let`. Notice that you have to write `let` twice if the enum member has multiple associated values. Of course, there is a shorthand way to write this without writing `let` twice. Here's a more concise way:

```
switch tech {
case let .Desktop(ram, processor):
    print("We chose a desktop with \(ram) and a \(processor) processor")
case let .Laptop(screensize):
    print("We chose a laptop which has a \(screensize) in screen")
default:
    print ("We chose some other unimportant computer.")
}
```

By placing the keyword `let` after the keyword `case` and before the member, you can declare two constants at once. This makes for cleaner code.

Raw Values

Raw values are different from associated values. You cannot have two of the same raw values in an enum. Raw values also all use the same type. You can use `strings`, the `ints`, or any floating-point types. When you use `ints`, the value automatically increments for you. For example, say that you use `ints` as the raw value type. Since the raw value will automatically increment, you can use a shorthand way of declaring enum members on one line:

```
enum Suit:Int {
    case Clubs = 1, Hearts, Diamonds, Spades
}
var chosenSuit = Suit.Diamonds
```

Here you declare the raw value type by adding a colon (:) next to the enum name and writing the type. This is similar to declaring a type for a variable or constant. This example uses `Int` so the value will auto-increment. When you declare a raw value for the enum, you can grab that raw value out of the variable by using `.rawValue`:

```
chosenSuit.rawValue // 3
```

The raw value of Diamonds is 3 because of the auto-increment. Clubs is 1, Hearts is 2, Diamonds is 3, and Spades is 4.

Play around with this and change Clubs to any integer you want. Try changing it to 100, or -10, or 0. It still auto-increments perfectly.

You can use the constructor Suit(rawValue: n) to do the opposite of rawValue by getting the raw value from an integer (or whatever type your enum is). Suit(rawValue: n) returns an optional of type Suit. Why is it an optional? You might try to grab the member with a raw value of 4000, and that would not exist. However, because Suit(rawValue: n) gives a suit (in an optional), it's helpful to compare it to *something* rather than just printing it out. Here's what it looks like:

```
Suit(rawValue: 3) == chosenSuit // true
```

You can then use value binding to find the member for the raw value:

```
enum Suit:Int {
    case Clubs = 1, Hearts, Diamonds, Spades
}
var result = "Don't know yet."
if let theSuit = Suit(rawValue: 3) {
    switch theSuit {
    case .Clubs:
        result = "You chose clubs"
    case .Hearts:
        result = "You chose hearts"
    case .Diamonds:
        result = "You chose diamonds"
    case .Spades:
        result = "You chose spades"
    }
} else {
    result = "Nothing"
}
result // You chose diamonds
```

Here you have to do value binding for Suit(rawValue: 3) because it is an optional and could have been nil. After you get theSuit out of the value binding, assuming it's not nil, you can use your normal switch statement to find the chosen suit. Notice that the result variable was successfully changed even though you scoped it through the if and switch statements.

Structs

Structs (which is short for *structures*) are copied when they're passed around. Classes are passed around by reference. This means that you will never have the same instance of a struct. Conversely, you can have multiple instances of the same class.

Here is what classes and structs have in common:

- Both define properties to store values.
- Both define methods to provide functionality.
- Both provide subscripts to give access to their values.
- Both provide initializers to allow you to set up their initial state.
- Both can be extended to provide additional functionality beyond a default implementation. (This is different from inheritance.)
- Both have the capability to conform to protocols (which you will learn about in Chapter 8, "Expanding Your Reach: Protocols and Extensions").

> **Note**
>
> Do not worry too much if you don't understand everything in these lists. You will understand it all by the end of this chapter or in later chapters.

The following is the difference between classes and structs:

- Classes have inheritance.
- Classes have type checking.
- Structs have deinitializers so you can free up unused instances.
- Structs have reference counting. You can have more than one reference to a class instance.

Here's an example of a simple struct:

```
struct GeoPoint {
    var lat = 0.0
    var long = 0.0
}
```

This defines a new struct of type `GeoPoint`. You give the struct two properties and declare them as `doubles`. (Even though you don't see any explicit type declaration, it is happening because `0.0` is inferred as a `double`.)

Now you can use the new struct. If you want to interact with the `GeoPoint` struct, you must create a `GeoPoint` instance:

```
var somePlaceOnEarth = GeoPoint()
```

Now you can interact with the new `GeoPoint` struct, using the dot syntax:

```
somePlaceOnEarth.lat = 21.11111
somePlaceOnEarth.long = 24.232323
```

Notice that when you created a new `GeoPoint` struct, the code completion gives you the option to initialize it with properties (see Figure 4.1).

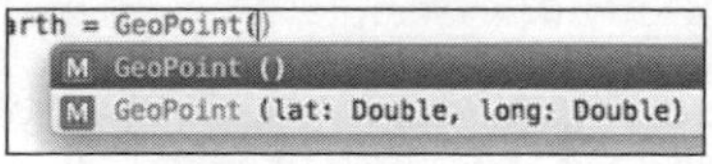

Figure 4.1   Code complete for GeoPoint shows multiple initializers

You can also write the last three lines as one line:

```
var somePlaceOnEarth = GeoPoint(lat: 21.1111, long: 24.23232)
```

Defining Methods in Structs

When we say *methods,* we are talking about the functions within structs. Methods are just functions that are going to be associated with the structs. By defining a method within the curly brackets of a struct, you are saying that this function belongs to this struct.

Here's an example of a struct with `Point`, `Size`, and `Rect`, which will be based on `CGRect`:

```
struct Point {
    var x:Int, y:Int
}

struct Size {
    var width:Int, height:Int
}

struct Rect {
    var origin:Point, size:Size

    func center() -> Point {
        let  x = origin.x + size.width/2
        let y = origin.y + size.height/2

        return Point(x: x, y: y)
    }
}
```

There are a couple of things to note here. The first thing you might notice is that you declare all the variables on one line. You can use this simplified version of declaring variables where it makes your code more readable. For example,

```
var one = 1,two = 2, three = 3
```

is the same as this:

```
var one = 1
```

```
var two   = 2
var three = 3
```

You might also notice that you set types for the properties explicitly (for example, `origin:Point, size:Size`). You did not give your properties any default values so Swift would be unable to determine the types of these properties.

However, because you did not give `Rect` any default value, Swift will complain. If you try to make a new `Rect` without any default values in the initializer, you will get an error:

```
var rect:Rect = Rect() // error: missing parameter for 'origin' in call
```

Swift does not like that you did not initialize the properties in the struct itself and did not initialize the properties upon making a new `Rect`.

The initializer included with every struct is called a *memberwise initializer*. Memberwise initializers are part of a much larger concept that we won't cover here. When creating a `Rect`, you can use the memberwise initializer to get rid of the error:

```
var point = Point(x: 0, y: 0)
var size = Size(width: 100, height: 100)
var rect:Rect = Rect(origin: point, size: size)
rect.size.height
rect.center()
```

That's better! Since you used the memberwise initializers when constructing `Point`, `Size`, and `Rect`, you no longer get errors. Here you also used the `center()` method of the `Rect`, and it told you that the center of the `Rect` is {x 50 y 50}.

Structs Are Always Copied

Earlier we talked about how structs are always copied when they are passed around. Let's take a look at an example that proves this, using the `Point` struct because it's supersimple:

```
var point1 = Point(x:10, y:10)
```

Now you can create `point2` and assign it to `point1`:

```
var point2 = point1
```

You modify `point2`:

```
point2.x = 20
```

Now `point1` and `point2` are different:

```
point1.x // 10
point2.x // 20
```

If `point1` and `point2` were classes, you would not get different values because classes are passed by reference.

Mutating Methods

If a method inside a struct will alter a property of the struct itself, it must be declared as mutating. This means that if the struct has some property that belongs to the struct itself (not a local variable inside a method) and you try to set that property, you will get an error unless you mark that method as mutating. Here's a struct that will throw an error:

```
struct someStruct {
    var property1 = "Hi there"
    func method1() {
        property1 = "Hello there"
        // property1 belongs to the class itself
        // so we can't change this with making some changes
    }
    // ERROR: cannot assign to 'property1' in 'self'
}
```

The fix for this error is simple. Just add the word mutating in front of the func keyword:

```
struct someStruct {
    var property1 = "Hi there"
    mutating func method1() {
        property1 = "Hello there"
    }
    // does not throw an error! YAY
}
```

Now that this is fixed, let's take a look at what this error means:

```
cannot assign 'property1' in 'self'
```

Well, it is property1 that you are trying to modify. This error says that you cannot assign property1 to self. What is self? self in this case is the struct's own instance. In this struct, property1 belongs to an instance of the struct. You could rewrite the line with property1 to be self.property1. However, self is always implied, so you don't need to write it. Also notice that the following code works without the mutating keyword:

```
struct someStruct {
    func method1() {
        var property2 = "Can be changed"
        property2 = "Go ahead and change me"
    }
}
```

The reason you can set property2 is because it does not belong to self directly. You are not modifying a property of self. You are modifying a local variable within method1.

Classes

In the following example of creating a class, notice that it looks just like a struct but with the word `class`:

```
class FirstClass {
    // class implementation goes here
}
```

You create a class exactly the same way you create a struct, but instead of using the word `struct`, you use the word `class`. Adding properties to a class is very similar. For example, the following `Car` class has properties for the make, model, and year (and you will define a default value for each property):

```
class Car {
    let make = "Ford"
    let model = "Taurus"
    let year = 2014
}
```

In this example, there are three immutable properties of the `Car` class. Remember that when you make a struct, you are able to leave these properties blank. If you do the same for a class, you get an error:

```
class Car {
    let make:String
    let model:String
    let year:Int
}
// error: class 'Car' has no initializers
```

If you want to fix this error, you must create an initializer for the `Car` class and initialize all the uninitialized properties. Classes in Swift don't have automatic initialization (that is, memberwise initializers). If you leave the properties without default values, you must provide an initializer for the class. Each of the uninitialized properties must be initialized.

Swift provides a global function `init()` for this very purpose. Some languages call this a *constructor.*

Initialization

Initialization is the process of getting the instance of a class or structure ready for use. In initialization, you take all things that do not have values and give them values. You can also do things like call methods, and do other initializations. The big difference between Objective-C initializers and Swift initializers is that Swift initializers do not have to return `self`. The goal of Swift initializers is to give a value to everything that does not have a value. Structs can define initializers even though they have their own memberwise initializers. You can also define multiple initializers for a class or struct. The simplest type of initializer is one without any parameters. Initializers without parameters are used to create new instances of the class's type. Here's an initializer for the `GeoPoint` class you created earlier:

```
struct GeoPoint {
    var lat:Double
    var long:Double
    init() {
        lat = 32.23232
        long = 23.3434343
    }
}
```

Here you are initializing `lat` and `long` with default values. You could put anything you want in that `init` method.

You can also make multiple initializers so that the user can create a `GeoPoint` however he wants:

```
struct GeoPoint {
    var x = 0.0
    var y = 0.0
    var length = 0.0
    init() {

    }
    init(x:Double,y:Double) {
        self.x = x
        self.y = y
    }
    init(length:Double) {
        self.length = length
    }
}
var regularPoint = GeoPoint()
var pointWithSize = GeoPoint(x: 2.0, y: 2.0)
var otherPoint = GeoPoint(length: 5.4)
```

Now you can initialize `Point` in three ways. If you want to create a `Point` by using x and y, you can use the initializer `Point(x:Double,y:Double)`. If you want to create a `Point` by length, you can initialize it with `Point(length:Double)`. If you just want to make a standard point, you can initialize it with no parameters to the `init` method. You would probably add more calculations than shown here, but this is the gist of making multiple initializers. As long as the parameters are different, you can make as many different initializers as you need. SpriteKit's `SKScene` has multiple initializers for multiple situations (see Figure 4.2).

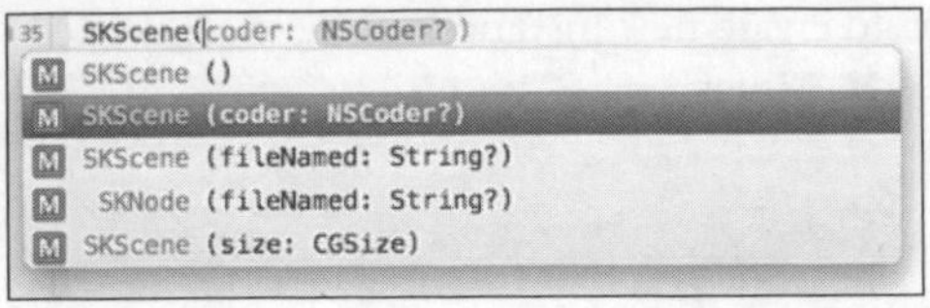

Figure 4.2   `SKScene` has multiple initializers available

Here you can see that you can initialize `SKScene` by filename, by size, and by coder. All this information about multiple initializers applies to both classes and structs. It just so happens that all the examples here use structs.

What Is a Reference Type?

Earlier we said that structs are copied when they are passed around. The other way to say this is that structs are *value types,* and classes are *reference types*. This means that when you assign a variable to a new instance of a class and then reassign that variable to another variable, you have the same reference in each copy of the class. Here's an example:

```
class Car {
    var name = "Honda"
}
var car1 = Car()
var car2 = car1
car1.name = "Dodge" // Dodge
car2.name // Dodge
```

Cool! Notice that when you change `car1.name` to `"Dodge"`, `car2.name` is also changed. That is because both `car1` and `car2` have a reference to the new instance of the `Car`. If you had done this with a struct, `car1` and `car2` would have different values for `name`.

Do I Use a Struct or a Class?

Whether you need to use a struct or class depends on a few factors, summarized here:

If You Say . . .	You Should Use a Struct	You Should Use a Class
I am storing a few simple data values—maybe some primitives	×	
I want values to be copied when passed around	×	
I want the properties of my object to also be copied when passed around (aka value types)	×	
Anything else		×

You can see that you will mostly be using classes for your data structures. Here are a couple examples of good uses of structs:

- A geometric point that contains an x and y and maybe a length
- A geolocation that defines latitude and longitude
- A geometric shape (like `CGRect`) that will contain width and height

All these structs are simple and contain only a few simple data values (you are not limited to geometric data). They often represent single values like a point or a rectangle.

Forgot Your Pointer Syntax?

When working with C, C++, or Objective-C, you know that you use pointers to reference the address (that is, the location in memory) of some value. You do this in Objective-C by using an asterisk (`*`). When you create a variable or constant in Swift that references some instance you created, you are not directly accessing that memory address. It is similar to a pointer but not exactly the same. Either way, you never have to reference anything using a pointer syntax when writing Swift.

The reason value types are called *value types* is that they are passed around as actual values. Reference types are called so because they are passed around as references that point to the actual objects. It's the difference between using cash and using checks. When you use cash, you are handing the person actual money (analogous to using value types). When you give someone a check, you are giving him not the cash itself but a piece of paper telling where to get the cash (analogous to using reference types). If you think about it, most people pass around money by reference rather than by value. They don't usually deal with the cash itself; they deal with some reference to money.

Property Observers

Property observers are a super-awesome feature built directly into Swift. They allow you to track and reply to changes of a property. You can add property observers to any property except lazy properties, which you won't learn about here. Here's how you create a basic property observer:

```
class Car {
    var name:String = "Honda" {
    willSet(newName) {
        print("About to set the new name to \(newName)")
    }
    didSet(oldName) {
        print("We just set 'name' to the new name \(name)
            from the old name \(oldName)")
    }
    }
}
var car1:Car = Car()
```

```
car1.name = "Ford"
// About to set the new name to Ford
// just set name to the new name Ford from the old name Honda
```

Notice that you add a pair of curly brackets at the end of the variable. Inside those curly brackets you add willSet and didSet. willSet will get called before the property is set. The parameter passed into the function is the new value that the property will be set to. didSet will get called after the property is set. The parameter passed into the function is the old value that the property had before it got changed. Obviously, you can access the new value now because it has already been changed.

Methods in Classes

A method and a function are very similar except for a couple of differences (aside from scope issues):

- A method has a reference to the object that it belongs to.
- A method is able to use data contained within the class it belongs to.

A method is identical to a function in syntax. Type methods in Swift are similar to Objective-C class methods. A big difference between both C and Objective-C and Swift is that in Swift you can define methods on classes, structs, and enums. This gives you great flexibility and strength. In Swift you have a couple of types of methods available to you. Let's start with instance methods.

Instance Methods

Instance methods are likely the type of methods you will be creating most of the time. An instance method belongs to an instance of a struct, a class, or an enum. It has access to information about that specific instance. It provides functionality to that instance. The Car class you made earlier has a property name. You can provide it with an instance method to make it go. Then each car you create (or instantiate) will have its own distance that it has traveled. Here's what it will look like:

```
class Car {
    var name = "Ford"
    var distance = 0
    func gas() {
        _spinWheels()
    }
    func _spinWheels() {
        //some complicated car stuff goes here.
        distance += 10
    }
}
var car1 = Car()
```

```
print(car1.distance) // 0
car1.gas()
car1.distance // 10
```

Just as in a real car, in this example the details of how a car works are hidden away in a private function. For example, you don't know how the gas pedal on the car works, but you know that if you press it the car will go. Obviously, this is not truly necessary in this case, but you can imagine how the details of making a car move forward could get much more complicated. gas and _spinWheels are both instance methods that belong to this specific instance of Car. You know this is true because if you create another car and check the distance, it will not be at the same distance as car1. These methods are acting on *this* instance. For example, here is a new car:

```
var car2 = Car()
print(car2.distance) // 0
```

Property Access Modifiers

In the preceding example you marked a method with an initial underscore to say, "Don't use this method outside this class." Swift has three property access modifiers—that is, three ways of forcing the use of a method into a context:

- private entities can be accessed only from within the source file in which they are defined.

- internal entities can be accessed anywhere within the target where they are defined.

- public entities can be accessed from anywhere within the target and from any other context that imports the current target's module.

Without a property access modifier applied, functions are internal. Meaning that if you don't write public or private or internal on the function, it will operate as if you wrote internal.

In the earlier example it would be more appropriate to change the method _spinWheels to be private and change the name to just spinWheels. You should do this even though you are working in the playground so that private won't restrict access because it's all in the same file.

Type (Static) Methods

In Swift you have instance methods, and you have type methods. Whereas instance methods work on the instance of class, type methods work on the class itself. If you made an instance of the Car class and you created a type method, you would not be able to use it on the instance of the Car class. These methods are only for the class itself. To add a type method to a class, you use the keyword class. To add a type method to a struct, you use the keyword static, as shown here:

```
class Car {
    var name = "Ford"
```

```
    var distance = 0

    class func getCarVersion() -> String {
        return "5.0.1"
    }
}
var car1 = Car()
print(car1.distance)
Car.getCarVersion()
```

Notice that if you want to access the car version, you call the method on the Car class itself. You may see these types of methods used on utilities and in various other situations.

Get to Know Your Self

You use the keyword self quite often in Swift. self is available on each instance of an object. self refers to the current instance. You don't always have to write self because Swift implies it. For the Car class, you could instead write this:

```
func spinWheels() {
    self.distance += 10
}
```

By using self.distance to refer to the distance, you are saying, in effect, "distance that belongs to this instance of the class." However, Swift already knows that is what you want, so you can just leave it as distance. It is often helpful to use self to distinguish between a method parameter and a property of the class, as shown here:

```
class Car {
    var name = "Ford"
    var distance = 0
    func go(distance:Int) {
        self.distance += distance
    }
}
```

In this case, the function has a parameter that is the same as the property of the class. To distinguish between them, you use self.distance to mean the property that belongs to the class, and you use just plain distance to mean the parameter of the function.

Inheritance: Creating a Bichon from a Dog from an Animal

In Swift, a class (the subclass) can inherit methods and properties of another class (the superclass). In our Bichon example, animal is the superclass, and dog is a subclass of animal. Then dog is a superclass of Bichon Frise, which is a subclass of Dog, which is a subclass of Animal. In Objective-C, everything eventually inherits from NSObject. It's like NSObject is 42 (the answer to life, the universe, and everything). It's the base of all superclasses. Swift does not have one grand base class. Defining a class that doesn't inherit from anything makes that class the base class for all other classes that inherit from it. In the following example you create a `Bichon` class, which inherits from the `Dog` class, which inherits from the `Animal` class. In this example, the `Animal` class has its own properties and methods that all its subclasses inherit:

```
class Animal {
    var name:String
    var numberOfLegs:Int
    func move() -> String{
        return "\(name) is moving."
    }
    init(name:String,numberOfLegs:Int) {
        self.name = name
        self.numberOfLegs = numberOfLegs
    }
}


class Dog:Animal {
    var breed:String
    override func move() -> String {
        return "\(name) the \(breed) is moving."
    }
    init(name: String, numberOfLegs: Int,breed:String) {
        self.breed = breed
        super.init(name: name, numberOfLegs: numberOfLegs)
    }
}
class Bichon:Dog {
    var fluffynessLevel:Double
    init(name: String, numberOfLegs: Int, breed: String, fluffynessLevel:Double) {
        self.fluffynessLevel = fluffynessLevel
        super.init(name: name, numberOfLegs: numberOfLegs, breed: breed)
    }
}
var penny = Bichon(name: "Penny", numberOfLegs: 4, breed: "Bichon",
    fluffynessLevel: 100.1)
penny.move() // "Penny the Bichon Frise is moving."
```

This example introduces a couple of new concepts. First is `super`. Calling `super` is like calling `self`, except instead of it referring to the instance of the current class, it refers to the instance of the parent class. So if `Bichon` inherits from `Dog`, then `self` would be `Bichon`, and `super` would be an instance of `Dog`.

If you are going to have a class inherit from another class, you should call the initializer of that class along with your class's initializer. `Bichon` is the not the one doing the initialization of name; rather, `Animal` is. So you call `super.init`, which calls the initialization of the parent, which needs to be called again from `Dog` to initialize `Animal`. It is as if you are instantiating the `Dog` class from the `Bichon` class and the `Animal` class from the `Dog` class. You are in fact doing just that, except you won't wind up with three classes in the end. You'll wind up with three parts that make up the `Bichon` class. Kind of like in real life. There are parts of you that are unique to you. Some parts you got from your father. Some parts you may have even gotten from your grandfather, and you made them unique. This is the purpose of overriding. You take something that existed in the parent class and override it with your own implementation. In this case, you just overrode the `move` class to give it a more appropriate implementation from the `Dog` class. It makes sense to add more details to `move` since you are no longer just talking about any kind of `Animal`. You are talking about a `Dog`. As it turns out, for this small program, the dog implementation of `move` is good enough that you don't have to override it in the `Bichon` class.

Summary

In this chapter you've learned how to write enums, structs, and classes. You've learned how to instantiate those classes and how each reacts differently to being passed around. You learned about passing by reference as opposed to by value. You also took a look at the difference between methods and functions.

5

SpriteKit

At this point we've covered the basics of Swift. We've learned enough to start building a game. This game will contain ideas and concepts that may not have been covered yet, but we will cover them as we go, and in much more detail in their dedicated chapters. Building a game in iOS using Swift is easy when you use an awesome framework like SpriteKit. SpriteKit allows you to make games easily, with the power of OpenGL and the ease of a simpler game framework. If you haven't ever used OpenGL in the past, let me tell you that it's not considered easy or quick to learn. Of course, OpenGL is not impossible, but the goal behind SpriteKit was to take the power of OpenGL and reduce it to a game-making framework that had all the typical game making tools already available. Things like a timer that is based on a number of frames. Things like a full-fledged physics engine and collision detection. All the items that would stop you in the past are now available right from the get-go.

Introducing SpriteKit

SpriteKit is a game-making framework that is available in Objective-C or Swift. You can use all of its built-in beauty and organization to build a game in an organized and thought-out way. SpriteKit is not going to organize your code for you, and you are allowed to write the game in any way that you want. After about a year of playing around with SpriteKit, I have come up with a couple of solid ways to organize code and put together a game that seems to work well for me, so let's get started!

The `SKNode` and `SKSpriteNode`

If you've ever made a game before, or even if you haven't, there is this idea of a stage, a place where things are visible to the player of the game. Items can be offstage or onstage, and when they are onstage they can be temporarily hidden. Items can be removed from the theater completely or created. All of these "items" will be based off of one base class, which is the `SKNode`. Anything that will be added to your metaphorical stage or taken off of your stage, or moved around on your stage, will be at its most basic an `SKNode`. You can think of the `SKNode` as anything that can exist in your game. Even the stage itself.

From there we move on to many other types of SKNodes. You have camera nodes for moving the camera around; you have SKShapeNodes for when you want to draw shapes on the screen/ stage. Let's focus for right now on one node that you may find to be the most important type of SKNode, and that is the SKSpriteNode. With this type of SKNode you can do many things, most important of which is adding an image (also known as a *sprite*) to your node so that something is visible on it. This is how you would create the visual representation of your main character. When you want to move that character around the stage, you use SKActions to perform the frame-based animation. You will not have to calculate how to move your character a certain distance over *n* frames. SpriteKit takes care of all the complicated math processes involved in moving your character, and in turn your character will move extremely smoothly. When you want to move your character along a path, you just pass the SKAction a path and it moves it along that path. It's all super easy-peasy. Let's create our game.

Creating a Game

The first step in creating a game is to open up your latest version of Xcode. In Xcode you can open up File, New, Project. You can also press Command-Shift-N to get to the new project screen.

The New Project Screen

At the new project screen you will notice that you have a bunch of choices for types of projects. If you have ever downloaded an app from the app store, you will be familiar with all of these types of projects. The only type of project we will be concerned with is the Game project.

When you choose one of these projects, that does not stop you from creating whatever you'd like. In other words, when you choose one of these projects to start with, Xcode will populate the project with settings that give you that type of working project from the start. For a "Game" type project, Xcode will populate your project with some Swift files that are the main files of your game. It will populate the user interface with a game scene so that your game can be put into a container for viewing. Choose the game project and click Next.

At the next screen you will have the options of choosing which language you want as well as naming the project.

> Project Name: My Kye
>
> Organization Name: [Your real or fake organization name]
>
> Organization Identifier: [com.yourOrganizationName.myKye]
>
> Language: Swift
>
> Game Technology: SpriteKit
>
> Devices: iPhone
>
> YES Include Unit Tests
>
> YES Include UI Tests

Next Xcode will ask you where you would like to save your project. If you don't have a typical place for saving your projects, I suggest you make a folder called `projects` in your home directory. If you already have a place for creating your project, just navigate there and click Create. You can skip the next couple of paragraphs and go to the section "Creating the Game."

You can find your home directory from this point by pressing Command-Shift-G. This brings up a directory selector. From here you can type in the location you want to visit.

In the Go to the Folder input, type ~. This will take you to your home directory. If you didn't already, create a `projects` directory in your home directory by selecting New Folder at the bottom of the screen and typing `projects` into the input. Anytime you create a new Xcode project, you can put it in your projects directory. If you work with multiple languages like I do, you can further subdivide this into different languages. Go into your new `projects` directory and click the Create button to save your game here.

Creating the Game

Believe it or not, you now have a working game. You went from zero to game in a few minutes. At this point you can run the game by selecting the Run button or pressing Command-R. When your game runs, you will see some words on the screen "Hello World", and you'll notice that when you click on the screen (if you are running this through the simulator, or tap on the screen if you are running this on your own device), you will see spaceships on the screen and also notice that those spaceships are spinning. Every time you click on a spaceship, a new `SKNode` is added to the screen. You can see the details of what has been added to the screen/ scene by looking at the bottom of the simulation. At the bottom of the screen, you should see "Nodes: 0 FPS: 59.0." The number of nodes should be the number of spaceships on the screen plus the label. If there are three spaceships on the screen, you should have four nodes. The reason the number is four nodes is that you now have one `SKLabelNode`, the "Hello, World!" label, and three `SKSpriteNodes`. Let's briefly talk about three types (of many) nodes you will encounter, which should give you enough supplies to make as many games as you want. Remember that all of these nodes are based off of the base class `SKNode`. Also notice that all the classes for SpriteKit will start with the letters `SK` for SpriteKit.

SKSpriteNode

The `SKSpriteNode` is a special `SKNode` that allows you to attach an image to a node.

SKLabelNode

The `SKLabelNode` is a special `SKNode` that allows you to create a node filled with text. You can use any of the typical available iOS fonts, or you can use a custom font.

SKShapeNode

The `SKShapeNode` allows you to create a special node that is a shape. Visually it will appear as a shape of any path with a stroke of any width and color, and/or a fill of any color and opacity. You can use a basic shape like a circle or rectangle, or you can create your own custom shape based off of a path.

With these basic node types you can build almost any game. There are, of course, other node types available, which you will be able to explore, but these node types will get you through your game.

What Is a Node?

After all of this talking about nodes and different node types, you might still be wondering what a node is. After all, so far it has been described as a kind of abstract concept. A node is anything in your game that can be added to your game. To understand this better, we should take a look at some of the code.

Remember that all of these SK classes are based off of the main SKNode.

Finding the Base

From the new project you created, open up GameScene.swift. This class contains the main entry point into your game. It has its own class named GameScene, which you can see on line 11.

```
class GameScene: SKScene {
```

This means that the base of GameScene is the SKScene. At this point we have not talked about SKScene yet. What we did say was that everything you add in your game will be (at its most basic) an SKNode. Is SKScene an SKNode, and how can we find out whether it is?

There are two basic ways of finding the base for a particular class. The first way is to check the online documentation. When you try to google, what you are looking for is the language reference. We are not looking for a tour of Swift 2 or any tutorials on Swift 2; we are looking for specific references to each class available in Swift 2. I googled "SpriteKit Framework Reference" and got to this documentation link, which may change in the future:

```
https://developer.apple.com/library/ios/
documentation/SpriteKit/Reference/SpriteKitFramework_Ref/
index.html#//apple_ref/doc/uid/TP40013041
```

On this page you can see at the top a link to some classes. Because of the changing nature of this documentation, I won't reference specific things on the page other than to say we are looking for a list of SpriteKit's classes. I was able to find the list of classes at this link, which may have changed at this point.

```
https://developer.apple.com/library/ios/
documentation/SpriteKit/Reference/SpriteKitFramework_Ref/index.html#classes
```

In this list of classes you can search for the SKScene class and click on its link. I was able to find the SKScene link here:

```
https://developer.apple.com/library/ios/
documentation/SpriteKit/Reference/SKScene_Ref/
index.html#//apple_ref/occ/cl/SKScene
```

On this page you should see an inheritance list. You can see that SKScene inherits from SKEffectNode, which inherits from SKNode, which in turn inherits from UIResponder, which inherits from NSObject.

The question is "Does SKScene inherit from SKNode?" Yes, it does.

Try doing this same class inheritance search for the SKSpriteNode, SKShapeNode, and SKLabelNode.

The other, faster way to find out what the base class of a particular SpriteKit class is to click on the class itself while pressing Command.

Go into your GameScene.swift and find the SKScene reference on that page. While holding the Command key on the keyboard, hover your mouse over the word SKScene. You should see the SKScene turn blue (like a link on a web page). When you click on that link, it takes you to a page that has a skeleton of the SKScene class. It isn't the real code to the SKScene class, just a skeleton of that class. This code does, however, contain the list of inheritance. If you click the SKScene class, you should now see somewhere on the page that SKScene inherits from the SKEffectNode.

```
public class SKScene : SKEffectNode {
```

You can then follow the chain by holding Command and clicking the SKEffectNode. This should take you to some code which says that SKEffectNode inherits from SKNode.

```
public class SKEffectNode : SKNode {
```

At this point we know that SKScene does in fact inherit from the SKNode.

At this point we can conclude that your game will work like this:

An SKScene will be added to the screen.

The rest of your game assets will be added to that SKScene.

Therefore, SKScene is the base of the node tree that will make up your game. When we say node tree, we mean that your game will have items that are added to the SKScene, that have items that are added to it. It is not a flat line of lineage but more like a family tree. In the sample of the game, you will see only items added to the base SKScene. You should know that things don't have to be that way and that we can even improve performance by working in node trees that have branches instead of a flat node tree.

GameViewController.swift SKView

Next let's take a step into our GameViewController.swift. The whole purpose of the GameViewController is to set up our SKScene and connect it to the SKView. The SKView is what sits in your Storyboard. Your SKScene is presented by your SKView. Where is this SKView? Let's check it out. Open up your Main.Storyboard in the project navigator. In the Storyboard you should see a blank black view on the screen. At the top you'll notice it is labeled Game View Controller. If you click on that black area to select it, you can view details about it. Before you can see any details about it, you must make sure that you have the correct columns open to view data. At the top right of the screen, you can hide and show different sections of Xcode. Hover over those buttons, and the one to the far right says "Hide or show the Utilities." Make sure that is selected and a third column will open up on the right. You'll find these utilities helpful only when building or using user interfaces in the Storyboard. Otherwise, when writing code you'll want to hide it. With the Utilities open you now have six sections of the utilities to help you gain information and change settings for the currently selected item in the Storyboard. So with your black area selected, you can hover over each of the six tools in the header, and each will give a tooltip about what it does.

Click the one with the tooltip labeled "Show the Identity Inspector," the one that is highlighted in Figure 5.1. It is the one that looks like a square newspaper.

Figure 5.1   Identity Inspector on the Utilities bar

With that selected and the black area clicked, you can see that you can assign a "Custom Class" to the selected area. And that area has a custom class attributed to it. This black area is assigned an SKView (see Figure 5.2).

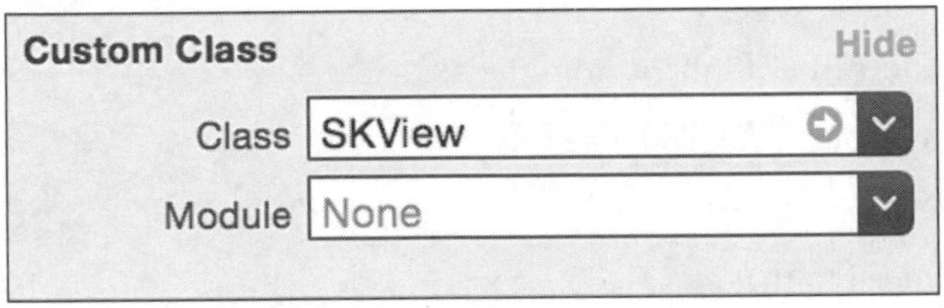

Custom Class   Hide

Class SKView

Module None

Figure 5.2   Custom Class assigned to SKView

The view controller for this SKView is our GameViewController. We can prove this by clicking the controller icon at the top of the black area.

Clicking that yellow circle selects the controller for the view that it controls (see Figure 5.3).

Figure 5.3   Controller Icon

Looking in the utility area with the identity inspector once again selected, you can see that the custom class is our GameViewController (see Figure 5.4).

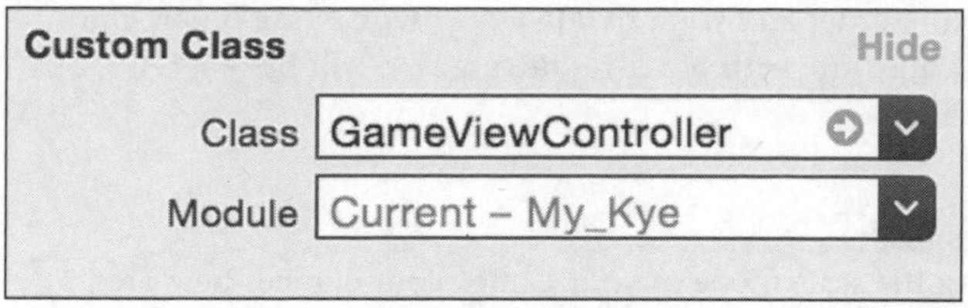

Custom Class   Hide

Class GameViewController

Module Current – My_Kye

Figure 5.4   Custom Class is `GameViewController`

Next to the class name (next to `GameViewController`), you can see a little gray arrow. If you click that little gray arrow, it will take you to the code for that `GameViewController`.

This shows you that our `GameViewController.swift` controls our `SKView`. Heading back into our `GameViewController.swift`, you can see that the `SKView` we are talking about comes from our Storyboard.

GameViewController.swift ignoresSiblingOrder

Here we can also set some debug information such as showing the node count, which you were able to see in the bottom-right corner of your simulator the last time you ran the game. You can also add the debug info for the FPS (frames per second). You also have the option of turning off `ignoresSiblingOrder`.

`skView.ignoresSiblingOrder = true`

Ignoring sibling order will significantly improve the performance of your app. This has to do with the z index of the items you add to the screen. Remember that the root node of our app is our `SKScene`. When you add things to that `SKScene` node, you are essentially creating children. The scene is the parent node and anything added to those nodes will be the children. Therefore, one can conclude that each label and spaceship added to the screen is a sibling of the others. The hierarchy thus far will look something like what's shown in Figure 5.5 (assuming you tapped the screen twice to add two spaceships to the screen).

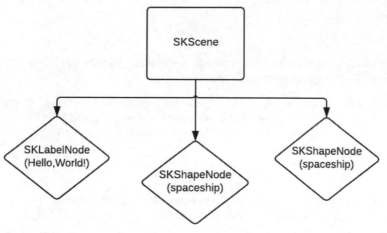

Figure 5.5   The hierarchy so far

If you tell SpriteKit to ignore the sibling order and you provide your own sibling order, you will make your game run at a faster frame rate with fewer resources. This will be one less computation that SpriteKit has to make.

GameViewController.swift scaleMode

You also have the choice of changing the scale mode of your game. Your choices here are going to depend on the type of game you are making and of course your personal preferences. This setting may be one of the most confusing settings available in SpriteKit. You have a couple of choices here. Notice that the selection is an enum so you can write this shorthand or longhand. To get the code completion and the full choices of available topics, you can write the full class name: SKSceneScaleMode.

When you press control + spacebar to code complete, you get the following code completion options:

```
AspectFill
AspectFit
Fill
ResizeFill
```

Of course, other options are available in the list of the code completion, but those have to do with the enum and not the scale mode.

The difference between these scale modes has to do with how you want your scene to appear to the user if it is not the same exact size as the view that presents it. In other words, your scene may need to be resized so that it fits in its view. How do you want it to be resized or scaled? That is the question that the scaleMode answers.

The best way to see what each of these settings does is to trace out the result and look at the result yourself. In your GameViewController.swift you can trace out the size of two things: the size of the SKView and the scene you are presenting to the view. Right below the line where it presents the scene (which should be line 29: skView.presentScene(scene)), add the following code:

```
print(skView.frame.size)
print(scene.size)
```

This way we can tell you the size of the view (which should not change) and the size of the scene, which may or may not change, depending on the scaleMode.

Only one of these modes resizes the scene itself. ResizeFill will modify the scene's size so that it is the same size of the view that presented it. All the other scale modes will not resize the view. Let's try this out. Right now you should have your scene scale mode set to AspectFill.

AspectFill

AspectFill will scale your scene to fill the view while preserving the scene's aspect ratio. The big thing to remember with this choice is that cropping may occur. The real calculation that happens behind the scenes is that a scaling factor is calculated for each width and height and the larger of the two is chosen. Because the larger of the two is chosen, your scene may be cropped. Therefore, only choose this if you are okay with things not being fully visible onscreen.

Make sure your scene is set to `AspectFill` and run your app. You will notice (if you chose the iPhone 6s Plus for the simulator) that the view has a size of (414.0, 736.0) meaning 414 width and 736 height. Of course, this is points and not pixels. If you change the simulator to the iPhone 4s, the results are similar but different. Because `AspectFill` does not change the size of the scene, the scene stays the same width and height. The scene is scaled but not resized. The view is now (320.0, 480.0) meaning 320 width and 480 height. Where do these view numbers come from?

Each phone has a default coordinate space defined in points. With points instead of pixels we can forget about the number of pixels it is rendering (may be doubled because of retina) and think about the number of points on the screen. Otherwise, retina and other screens would be an even bigger nightmare to write code for. The list of points for the screen is as follows:

iPhone 4s 320×480

iPhone 5 and 5s 320×568

iPhone 6 and 6s 375×667

iPhone 6 Plus and 6s Plus 414×736

So if these are the sizes of your iPhone screen, where is the size of the scene set? The answer is that you can set the size of the scene yourself programmatically; however, Xcode now has a visual graphical user interface for building the scene with.

If you look in your file navigator, you will see a `GameScene.sks` file. This `sks` file is the equivalent of the Storyboard. Whereas the Storyboard is for user interfaces, the `sks` file is for SpriteKit scene building.

Click on that `sks` file and it will open up the SpriteKit scene user interface builder. Again make sure that you have the utilities column open and select the third icon, which shows sizing handles (see Figure 5.6).

Figure 5.6   Sizing icon

When you select that icon, you will see that one of the parameters you can edit is the size of the scene. It is currently set to 1024×768. If you change the height to 767 and run the app again, you will notice that it did in fact change the size of the scene. We print out the size of the scene and the size of the view, and the size of the scene now reads (1024.0, 767.0). You were able to change the size of the scene through this editor. The reason this works is that we did not choose `ResizeFill` as our scale mode. All the other scale modes will not change the size of the scene, but `ResizeFill` does.

The other way to change the size of the scene is to do it programmatically. Go into your `GameScene.swift`. In your `GameScene` you will notice a method called `didMoveToView`. In our `GameViewController.swift` we present this scene by calling `skView.presentScene`. Immediately after `presentScene` is called and the scene is presented, `didMoveToView` gets called. In this method we can change the size of the scene. We changed the size of our scene in our sks file. We can also change the size of the scene in our `GameViewController.swift` right before we present the scene. The best place to do this would be before we present the scene so that no extra calculation needs to take place. In your `GameViewController.swift` right before the line that presents the scene, add the following code:

```
scene.size = CGSize(width: 1024, height: 766)
```

The size of the scene uses a `CGSize`. A `CGSize` is built specifically for this purpose of providing a width and a height in one object. You will notice that we use a lot of `CG` classes when using SpriteKit. For example, when you set the values of `CGSize`, by default it takes two `CGFloats`. However, `CGSize` also has initializers for `Int` and `Double`. This makes it easy to write

```
scene.size = CGSize(width: 1024, height: 766)
```

instead of

```
scene.size = CGSize(width: CGFloat(1024), height: CGFloat(766))
```

SpriteKit didn't always have all these niceties built in. When Swift first came out, the width and height of `CGSize` needed to be a `CGFloat`, so your game was one enormous conversion-fest `Ints` to `CGFloats`, `Doubles` to `CGFloats`, and everything to `CGFloats`.

AspectFit

Like `AspectFill`, `AspectFit` also preserves the aspect ratio of the scene, this time by taking the smaller of the two sizes deemed perfect for scaling. Instead of cropping occurring, letterboxing may occur because the smaller side may be too small to fit perfectly in the screen and you'll get letterboxing instead. This is good when you want all the stuff in your scene to be visible and you are okay with some black areas appearing on the screen.

Fill

`Fill` scale mode will just scale the scene to fit the view. `Fill` will not choose a smaller or larger side; it just scales it. That's just the way `Fill` works. This is good when your scene can be any old aspect ratio. Things may look funky, but you are guaranteed it will fill the entire screen.

Lastly, let's talk about `ResizeFill`.

ResizeFill

Lastly, let's talk about `ResizeFill`. `ResizeFill` is the odd one out. Whereas all the other scale modes will scale the scene, `ResizeFill` does not scale the scene; it resizes the scene to be the same size as its containing view.

The Game

The first step in making your game is to delete all the sample code so you can make your own game.

In your `GameScene.swift` you can remove all the sample code, and your `GameScene.swift` should look like this following the extraction:

```swift
class GameScene: SKScene {
    override func didMoveToView(view: SKView) {
    }

    override func touchesBegan(touches: Set<UITouch>, withEvent event: UIEvent?) {
        /* Called when a touch begins */

        for touch in touches {
            let location = touch.locationInNode(self)
        }
    }

    override func update(currentTime: CFTimeInterval) {
        /* Called before each frame is rendered */
    }
}
```

The end result is that your game scene is ready to have someone tap the screen with as many fingers as they want, and the `touchesBegan` will get run.

The `update` method will run at the *x* number of frames-per-second rate. You will get the `currentTime`, which works similarly to a Unix timestamp. You can know how long something has been running by comparing it to another `currentTime` time that has passed.

The Game Manager

Here is where we start organizing our game into nice little chunks of code to keep things simple and understandable. If we were to write everything in one giant file (the `GameScene.swift`), it would quickly get hard to manage. Also, if we created a character in that one file and we wanted to replicate it multiple times and even change it one of the many times, it would be difficult because we would have to duplicate a lot of code.

To fix this problem of all the code in one file, we will separate our code into multiple files. Our method consists of creating so-called "Managers" and individual object classes. If you are going to have a game in which you have heroes and enemies and many balloons floating around, then you want to create a Hero class, an Enemy class, a Balloon class, and a balloon manager class. This way you can manage your balloons in their own array in their own class. You can rapidly create many balloons by replicating the balloon class. You can even go further and create a enemy manager class. You'll also want to use the delegate design pattern to tell other classes when something is happening in your classes. For example, if the enemies are moving around based on the number of balloons, you'll want to let the enemies manager know when a balloon has been popped.

Before we build anything else we need to figure out how to build our assets.

The Point System

The point system that Apple uses for drawing things and measuring things is a really good idea. The problem they are solving has to do with the screen resolutions. There is this notion of 1x, 2x, and 3x resolutions, which means in the most basic terms that some resolutions pack in more pixels than the other ones did before. This makes for a fantastic-looking display but for some massive confusion when you are making assets and moving things around the screen.

This is where the point system comes in. You can think of a point as 1 pixel in 1x, 2 pixels in 2x, and 3 pixels in 3x. So the idea is that the iPhone 6s Plus is 414×736 points for the screen size but it renders 3x the amount of pixels to the screen, which makes the rendered pixels 1242×2208. The iPhone 6 Plus screen can't handle that many pixels so it has to be down-sampled before it appears on the screen. It will be down-sampled to 1080×1920. All the math to do that is none of your concern, and that is why we have points. You simply provide Apple with an image 1x, 2x, and 3x, and it will take care of the rest of the calculations.

For example, let's say we have a 1x image that is 20×20 pixels. For the 2x image we will make that image 40×40 (20*2) pixels. For the 3x image it will be 60×60 (20*3) pixels. This means we can provide much more detail in the 60×60 image than we can in the 20×20 image. The way I design the assets is to start with the 3x and work my way down to the 1x.

In Figure 5.7 the 1x start is originally 60×60 pixels. The 2x is 120×120 and the 3x is 180×180. Xcode will automatically figure out which resolution is which if you name them with @2x and @3x, respectively. The names of these icons would be star.png, star@2x.png, and star@3x.png, respectively.

Figure 5.7   A 1x, 2x, and 3x star

The question then becomes how does one make a background image, assuming this is for a title screen on which the background does not move and we just want one image that fits the background of the screen. Well, that all depends on the scale mode. If your scale mode changes the size of your scene (which only one scale mode, ResizeFill, does), you need to know the final size of your scene, which would be the size of the view in the case of ResizeFill. If your scale mode does not change the size of your screen, you can just go with the size of your scene and assume that it is 1x.

Remove the line that changes the size of your view programmatically in `GameViewController.swift`:

```
scene.size = CGSize(width: 1024, height: 766) // remove this line
```

In your `GameScene.sks` file change the size of the scene back to 1024×768 (see Figure 5.8).

Figure 5.8   Set the size of the scene to 1024×768

Let's also set up this project to be a landscape mode game instead of the default portrait mode game. In your file explorer choose the main blue project icon (see Figure 5.9).

Figure 5.9   Choose the main project icon

Make sure the General tab is selected.

Under Device Orientation select only Landscape Left (unselect all the other options).

Now the scene size will fit the screen size better since our screen size will be wider than it is tall. The content should fit better.

If we want a background picture to fill the scene, we need to make our background image 1024x768 points. That means that it will be 1024x768 at 1x, 2048x1536 at 2x, and 3072x2304 at 3x. That's a very large image. Sounds great—let's make one.

You can get a link to all three images here: http://imgur.com/a/7IRwU.

Figure 5.10 shows our beautiful sample background image.

Figure 5.10   Our background image

With this image we will be able to see what is going on with the scale mode. We have four hearts, one in each corner, and we will know based on the placement of these images whether the entire image shows. Which scale mode would be the best if we want to keep the aspect ratio of our image and we want to make sure the whole thing shows? `AspectFit` guarantees us that our scene will fit and not be cropped, but it might be letterboxed. `Fill` also guarantees this, but it will not keep the aspect ratio. Let's try `AspectFit` first and see what happens. In the project file explorer open up `Assets.xcassets` and remove the spaceship image set by selecting it and pressing Delete on your keyboard. Select all three images and drag them into the library. Your asset library should now look something like what's shown in Figure 5.11.

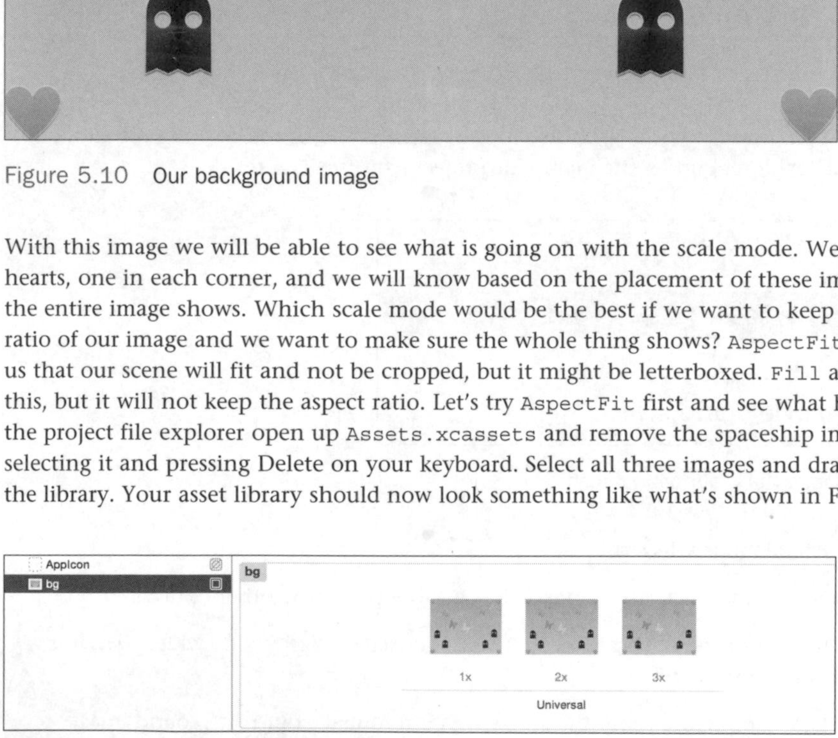

Figure 5.11   Asset library with three images

Because we named the files `bg`, `bg@2x`, and `bg@3x`, Xcode knows what each file is. Of course, you can drag in files manually, but this works in one fell swoop.

Adding the Background

At this point we can add the background to our `GameScene` and see what happens. Go into your `GameScene.swift` and change your `didMoveToView` to be as follows:

```
override func didMoveToView(view: SKView) {
    let xy = 0.5;
    anchorPoint = CGPoint(x: xy, y: xy)
    let background = SKSpriteNode(imageNamed: "bg")
    addChild(background)
}
```

Here we are adding our background to the screen. We use the `imageNamed` initializer to pull straight from the asset library. In the asset library our image is named `bg`. We also have to do one quick thing by changing the anchor point to 0.5 for x and y. The reason we do this is so that when we add the background to the screen we won't need to apply any positioning for it. By setting the coordinate 0,0, we will be in the middle of the screen. We can talk more about that later. Most important, we add the background to the screen with `addChild`.

With the scale mode set to `AspectFit`, we get get something that looks like the image shown in Figure 5.12.

Figure 5.12   Scale mode set to `AspectFit`

There is the letterboxing we were talking about. The good thing is that all the scene fits in the view. The bad thing is that we get some blank black area around the sides.

With the scale mode set to `AspectFill`, we get an image that looks as shown in Figure 5.13.

Figure 5.13   Scale mode set to `AspectFill`

Notice that the image fills the whole screen, but unfortunately we are missing our place-marker hearts, which got cropped just as expected.

With the scale mode set to `Fill`, we get an image as shown in Figure 5.14.

Figure 5.14   Scale mode set to `Fill`

The good thing here is that the whole image fits and nothing is getting cropped. The bad thing is that the image is stretch and skewed. You may not mind that if your background is something more abstract or nondescript.

If we want to change the background to be ResizeFill, we will need to make the background image the same size as the view. The view will change size depending on which phone is being used. That gets a little trickier because to accommodate the various phones, we would need to make a background image for each phone in multiple sizes and then detect each phone size.

Anchor Points

Lastly, let's talk about anchor points because I've been anchoring to talk about it all day.

With the anchor point we can set where the 0,0 point will be on the screen. With our background image we want to make sure that it is in the center of the screen. There are a couple of ways to accomplish this. The easiest way is to set 0,0 as the center of the screen. When you add the background to the screen, it will be in the center. Which way do x and y go? Which way is positive and which way is negative? In your GameScene in the didMoveToView, you can move the position of the background by 10 points for x and y and see where the background goes, and that will tell you which way x and y go.

Change your didMoveToView to add 10 to your x and y positions and run the game.

```
override func didMoveToView(view: SKView) {
    let xy = 0.5;
    anchorPoint = CGPoint(x: xy, y: xy)
    let background = SKSpriteNode(imageNamed: "bg")
    background.position.x += 10
    background.position.y += 10
    addChild(background)
}
```

When we run this, we see see something that looks like what's shown in Figure 5.15.

Figure 5.15   Image with x and y positions added

Notice the little gray on the left and bottom sides. That means that x is positive to the right and y is positive going up.

Summary

In this chapter we introduced all the most important starting concepts about SpriteKit. SpriteKit is easy to get started with but tricky to master, especially when it comes to aspects, points, pixels, and anything having to do with positioning. If you don't read all the documentation, you can get yourself in a pickle quickly because SpriteKit does things a little differently than other game frameworks. When you read though this chapter, hopefully you will have greater understanding of how to set up your game for success.

6

Reusable Code: Closures

Closures in Swift have their own special syntax. When relating closures to Objective-C, you can think of closures as self-contained blocks of functionality. When you use them, you often directly replace an Objective-C block. You use them for things like creating a callback after a URL has been fetched from a server or calling a function when an animation is done. You use them for things like sorting when you need to pass a special sort function.

What Are Closures?

Closures are a familiar concept in many languages. Closures can be created when an environment is enclosed in a referencing unit of scope. We often say "a function within another function" when we're talking about closures. But the real closure itself happens *because* you put a function within another function. When you put that function within the other function, the inner function has a reference to the outer function.

In languages other than Swift, closures are not often defined as a special syntactic structure. This is usually what makes them a difficult concept to grasp. For example, in JavaScript, you can create a closure by just putting one function inside another. The inner function will have access to all the local variables of the outer function. If the outer function returns the inner function, you now have a permanent reference to the inner function, which still has access to the outer function's local variables. This works in Swift as well.

In short, closures are functions that refer to independent variables. Functions defined in a closure remember the environment in which they were created—even after everything has run. This is interesting because local variables are usually trashed after a function has run.

Things get really interesting when you realize that operators in Swift are implemented as functions themselves. Take, for example, the less-than sign (<). It takes two parameters: a left-hand parameter and a right-hand parameter. So you see, closures can be written in extremely simple and concise ways.

Closures in Other Languages

It may be helpful to see closures in a broader context. A closure itself is relatively the same in all languages. However, Swift provides extra-special syntax for closures, which makes their implementation a bit different. In JavaScript you can create a closure by writing a function within another function. That inner function does not exist outside the outer function and therefore is "enclosed" (thus the name *closure*) in the outer function. The outer function can then return the inner function and make it available to all. Now the outer function has finished running, and all of its local variables should be dumped. But they aren't because the inner function is now available globally and still has references to the outer function's local variables. Let's look at some code to see how this works. This is code written in JavaScript, not Swift:

```
function nameClosure() {
    var name = "Skip Tastic"
    function sayYourName() {
        console.log(name);
    }
    return sayYourName;
}
var yourName = nameClosure()
yourName()
```

When `nameClosure` is called, it returns `sayYourName` and therefore is the inner function itself. Now you have a reference to the inner function `sayYourName`. The inner function has a reference to the local variable name even though `init` has been called and passed. So when you call the variable you set as `yourName`, you get the console to log the local variable. This is actually similar to summoning the dead. Try this example:

1. Open Google Chrome.

2. On any tab, right-click the screen and click Inspect Element.

3. When the developer tools open, choose the Console tab, which is like a dumbed-down JavaScript playground.

4. Type in the preceding JavaScript code.

You could write this same example in Swift. Here's how:

```
func nameClosure() -> () -> () {
    var name = "Skip Tastic"
    func sayYourName() {
        print(name)
    }
    return sayYourName
}
var yourName = nameClosure()
yourName()
```

You can see that this code is almost exactly the same as the JavaScript code. One change is that you replace `function` with `func`. In Swift, you have to be a little more specific if you are going to return a function. You need to tell Swift that this function returns its own function. Because functions on their own have types, you need to return a function that returns `Void`. The way you express a function that returns nothing or `Void` is to say that the function returns an empty tuple, which is essentially void. So the type of return value of `nameClosure` is `()->()`. This is because `sayYourName` does not return anything.

In the end, you will see that the Swift code prints out the result of the local variable, as promised. This is good because after you understand closures, you can apply them to any language. Swift happens to be a great place to learn closures, and the excitement doesn't stop with what you've seen so far. In fact, it goes so much further that I think your mind will be blown by the end of the chapter.

How Closures Work and Why They're Awesome

Swift defines a closure syntax that is different from the regular function syntax. This syntax allows you to do a couple things: It allows you to infer the type of the object from the context, and it allows you to return a value without actually writing `return`. There are several ways to write closures in Swift, and some of them take very little code. If you are used to replacing or rewriting Objective-C syntax, you may have seen blocks as the last parameter of a function. Swift allows you to write closures outside functions when they are the last parameters. This gives you a nice, clean-looking syntax.

Let's take a look at the `sort` function in Swift. For this example, you are going to pass two parameters to the `sort` function. The first is an `inout` parameter of the array you would like to sort. The second parameter is the function you would like to use to sort the array. The function must take two `Strings` as parameters and return a `Bool`. You will check whether each string is less than the other string in order to sort the string alphabetically. (When you compare two strings with a less-than or greater-than operator, Swift sorts strings alphabetically in either a reverse or a forward direction.) The following code sorts the array alphabetically:

```
var names = ["john","sam","zed","bob","harry","noa"]
func alphabetical(s1:String,s2:String) -> Bool {
    return s1 < s2
}
names.sort(alphabetical)
```

The `sort` function takes each of the strings in the array, one at a time, and compares them to each other by running them through the function. Notice that there is a global function to do the sorting. You pass this function into `sort`. We talked previously about the type of a function. In this case, the function is of type `(s1: String, s2: String) -> Bool`. You can find this out by three-finger-clicking the function name. If you three-finger-click the `sort` function, you see what it needs in order to work: `func sort<T>(inout array: [T], predicate: (T, T) -> Bool)`. This syntax may look a little foreign at this point because we haven't covered anything like it. This is the syntax for generics, which you'll learn about in Chapter 9, "Becoming Flexible: Generics." You can think of the T as standing for anything you want. It could be a `String`, an `Int`, a car, a cat, or whatever. So the `sort` function takes an `inout` array with any type in it. It also takes a function/closure that has two parameters of the same type and then returns a `Bool`. Note that T is different from `AnyObject`. Whereas `AnyObject` can be a `String` or an `Int`, T must be of one type. Using T is like saying you don't know the type yet but we will choose it later. Using `AnyObject` allows you to have a mix of a bunch of types.

The Closure Syntax

You can rewrite that last alphabetical function to be an inline closure. It would look like this:

```
var alphabetical = {(s1:String, s2:String) -> Bool in s1 < s2}
```

You remove the `func` keyword and the name of the function. You put the whole thing in some curly brackets, put the actual content after the word `in`, and remove the keyword `return`. The closure knows that it should return stuff. The closure by itself doesn't do much. You need to either save it to a variable or pass it directly into the `sort` function. Notice how it still matches the signature of the previous function you used. It takes two `Strings` and returns a `Boolean`. Now you can pass this into the `sort` function:

```
sort(&names,{(s1:String, s2:String) -> Bool in s1 < s2})
```

What is so cool about this is that you can define a whole reusable functionality within the `sort` function itself. The `sort` function does not have to go anywhere else to get the closure it will use to sort the array.

Inferring Using Context

The `sort` function must take an array and a function with a specific signature. In the example we've been working with, the function must take two parameters that are `Strings`. You cannot use any other types in this case. You and I know this, and Swift does, too. You can shorten the closure syntax because you know that s1 and s2 are `Strings`. You can also shorten the closure because you know that the return type must be a `Bool`. Who the heck needs to write a return type when you already know it must be a `Bool`? Here is a shorter closure you can pass to the `sort` function:

```
names = names.sort({s1, s2 in s1 < s2})
```

Now you have a much shorter, easier closure. Let's review what has happened so far: You first took a regular old function and passed it to the `sort`. Then you rewrote the function as a closure and passed it to the `sort`. Then you realized you didn't need to do any typing because Swift can infer types from the context. So you rewrote the closure by removing the types and parentheses. Notice that you never had to write the `return` keyword because it is also inferred.

Arguments Have a Shorthand, Too

As it turns out, you don't even have to declare s1 and s2 as the parameters. You can use a special syntax to get the *n*th parameter. You can write $0 to get the first parameter and $1 to get the second parameter and so on. Now the closure gets even shorter because you no longer need to declare the names of parameters. You can pass the closure to sort like so:

```
names = names.sort({$0 < $1})
```

You are able to write this because of all the things mentioned before plus the fact that you don't have to declare parameters if you use a special argument shorthand. Why declare something that does not need to be declared? You don't need the return keyword, and you don't need to declare a type for the parameters because it is inferred. This closure does return a Bool because it is comparing two things together. This is an extremely flexible closure because it does not declare any types. If your array contained Ints, Doubles, Floats, or your own custom type, then this closure would still work just fine.

Sorting a Custom Car Class

To sort a custom class, you need the class to inherit two protocols: Comparable and Equatable. Here's how you could define a short Car class that just has a name property:

```
class Car:Comparable,Equatable {
    var name:String

    init(name:String) {
        self.name = name
    }
}
```

To implement Comparable and Equatable, you must teach Swift how to compare two cars. Because the name of the car is a String, you can use the name. You need to write global functions that define the <, >, <=, >=, and == signs. One caveat is that you should not write these functions within the Car class; rather, you should write them globally. Here's an example of how to do that:

```
func ==(lhs: Car, rhs: Car) -> Bool{
    return lhs.name == rhs.name
}
func <=(lhs: Car, rhs: Car) -> Bool{
    return lhs.name <= rhs.name
}
func >=(lhs: Car, rhs: Car) -> Bool{
    return lhs.name >= rhs.name
}
func >(lhs: Car, rhs: Car) -> Bool{
    return lhs.name > rhs.name
}
```

```
func <(lhs: Car, rhs: Car) -> Bool {
    return lhs.name < rhs.name
}
```

Here you are naming the functions with the signs they represent. Notice that you could redefine these functions for comparison of other classes.

Finally, you can create a cars array and sort it, like this:

```
var cars = [Car(name:"Ford"),Car(name:"Mercedes")]
cars.sort({$0 < $1})
print(cars)
```

Here you create two cars in an array of cars. Then you sort the array, which uses the comparison functions to compare the two cars. If you ever needed to compare other types of classes, you could rewrite the > and < functions to accommodate those other types. Remember that you can have two functions with the same name as long as the method is different in some way. That is what makes it legit to make multiple less-than functions. Also note that you could create the comparison functions on a protocol or base class. This would give you the option of comparing multiple classes with the same comparison. It's a win–win for everybody. Here is our shortest closure yet:

```
names = names.sort(<)
```

Okay, now this is impressive. I would say that this is the ultimate in refactoring.

Closures Are Reference Types

Chapter 4, "Structuring Code: Enums, Structs, and Classes," talks about reference types and value types. It talks about the difference between things being copied and things being referenced when they are passed around. If you think about it, it makes a lot of sense for closures to be reference types rather than value types. Closures capture values in their context. If a closure was copied every time it was passed around, it would lose context that it has access to. In other words, it would lose access to those local variables. Here's an example:

```
func increment(n:Int)-> ()->Int {
    var i = 0
    let incrementByN = {
        () -> Int in
        i += n
        return i
    }
    return incrementByN
}
var inner = increment(4)
inner() //4
inner() //8
inner() //12
```

This example changes things up a little bit. In the end, you use the inner closure that holds a reference to i, incrementByN, to increment that local variable i by 4. The main point is that the inner closure has a reference to that local variable after the function has returned, and the closure you use is passed by reference, which makes the number increment each time.

Automatic Reference Counting

Now is a good time to talk about Automatic Reference Counting, otherwise known as ARC. If you are an Objective-C programmer, you know all about ARC. If you were one of the first iPhone programmers, you know that you used to have to do your own reference counting. You will be happy to know that for the most part, you can let Swift worry about the management of memory.

When you create instances of classes, those classes exist by reference. When those instances are no longer needed, Swift cleans them up for you.

ARC works by keeping track of the instances of classes that you create and where those instances are referenced. Every time you create a new instance of a class, ARC finds some free memory available where you can place the new instance. You don't need to worry about how this works; just know that it works. (Of course, those details are available if you feel like diving in; go to https://developer.apple.com/library/ios/documentation/swift/conceptual/ swift_programming_language/AutomaticReferenceCounting.html.) When you no longer need that instance of the class, ARC takes back that memory it gave you and deallocates your instance. If Swift was not smart and accidentally deallocated an instance you were still using, then you would no longer be able to access your class and all its properties.

To tell Swift "I'm using this; don't deallocate it," you assign that class reference to a variable or constant. When you do this, you are creating a strong reference. Swift won't deallocate that memory associated with your class instance because you said you needed it. Imagine Rose in *Titanic,* saying she would "never let go." Well that's a bad example because eventually Rose did let go. But it's actually a good example because Rose only let go when she was sure Jack was dead and gone. Swift will not allow it to be deallocated as long as the strong reference remains. You can deallocate that instance by assigning it to nil. Take a look at this example, using the Car class from earlier:

```
var c1:Car? = Car(name: "Ford")
```

Here you create a new instance of the Car class. ARC allocates some memory for a new instance of Car. You have one instance of the Car class allocated; let's reference c1 a couple more times:

```
var c2 = c1
var c3 = c2
```

Now you have three references to the one instance of the Car class. But these are not just any references; they are three strong references. For Swift to deallocate the single instance of Car, you need to assign all three of these references to nil. If you were to assign two out of three to nil, the instance would remain in memory because it would be still in use. You can assign `c1` and `c2` to `nil`:

```
c1 = nil
c2 = nil
```

You now have one reference of the `Car` class still out there. ARC is counting this instance of the `Car` class, so it remains allocated in memory. You can assign `c3` to `nil` to completely remove all references to the instance of the car:

```
c3 = nil
```

Now the single instance of `Car` is deallocated because all three references have been unreferenced by being set to `nil`. By the way, if you create an optional property, that property is initialized with `nil` and not any instance of a class. You can rewrite the `Car` class a tad and add a new class for a driver as well:

```
class Driver {
    var car:Car?
}
class Car {
    var name:String
    var driver:Driver?
    init(name:String) {
        self.name = name
    }
}
```

When you create a new `Car` instance, `driver` is created and set to `nil`.

Strong Reference Cycles

By letting ARC do its thing, you can pretty much sit back and relax because ARC allocates and deallocates memory when it is needed. However, there are situations in which you've created a permanent bond between two classes. Consider the new `Car` and `Driver` classes. Notice that when you create a new `Driver` and new `Car`, your driver's car will be `nil` and your car's driver will be `nil`. You can see what I mean when I create a new car and driver:

```
var car = Car(name: "Ford")
var driver = Driver()
```

Now you have a new `car` and new `driver` that ARC has reference counted. `driver` has a car that is `nil`, and `car` has a driver that is `nil`. Now you can assign `car`'s driver to car and driver's car to car:

```
car.driver = driver
driver.car = car
```

You have now created a permanent strong reference between those two instances that can never be resolved. If you set `car` to `nil` and `driver` to `nil`, neither will ever be deallocated.

The way you can tell is by using the special `deinit` function. This function is called when the class is deinitialized. You can add it to both the `Car` and the `Driver` classes. To see `deinit` in action, you must run your code in a project instead of in the playground. You can start a new game project and create your `Car` and `Driver` classes directly in `ViewController.swift`. Then in `viewDidLoad`, you can initialize and deinitialize your `car` and `driver` classes:

```swift
class Car {
    var driver:Driver?
    init() {
        print("INITTING Car")
    }
    deinit {
        print("DEINITTING Car")
    }
}
class Driver {
    var car:Car?
    init() {
        print("INITTING Driver")
    }
    deinit {
        print("DEINITTING Driver")
    }
}
```

Now in your `didLoadView` function, you can test `init` and `deinit` by creating an optional `car` and then setting it to `nil`. When you create the `car`, the `init` method runs. Then setting the `car` to `nil` calls the `deinit` method. You must set the car to be optional so that you can later send it to `nil`:

```swift
override func viewDidLoad() {
    super.viewDidLoad()
    var car:Car? = Car()
    car = nil
}
```

Now when you run this, you see that the `car` was first initialized and then deinitialized. Now let's get back to the strong reference cycle. If you create a new `driver` and the new `car` and assign the `car`'s `driver` to the new `driver` and vice versa, and if you then try to set the `car` and the `driver` to `nil`, you see that neither gets deinitialized:

```swift
override func viewDidLoad() {
    super.viewDidLoad()
    var car:Car? = Car()
    var driver:Driver? = Driver()
    car!.driver = driver
    driver!.car = car
    car = nil
    driver = nil
}
```

You have created a strong reference cycle and a memory leak. In this case, car and driver will never be deallocated.

unowned Versus weak

Swift provides a solution for strong reference cycles by allowing you to use the keyword weak or the keyword unowned. You use the keyword weak when it is possible for your reference to have no value at some point. If this isn't the case, you use unowned.

The weak Keyword

A weak reference does not keep a stronghold to the instance that it refers to. When you assign a reference as weak, you are saying that it may at some point have "no value." Therefore, you must assign a weak reference as an optional. It is possible that a weak reference may be deallocated before you are done with it. ARC automatically sets weak references to nil when they are deallocated. You can then easily check this with an if statement.

To see how this works, you can rewrite the car and driver example and set one of the variables to weak. You don't need to set both to weak, just one, because when there are no more strong references to the car or driver, it will be deallocated. The only change you really need to make is in either the car or the driver class. You just need to mark the variable as weak in one of the classes. For now, do this in the driver class. Edit your driver class to look like this (and notice I am adding only one word here).

Run the code, and you'll see that car and driver both get initialized and deinitialized:

```
//INITTING Car
//INITTING Driver
//DEINITTING Car
//DEINITTING Driver
```

The unowned Keyword

Instead of using weak, you can use unowned. The big difference between unowned and weak is that unowned is assumed to always have a value. Therefore, it does not need to be an optional. You have to be super-duper careful when using unowned because whereas weak sets your variable to nil after it has been deallocated, unowned does not. If you try to reference an unowned variable after it has been deallocated, your program will reliably crash. Therefore, you want to use unowned only when you are absolutely positive it will always have a value. Here's how you can rewrite the driver class to use unowned instead of weak:

```
class Driver {
    unowned var car:Car
    init(car:Car) {
        self.car = car
        print("INITTING Driver")
    }
    deinit {
        print("DEINITTING Driver")
    }
}
```

You must now add an initializer for `driver` because `car` is no longer an optional. You also have to change `viewDidLoad` because you are no longer dealing with an optional car. Update your code like so:

```
override func viewDidLoad() {
    super.viewDidLoad()
    var car:Car? = Car()
    var driver = Driver(car: car!)
    car!.driver = driver
    driver.car = car!
    car = nil
}
```

When you run this code, notice that you get the same result. `car` and `driver` are both deinitialized properly. Why does this work now, when it didn't work before? Well, remember that when you have a strong reference, ARC cannot deallocate the instance. When you have a strong reference cycle (when we don't use `weak` or `unowned`), it goes in both directions. `car` strongly·references `driver`, and `driver` strongly references `car` (see Figure 6.1). When you mark one of the references as weak, you get rid of that strong reference that was going bidirectionally. The same goes for unowned: Swift is no longer able to have a bidirectional strong reference.

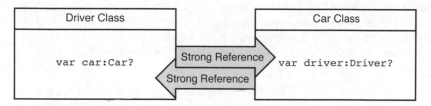

Figure 6.1   Strong references in both directions

When you mark the `driver` of the `car` class as `weak` or you no longer have a strong reference, ARC can deallocate that instance (see Figure 6.2).

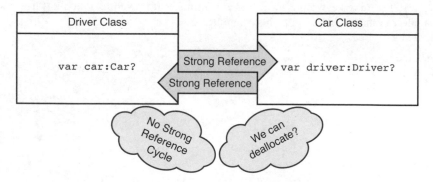

Figure 6.2   No longer fused at the hip. ARC can deallocate

The same goes for unowned: When you mark the driver of the car class as unowned, you no longer have a strong reference, and ARC can deallocate that instance (see Figure 6.3).

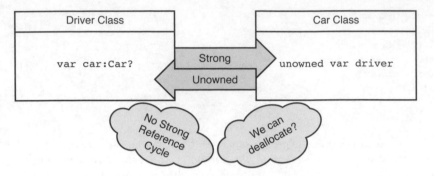

Figure 6.3   Once again not fused at the hip. ARC can deallocate

Thus sayeth the ARC.

Strong Reference Cycles in Closures

An important point in this chapter about closures is that you can create strong reference cycles in closures. This is the bottom line: If you have a closure as a property of a class, and that closure references self, then you have a strong reference cycle. The closure can reference any property of the class. Remember that closures are referenced types, so a reference will be created.

You need to run the next example in a project. So either reopen your last project or open a new project in Xcode. I am using a SpriteKit game setup for this project. In the view controller, you alter the car class from before. You also use a new keyword, lazy, so that you can use self within the closure. Lazy properties do not get evaluated until they are used. Therefore, by marking this closure as lazy, you know that self will exist, and we can use it. You will often use lazy when there are values that you want to use that will not be available until after initialization. You can only use values in properties that are available before initialization unless you use lazy. The lazy keyword is evaluated at runtime, if it is even used at all. If it is never used, it is never evaluated. Check out this example:

```
class Car {
    var make:String
    var model:String
    var year:Int

    init(make:String,model:String,year:Int) {
        self.make = make
        self.model = model
        self.year = year
```

```
        print("INITTING Car")
    }

    lazy var fullName:() -> String = {
        return "\(self.year) \(self.make) \(self.model)"
    }

    deinit {
        print("DEINITTING Car")
    }
}
```

Here you have created a closure with a strong reference cycle. You can now initialize this class and attempt to deinitialize it, which will be unsuccessful because of the strong reference cycle. Because you are using SpriteKit, you can do this in the `viewDidLoad` function:

```
override func viewDidLoad() {
    super.viewDidLoad()
    var car:Car? = Car(make: "Ford", model: "Taurus", year: 1997)
    print(car!.fullName())
    car = nil
}
```

Run this code by pressing Command-R or by selecting Product, Run. You should see that everything works except the `car` is never deinitialized.

To prevent strong reference cycles for closures, you define a *capture list* when writing your closure. You create these in the same way that you create weak and unowned references for other variables. Creating a capture list allows you to capture different class instances and make sure they are no longer strongly referenced. You can mark `self` or any other class property as `weak` or `unowned` to allow ARC to deallocate instances when necessary.

To fix the `car` class so that you no longer have a strong reference cycle, you only need to add one line of code, shown in bold in the following:

```
class Car {
    var make:String
    var model:String
    var year:Int

    init(make:String,model:String,year:Int) {
        self.make = make
        self.model = model
        self.year = year
        print("INITTING Car")
    }

    lazy var fullName:() -> String = {
        [unowned self] in
```

```
        return "\(self.year) \(self.make) \(self.model)"
    }

    deinit {
        print("DEINITTING Car")
    }
}
```

Now if you run this code, you will notice that the `car` class is properly deinitialized. You can add multiple properties to the capture list; just separate them using commas.

Trailing Closures

When you write a closure as a parameter of a function, the closure is often the last parameter. You see this often in Objective-C as well as with blocks. In Objective-C, you write something like this when animating:

```
[UIView animateWithDuration:1.50 delay:0
options:(UIViewAnimationOptionCurveEaseOut|
UIViewAnimationOptionBeginFromCurrentState)
animations:^{
    //do animations here.
}];
```

Notice that this function takes two blocks, and you have one block at the end. You could write the last block as a trailing closure. This means you could write the closure outside the function's closing parentheses. You could rewrite the last function in Swift like so:

```
UIView.animateWithDuration(1.50) {
    // do animations here.
}
```

Here you take advantage of the capability to write closures outside functions. Without using the trailing closure, the preceding call would look like this:

```
UIView.animateWithDuration(1.50, animations: {
    // do animations here.
})
```

You don't have to write `animations:` explicitly with the trailing version because Swift automatically knows that `animations` is the last parameter and it is a closure. This makes your code cleaner because you don't have to keep track of the closing parentheses, and it also means less writing for you. Furthermore, in certain situations, you can even do away with the parentheses. If the closure is the function's only argument, you need not include the parentheses at all. For example, say that you have a function like this that takes only one argument:

```
func gimmeAClosure(yumClosures:()->()) {
  //some good stuff goes here
}
```

Then when you call this function, you don't need to include the parentheses at all:

```
gimmeAClosure {
    //some closure stuff
}
```

> **Note**
>
> This is superconvenient but it could have been potentially confusing if you had never read that you can call functions and pass in closures without parentheses. If you had run into this syntax while examining someone's code, you might have found yourself a tad confused.

Summary

In this chapter you have learned how closures work—how they "enclose" values in their context. You have learned that Swift provides specific closure syntax for writing them. Closures in the wild can be confusing if you aren't used to all the syntactic possibilities. In this chapter you have learned pretty much everything you might wind up running into.

Often when learning a new language, you find yourself trying to relate bits and pieces to other languages you already know. When converting Objective-C to Swift (which you're sure to do often), you'll notice that you can directly replace blocks with closures. When replacing them, you often have multiple syntax choices that can make your writing even shorter.

7

Creating Your Own Syntax: Subscripts and Advanced Operators

Swift is such a powerful language that it allows you to create your own new full-fledged language. You will hear people talk about writing functional Swift and writing jQuery-like Swift. It is great to have such flexibility. With Swift you can take an existing syntax and apply it to other things. For example, subscripts allow you to provide functionality to the square-brackets notation. What you do with that square-brackets notation is up to you. You can provide subscripts for enumerations, structures, and classes. You can use subscripts to query a class to get some sort of information back.

You probably know subscripts from arrays and dictionaries. You use subscripts to access members of an array by using the square-brackets notation (for example, `myArray[5]` to get the sixth element of an array). You use the square-brackets notation in dictionaries as well to access values by their key. In both arrays and dictionaries, this implementation is written using subscripts. You can prove this by looking at the Swift source code. I'll show you how to do that in a second.

With advanced operators, you have the ability to program on the bit and byte levels. Swift gives you basic operators as well as advanced operators—operators like the bitwise AND operator, which combines the bits of two numbers.

I combined subscripts and advanced operators in one chapter because Swift allows you to write your own custom operators. This is obviously all a part of the master plan to describe your own custom language syntax. Often it's important to define your own custom operators in your custom classes, structs, and enums. Think of the custom `Car` class you have been using in other chapters. How would you add two cars together with the standard + operator? One thing is for sure: Swift doesn't know how to add two cars together for you. You have to tell Swift how to do this. And to do that, you need to define your own custom syntax for writing Swift.

Writing Your First Subscript

To create a subscript, you use the keyword `subscript` in your class, struct, or enum. A basic subscript looks like this:

```
class Hand {
    let fingers = ["thumb","index","middle","ring","pinky"]
    subscript(i:Int) -> String{
        return fingers[i]
    }
}
let hand = Hand()
print("I had to use my \(hand[2]) finger on the way into work today.")
```

Here you are creating a class called `Hand`, which has five fingers. You can access each finger by index. After you create a new instance of `hand`, you can access the thumb by using `hand[0]`. This directly accesses the `fingers` array. You can read and write to subscripts. You can mark them as read-only or read-write. Currently, the `hand`/`fingers` access is a read-only property. To make it writable, you have to tell Swift, like this:

```
class Hand {
    var fingers = ["thumb","index","middle","ring","pinky"]
    subscript(i:Int) -> String{
        get{
            return fingers[i]
        }
        set{
            fingers[i] = newValue
        }
    }
}
let hand = Hand()
//Not everyone calls it a pinky. Let's rename it to pinkie.
hand[4] = "pinkie"
print("I use my \(hand[4]) when I drink tea.")
```

You tell the subscript that you want it to be readable and writable by adding the `get` and `set` properties to it. You access the finger of the hand by using the getter. You have to explicitly write a getter for this subscript because you are adding a setter as well. If you are making a property read-only, you can leave out the getter because it is implied. Now with the setter, you are able to rename one of the fingers of the hand. You rename the pinky to `pinkie`. Now when you print the sentence, it says "I use my pinkie when I drink tea" instead of "I use my pinky when I drink tea." But you don't have to just use integers, and you don't have to return integers, either. You can use this subscript notation however you would like.

Let's take a look at the implementation of a Swift array and how it uses subscripts to access elements of the array. To do this, you can type the following into the playground:

```
let a:Array<String> = []
```

This declares an array using the more verbose syntax. You can now hold down the Command key on your keyboard and click the word `Array`. The actual implementation of the array is not included in the source code, but you can see a skeleton of how it was declared. You should see something like this:

```
subscript (subRange: Range<Int>) -> Slice<T>
```

This allows you to access elements of an array by using a range. You can see that the range must be made up of integers. This looks as though it's probably only a getter and does not include a setter as well.

You can use subscripts for many things. But you should think about their proper use. For example, you could use a subscript to mess around with a `String`:

```
class Candianizer{
    subscript(sentence:String) -> String {
        return sentence + " ay!"
    }
}
var candianizer = Candianizer()
candianizer["Today is a good day"] //Today is a good day ay!
```

In my opinion, this is not a good use of a subscript. Even though you can use subscripts this way, you generally use them to find elements of a collection, list, or sequence. But you can implement a subscript however you find most appropriate. In the preceding example you might be better off using a function for `candianizer`.

Dictionaries use subscripts to set and get values for particular instances. You can use subscripts to set a value, like so:

```
var beethovenByOpus = [67:"Symphony No. 5",
    53:"Waldstein",
    21:"Symphony No. 1 in C major"]
beethovenByOpus[67]
```

In this example, you create a dictionary to get some of Beethoven's works, by opus. Now you can access the works by using the subscript syntax. In this example, `beethovenByOpus[67]` prints `"Symphony No. 5"`.

Dictionaries are made up of key/value pairs. In this example, the key is `67` and the value is `"Symphony No. 5"`. Now the dictionary has the type `Int:String`. You could create a dictionary because you know exactly what you need, but you first need to learn about generics. After you get generics down, you can give it a whirl. For now, you should know that for dictionaries, a subscript is both a getter and a setter. You can make subscripts deal with any input types, and they can use any type for return values as well. However, you cannot use `inout` parameters, but you can use multiple parameters to grab any values you want.

Here is an example of creating a multidimensional array for a level of a game. In this example, you use the subscript syntax to grab a specific block from the game:

```
class Level {
    //[Array<Int>]
    var map = [[0,0,0,1,1],
               [1,1,1,0,0],
               [1,1,1,0,1]]
    subscript(row:Int,col:Int) -> Int {
        return map[row][col]
    }
}
var level1 = Level()
level1[0,4]
```

It is common to use multidimensional arrays to store game-level data. If you are making a tile-based game, maybe the 0s are walkable ground, and the 1s are nonwalkable walls. Say that you want an easy way to grab a specific tile. Normally, if you wanted to grab the first tile in the first row, you would use something like this:

```
level1.map[0][0]
```

This works well. But you can make the syntax even nicer by creating a subscript to grab the row and column right from the level:

```
level1[0,0]
```

Now you get back the tile straight from the level instead of having to access the map. The really great thing about this is that you could add in error checking to make sure the block exists before you try to access it. Also, this map should be read-only. You could add that at the subscript level, like this:

```
struct Level {
    //[Array<Int>]
    var map = [[0,0,0,1,1],
               [1,1,1,0,0],
               [1,1,1,0,1]]
    func rowIsValid(row:Int) -> Bool {
        return row < map.count
    }
    func colIsValid(row:Int,col:Int) -> Bool {
        return col < map[row].count
    }
    subscript(row:Int,col:Int) -> Int {
        get{
            assert(rowIsValid(row), "Row does not exist")
            assert(colIsValid(row,col: col), "Column does not exist")
            return map[row][col]
        }
    }
}
var level1 = Level()
```

Check out what happens here: It's supercool. You use Swift's `assert` method to check the validity of the game-level data you are trying to get. You have to send `assert` a `Bool` to say `true` (meaning yes, it is legit) or `false` (meaning no, it is not legit). You make `rowIsValid` and `colIsValid` functions to do that checking for you. The good thing about this is that if the user enters a row that is too high or a column that is too high, he will get an error message that is geared toward game-level data. Also, the user cannot set the game-level data directly but would have to go through the map, which you could set to be `private`.

That's all you need to know about subscripts for right now. It's all about the way that you want to implement them.

Next we will talk about advanced operators and why it is still important to know how to code on the bit level.

Bits and Bytes with Advanced Operators

Everything you do on computers boils down to bits and bytes, and it's important to be able to understand things on that level. Even though this seems like an old-school idea, it has many real-world and even future implications. For example, if you want to write code to connect to a Bluetooth low-energy device, such as a heart-rate monitor, then you need to look at the Bluetooth specifications for such devices (see https://developer.bluetooth.org/gatt/characteristics/Pages/CharacteristicViewer.aspx?u=org.bluetooth.characteristic.heart_rate_measurement.xml). Notice that to be able to get the heart rate out of the data from the Bluetooth device, you need to grab specific bytes and bits. This is a current technology and is growing with the presence of iBeacons.

This doesn't apply to just Bluetooth, either; another good example is file specifications. If you ever want to create a binary file specification or read a binary file, you need to know where different information is going to be in bytes of the file. Take the Photoshop file specification (see www.adobe.com/devnet-apps/photoshop/fileformatashtml/). Notice that it tells you exactly where to look in the file and how much data to grab. For example, the header info tells you that the length is 4 and the content should always equal 8BPS. This is an identifier for the file. If you read those first few bits of a Photoshop file, it should say 8BPS. This is similar to when you get a box of animal crackers that reads "Do not eat if seal is broken." (For me it's always the giraffe that's broken, maybe because of its tall stature and long neck.) Don't assume that it's a Photoshop file unless it has that signature at the beginning.

It's important to note that in Swift you can represent binary with a `0b` prefix, in the same way that you write hex with a `0x` prefix. Also, a great little trick for binary on a Mac is to open up the built-in calculator. When in the calculator, you can then choose View, Programmer to see binary representations of numbers. For example, in decimal, `0b00001111` is 15 (because 1 + 2 + 4 + 8 = 15; see Figure 7.1).

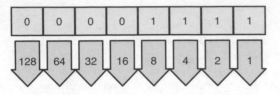

Figure 7.1   Each bit is represented by a square and can have a value of either 0 or 1

Notice that there are 8 bits here, and all 8 bits together represents 1 byte. For our purposes we are going to read the bits from right to left. Each bit (from right to left) is worth double what the last was worth. To find out what the whole thing is worth, you add the value listed below (values are listed in the arrow below each bit in Figure 7.1) only if the bit (the value in the square) is 1. If the value is 0 you do not add the value of the bit. After you have the value by calculating the 8 bits, you can perform different operations on them. Each of these operators is going to do something to the 8 bits of the byte. Some will shift the bytes and others will eliminate bytes. In the end you are left with 8 bits, which represent a byte, which can be translated into letters, numbers, or other stuff (it could be an individual pixel for a .png file). As we said before in the case of the Photoshop file, we could be looking for 8BPS to appear in the beginning of the file. Other file types have different signatures. The first advanced operator is bitwise NOT.

Bitwise NOT

You use the bitwise NOT operator when you want to invert all the bits. You write the bitwise NOT as a tilde (~). If you invert 0b00001111, you get 0b11110000, which is 240. You can try this out in the playground. You represent the 8 bits as 1 byte by using UInt8. The 8 in UInt8 stands for the number of bits. UInt8 represents 1 byte because it has 8 bits available to store things. This means you have values from 1 to 255 available to you with UInt8. This is the case because if you make all 8 bits set to 1, then 0b11111111 is equal to 255. If you use UInt16, then you have 16 bits available to you, and your max value is much larger, at 65,535. You can try this out in the calculator as we mentioned in the preceding section.

Let's get back to inverting bits, which you could do by first assigning your binary value to a variable and then inverting it. Using bitwise NOT takes everything that was a 1 and makes it a 0 and everything that was a 0 and makes it a 1 (see Figure 7.2).

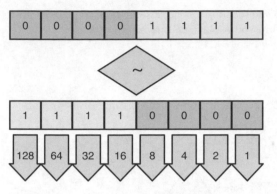

Figure 7.2   Inverting bits with bitwise not

Let's write some code that actually inverts some bits.

```
var b:UInt8 = 0b00001111 // 15
~b // 240
```

In this example we created the number 15 represented in bits. We assigned it to a variable that is of type UInt8 so we could store those 8 bits in the perfect container for it. You inverted it with the tilde (~) and you got back 240 because 0b00001111 inverted is 0b11110000 (128 + 64 + 32 + 16 = 240).

Bitwise AND

Bitwise AND is represented by a single ampersand: &. Whereas bitwise NOT inverts all the bits, bitwise AND changes the bits only if both bits are 1s. For example, say that you have something like what's shown in Figure 7.3.

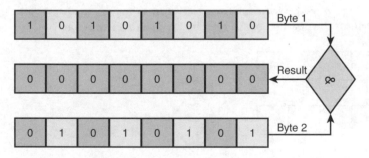

Figure 7.3   Performing a bitwise AND on two bytes

In this example, the result of the bitwise AND combination is 0 because there is no place where both bit 1 and bit 2 contain 1s in the same slot. You could code this example like so:

```
var a:UInt8 = 0b10101010 //170
var b:UInt8 = 0b01010101 //85
a&b //0
```

Figure 7.4 shows another example of a bitwise AND combination that has some *positive* results.

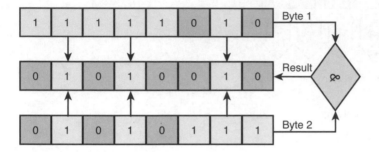

Figure 7.4   Another bitwise AND with more positive results

In this example, bits of the top byte (all the bits of the first byte) contain 1s where the bits of the bottom byte (bit 2) also do, so the result has some positive results—in spots 2, 4, and 7 from the left. In the playground, you could write this example like so:

```
var a:UInt8 = 0b11111010 //250
var b:UInt8 = 0b01010111 //87
a&b //82
```

Bitwise OR

Bitwise OR is written using a single pipe: |. Whereas bitwise AND returns the new number if both bits are set to 1, bitwise OR returns the new number if either bit is equal to 1 (see Figure 7.5).

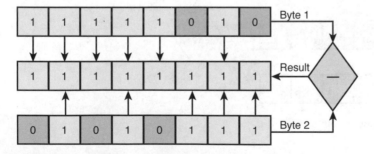

Figure 7.5   Performing a bitwise OR on two bytes with the result in the middle

When you use the bitwise OR operator, the result is all 1s (255). You can try this out with code like so:

```
var a:UInt8 = 0b11111010 //250
var b:UInt8 = 0b01010111 //87
a|b //255
```

Figure 7.6 shows another example in which both inputs are 0, so the resulting bit is 0 also.

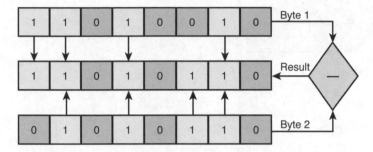

Figure 7.6   Another bitwise OR comparing two bytes

You could write this comparison as follows:

```
var a:UInt8 = 0b11010010 //210
var b:UInt8 = 0b01010110 //86
a|b //214
```

Bitwise XOR

Otherwise known as the exclusive OR operator, written as ^, bitwise XOR compares two inputs and returns 1 when the two inputs are different (see Figure 7.7).

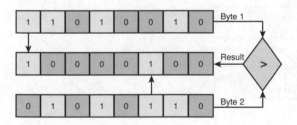

Figure 7.7   Performing a bitwise XOR on two bytes (one on top and one on bottom)

Notice in this example that only the comparisons in which input 1 and input 2 are different result in a 1. Matching 1s (1 and 1) returns 0, and matching 0s (0 and 0) returns 0.

Shifting Bits

You can take the 8 bits of a byte and shift them all to the left or to the right. You can do this using the bitwise left shift operator (<<) or the bitwise right shift operator (>>). Notice in Figure 7.8 how each shift is in its own box. You are essentially moving a bit to the next box over.

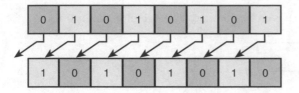

Figure 7.8   Shifting bits to the left

You could write this in code like so:

```
var a:UInt8 = 0b01010101 //85
a << 1 //170
```

Notice that this bitwise left shift had the effect of doubling the integer. Doing a bitwise right shift, on the other hand, halves the number:

```
var a:UInt8 = 0b01010101 //85
a >> 1 //42
```

Notice that because you are working with integers and not floating-point numbers, you end up with 42 and not 42.5. Also notice that if 1 was the leftmost bit, this does not necessarily multiply it by 2. This is because the first 1 winds up getting discarded when it moves off the left (see Figure 7.9). Here is an example of the 1 getting discarded:

```
var a:UInt8 = 0b11010101 //213
a << 1 //170
```

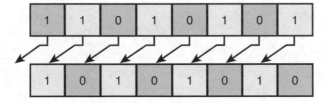

Figure 7.9   Shifting bits

Any bits that are moved outside the bits of the integer are thrown away. Also note that when a new space is created, as in Figure 7.9, a 0 is inserted. This method is known as *logical shifting*.

UInt8, UInt16, UInt32, Int8, Int16, Int32, and So On

There is a difference between signed and unsigned types. It has nothing to do with autographs. When you have a signed type, it can be positive or negative. The types that start with `Int` are signed and can be either negative or positive. How does Swift represent a negative value in 8 bits internally? The leftmost bit says whether the number is positive or negative. This is how it is represented internally. A 1 as the first bit means the `Int` is negative, and a 0 means positive. Any of the types that are `Int`s (`Int8`, `Int16`, `Int32`, and so on) use the first bit to say whether the number is negative or positive. If `Int8` has 8 bits available, it now has 7 to represent the number and 1 to represent the sign (see Figure 7.10). `UInt`s (unsigned integers) don't do this. For example, the max value of `UInt8` is 255, and the max value of `Int8` is 127. The leftmost bit was worth 128 so 255 − 128 and you are left with 127.

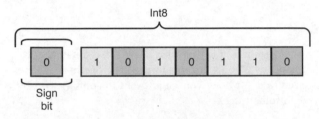

Figure 7.10   A signed byte: the `Int8`

In code, however, you can represent –4 in binary like so:

```
var a:Int8 = -0b100
```

Value Overflow and Underflow

If you try to fit too much into an `Int` that cannot handle it, you get an error. For example, the max for an `Int32` is 2,147,483,647. You don't have to do math to figure this out. You can figure it out like this:

```
Int32.max // 2,147,483,647
Int32.min // -2,147,483,647
Int16.max // 32,767
// etc....
var a:Int32 = 2_147_483_649 // ERROR: integer literal overflows
// when stored into 'Int32'
```

In this case, `Int32` is not big enough to hold the number you tried to assign it. It is a little too large (the max is 2,147,483,647 and you tried to use 2,147,483,649), and you get an error. It isn't always desirable or necessary to get an error. You can use value overflow and value underflow to fix this. When you reach the max value of an `Int`, and you add one more, value overflow causes the `Int` to circle back around to the minimum value. Let's watch that `Int` circle back around:

```
var a:Int32 = 2_147_483_647
a &+ 1 // -2,147,483,648
```

This would normally cause an error, but instead it loops around to the minimum value of the `Int`. The opposite happens when you use value underflow. If you are at the minimum of an `Int` and you subtract 1, in order to not get an error, you must use value underflow, like this:

```
var a:UInt8 = 0
a &- 1 // 255
```

This would normally throw an error, but instead it loops back around to the max value of a `UInt8`. We use that ampersand to say we want value underflow and value overflow.

Customizing Operators

Think about the custom `Car` class you've been working with in this book. It has a name, and you could easily add a price to it. What happens if you want to add two cars together? Swift does not know how to do this, so you need to tell it how. You might want to combine cars by name or by price, or you might want to do something else.

You can overload (that is, tell the operators to do something else) all the operators in Swift to do what you would expect for your custom types.

In the case of the custom `Car` class, you have to tell Swift how to add these two things together. Here is a full example of how you can define your own equality operator to see whether two "ingredients" are equal:

```
enum DrinkType:UInt8 {
    case Cognac = 1, Bitters, Gin, Dry_Vermouth, Absolut
}
struct Ingredient:Equatable {
    var quantity = 0.0
    var type:DrinkType = .Cognac
}
func == (a:Ingredient,b:Ingredient) -> Bool {
    if a.quantity == b.quantity {
        if a.type == b.type {
            return true
        }
    }
    return false
}

var someGin = Ingredient(quantity: 2.5, type: .Gin)
var someDryVermouth = Ingredient(quantity: 0.5,type: .Dry_Vermouth)
var someAbsolut = Ingredient(quantity: 2.5, type: .Absolut)
```

```
var dryMartini = [someGin,someDryVermouth]
var absolutGibson = [someAbsolut,someDryVermouth]
var availableDrinks = ["Dry Martini":dryMartini,"Absolute Gibson":absolutGibson]

class Drink {
    var contents = [Ingredient]()

    func serveIt() -> String {
        for (key,value) in availableDrinks {
            if contents == value {
                return "Serving \(key)"
            }
        }
        return "Drink not available."
    }
}
var drink = Drink()
drink.contents.append(someGin)
drink.contents.append(someDryVermouth)
drink.serveIt()
```

This is quite a significant example, but I want to make sure you get the gist of why you have to define your own operators. In this example, you define a bunch of ingredients for drinks in an enum. You create an `Ingredient` structure so that you can give a quantity and drink type. Now when you have those quantities and drink types together, you cannot compare them using `==`. Try it out. It will not work because you need to first say that the struct itself is `Equatable`. What this really means is that it can be used for comparison with a `==` operator. Without marking the struct as equatable (you should try this), you get an error when you try to compare two ingredients.

When the `Ingredient` is `Equatable`, you have to define how you are going to compare two ingredients. What you really want here is to make sure the quantity and type are the same. You make a global `==` function to define what happens when you compare two ingredients. You make it global because that's the way that Swift works. Don't worry: You can define as many of those `==` functions as you need, as long as you are comparing something other than ingredients. That will make the method signature different—and it will make it legit.

Now you can create a new drink by using the `Drink` class, and you can try to serve the drink. Swift is able to loop through the dictionary of available drinks and compare its current drink contents to see whether it matches a recipe for another type of drink. This example can compare only two ingredients because that is the functionality you wrote. You could also create other operators for this struct as well. Such operators are called *binary operators* because they take two parameters, one on each side of the operator (for example, a `==` b). You can also create *unary operators,* which operate on only one side (for example, `-a` or `a++`). When the operator is on the left, it is called a *prefix unary operator,* and on the right it is a *postfix unary operator.* You could define these for your `Ingredient` class to increase the quantity of the ingredient by 1. Here's how you write that function, which you can add right below your `==` function:

```
postfix func ++ (inout a:Ingredient) -> Ingredient {
    a.quantity += 1
    return a
}
var someGin = Ingredient(quantity: 2.5, type: .Gin)
someGin++
```

Now you can create an ingredient and increment its quantity by 1. In this case you are using a postfix operator because you put the operator after the instance of the struct. You use `inout` because you want to modify the object itself. Usually with these unary operators, you use an `inout` parameter. Also note that if you define multiple binary and unary operators, you can use them within each other's definitions. For example, if you defined a binary addition operator, you could use it to increase the quantity for the definition of the `++` operator.

The only operators you can't redefine are the assignment and ternary operators (that is, `a = b` and `c ? d : e`). That one with the question mark is the ternary operator.

Making Your Own Operators

In addition to redefining operators, you can make your own. Custom operators can start with these characters:

```
/ = - + * % < > ! & | ^ . ~
```

They can also start with Unicode math, symbol, arrow, dingbat, and line/box drawing characters. All characters after the first one can be any of the preceding characters and/or Unicode characters. In this section, you'll define the binary `~<*^*>~` operator, just to be extreme. (This arm-flailing-starry-eyed-looking-up operator won't do anything impressive or useful.)

To define an operator, you must use the keyword `operator` and define it as `prefix`, `infix`, or `postfix`, like this:

```
infix operator ~<*^*>~ {}
```

Here you are bringing the operator into existence. You haven't actually defined what it does yet.

Next, you define what the operator does. Note that because you use `sqrt` here, you need to import UIKit:

```
func ~<*^*>~ (a:Ingredient,b:Ingredient) -> Ingredient {
    let c = sqrt(a.quantity)
    let d = sqrt(b.quantity)
    let e = pow(c, d)
    return Ingredient(quantity: e, type: a.type)
}
```

```
var someDryVermouth = Ingredient(quantity: 0.5,type: .Dry_Vermouth)
var someAbsolut = Ingredient(quantity: 2.5, type: .Absolut)
var newIng = someDryVermouth ~<*^*>~ someAbsolut
newIng.quantity //0.578115871271409
```

What the operator actually does is up to you. At this point, the new operator is completely useless, but you can see that you can really name your operators however you like.

You have three options when creating operators: infix, prefix, and postfix operators. An infix operator has arguments on both sides of the operator, and the operator you just made is an example of this type. A prefix operator is placed before the argument. Here's an example of this:

```
prefix operator --- {}
prefix func --- (inout a:Ingredient) -> Ingredient {
    a.quantity -= 2
    return a
}
---someGin
```

Here you are creating a triple-minus decrement, which will subtract not 1 but 2. It is a prefix operator because you write the triple minus before the variable.

A postfix operator is used after the variable. Here's an example of a custom postfix operator:

```
postfix operator +++ {}
postfix func +++ (inout a:Ingredient) -> Ingredient {
    a.quantity += 2
    return a
}
someGin+++
```

Here you are creating a triple-plus increment, which will add not 1 but 2. It is a postfix operator because you write the triple plus before the variable.

Bits and Bytes in Real Life

In this section, you are going to pull in a file and read its bits and bytes. You should be able to decode the file according to the specifications. Let's see what you can do with it. If you are using a Mac, you already have Python installed, which means you can simply start a local web server without installing anything. You are going to host a GIF file and read it in. You can use any GIF you want, but I have prepared one for you at http://i.imgur.com/j74SykU.gif.

To start a new single-view application, follow these steps:

1. Select File, New, Project.

2. Make sure IOS, Application is selected and click on Single View Application.

3. Set Product Name to GIFReader and make sure Language is set to Swift.

4. Click Next.

5. On the Save screen, click Create. You now have `AppDelegate.swift`, `Main.storyboard`, and `ViewController.swift`.

6. Open `ViewController.swift` and edit the `viewDidLoad` function, like this:

```
override func viewDidLoad() {
    super.viewDidLoad()
    loadGIF()
}
```

7. Write the skeleton for the `loadGIF` function, like this:

```
func loadGIF() {

}
```

8. Create a new file that does the URL requesting. Call it `Service.swift` and add the following:

```
import UIKit
class Service {
    var url = "http://i.imgur.com/j74SykU.gif"
    func getGIF(callback:(NSData)->()) {
        request(url,callback: callback)
    }
    func request(url:String,callback:(NSData)->()) {
        let nsURL = NSURL(string: url)
        let task = NSURLSession.sharedSession().dataTaskWithURL(nsURL!) {
            (data,response,error) in
            callback(data!)
        }
        task.resume()
    }
}
```

Here you create a generic request method that requests any data from any URL and returns that data. It is a good amount of code, so you should abstract it away. You use `NSURLSession.sharedSession().dataTaskWithURL(url)` to grab some data from a URL. You could easily modify this to return JSON data as well. If you were writing a larger app, you could write a function like `getPosts`, `getComments`, or `getWhatever`, and all you would have to do is call `request(url,callback)`.

9. Save your file and go back to `ViewController.swift`. Right above the `viewDidLoad` method, as the first line in the class, instantiate your service so you can use it:

```
var service = Service()
```

10. In your new `loadGIF` function, load the GIF:

```
func loadGIF() {
    service.getGIF() {
        (data) in
        println("Got GIF: \(data.length)")
    }
}
```

11. Notice the brevity of the function to load the GIF. You have abstracted away all the messy loading and created a simple closure to load the GIF. You should now have the entire GIF in the `data` parameter, which is of type `NSData`. Now the bits and bytes can begin. Test your app by running it with Command-R. You should see a `trace` statement saying that it got the data and will print out the length. (You can be sure it's the right length if you inspect the real file with Command-I. When I did this, I saw that it was 1.97MB. The `println` command returned `"Got PSD: 1978548"` for me, which says that the length of the data is in bytes.)

12. Remove `println`. Now you need to take each byte from the data and place each byte into an array. You can use an array of `UInt8`s to divide everything up 1 byte at a time. After these few lines, you will have a new array containing 1 byte per array element. It's not always useful to load everything into memory, but the point of this example is to show you how to work with bits and bytes. You will use the `getBytes` from `NSData`, and you will provide the length of the whole thing. In real life, you might want to load a little bit at a time. Hopefully you aren't using a 300MB GIF. Change your code like so:

```
func loadGIF() {
    service.getGIF() {
        (data) in
        var bytes = [UInt8](count:data.length, repeatedValue:0)
        data.getBytes(&bytes, length: data.length)
        print(bytes.count)
    }
}
```

Here you create an array of 0 the length of the data. Then you take that array and make a buffer to fill with the data. You basically pass in the `bytes` array like an `inout` parameter, and it fills it up with the right bytes. You can now check the bits and bytes to see whether it conforms to the GIF file specifications. That isn't a whole lot of code, and most of it loads the file.

However, you don't need to store the bytes in an array. Sometimes you will need to do this, but not this time. There are even easier ways to read the data. You need to get the first 6 bytes and see whether they are equal to `"GIF89a"` or something else. You can do that with one line of code by rewriting `loadGIF()`:

```
func loadGIF() {
    service.getGIF() {
        (data) in
```

```
                    print(NSString(data:
data.subdataWithRange(NSMakeRange(0, 6)), encoding:
NSUTF8StringEncoding))
        }
}
```

Here you use NSString, which has an initializer to create a string from data. You don't want all the data; you just want to check the first 6 bytes, so you use NSMakeRange to create a range from 0 to 6. You set the encoding to NSUTF8StringEncoding. When you run this, the console should say "GIF89a" (or something similar). This means the GIF file is legit because version numbers as of July 10, 1990, are "87a" for May 1987 and "89a" for July 1989.

13. Get the width and height of the file at bytes 7 and 8 and at bytes 9 and 10:

```
func loadGIF() {
    service.getGIF() {
        (data) in
        var current = 0
        var newCurrent = 0
        print(NSString(data: data.subdataWithRange(NSMakeRange(0,
6)), encoding: NSUTF8StringEncoding))
        current = 6
        var width = [UInt16](count:1, repeatedValue:0)
        newCurrent = current + 2
        data.getBytes(&width, range: NSMakeRange(current, newCurrent))
        current = newCurrent
        print(width)
        var height = [UInt16](count:1, repeatedValue:0)
        newCurrent = current + 2
        data.getBytes(&height, range: NSMakeRange(current, newCurrent))
        current = newCurrent
        print(height)
    }
}
```

You keep track of where the current byte pointer is. Otherwise, you are going to have to keep a count in your head. You know that the width and height come right after the GIF signature. You get the width and height at the next 4 bytes, with 2 bytes each. You use a UInt16 to represent 2 bytes. Because UInt8 represents 1 byte, this means a UInt32 will represent 4 bytes.

14. Now you need to find out whether the GIF contains a global color table. And for that you can inspect the first bit of the next byte:

```
var packed = [UInt8](count:1, repeatedValue:0)
data.getBytes(&packed, range: NSMakeRange(current, 1))
var hasGlobalColorTable = false
```

```
if packed[0] & 1 == 1 {
    //odd first bit is 1
    hasGlobalColorTable = true
}
var restOfLogicalScreenDescriptor = 3
current = current + restOfLogicalScreenDescriptor
print(hasGlobalColorTable)
```

You grab the next byte by using UInt8. You can do a trick to find whether the first bit is a 0 or a 1. By using & 1, you can see whether that equals 1 and therefore the first bit is 1. You also need to take into account the rest of this block. You add 3 more bytes to account for the rest of the logical screen descriptor since you are not using it right now anyway.

As you can see, a lot of steps are involved in getting all the data out of a GIF file. Here you've seen the gist of reading binary data based on a specification. UInt8 represents 1 byte, UInt16 represents 2 bytes, and so on and so forth. Depending on your next size step in the specification, you can grab however large a piece you need (in bytes).

Summary

In this chapter you have learned how to create your own custom syntax. These features are super-duper powerful and can be combined in many ways. When you combine them with trailing closures and @autoclosures (which you will learn about in Chapter 9, "Becoming More Flexible: Generics"), the possibilities are endless. You can define your own way of processing data with your own custom operators using your own custom classes made of ASCII pandas and Hebrew letters. You can, technically, use the subscript syntax however you want, but remember that with great power comes great responsibility. You have to be careful not to use them as functions but to use them as element assessors.

You've also learned in this chapter that generics give you real power. You can now apply everything from this chapter and the previous ones to create your own dictionaries and custom arrays.

In this chapter, you've also learned how to program at the bit level. In this chapter you've learned how to pull data from a URL and then parse it. You can now take any specification and parse away, and you can also create your own specifications.

8

Protocols

Protocols are at the heart of the iOS architecture; they are first-class paradigms, right up there with classes and structs. They hold a special place because they are the backbone of design patterns such as delegates. Delegates are heavily used in iOS for notifying the programmer when application, UI, and other events happen. You can use a delegate to send a message to everyone who conforms to that protocol. When you use a protocol and all of its offerings, it is called *conforming* to the protocol.

Protocols themselves don't have any implementation at all—that is, you don't really write code in protocols that *does stuff*. You can use protocols as a checklist to say "I need you to write the following methods if you want this thing to work." Protocols describe what must be implemented and what that implementation should look like. You can use protocols with classes, structures, and enumerations. When a class, a struct, or an enum provides the functionality described in the protocol, you can then say that it is *conforming* to the protocol.

Writing Your First Protocol

To create a protocol, you start with the keyword `protocol` and then give it a name, followed by a pair of curly brackets. A basic protocol would look like this:

```
protocol MyProtocol {
}
```

You might notice that this newly created protocol is completely empty. Although it is empty, it is valid. The protocol doesn't currently have any functions that it wants you to conform to, but you can provide an implementation of it already. You'll create a class that conforms to `MyProtocol`. It won't be hard to conform to it because it doesn't have any functions to conform to yet. It's like if someone gave me a blank shopping list: I would drive to the supermarket and, when I got there, I would just turn around because there would be nothing to get. Here is the implementation, using a class:

```
class MyClass:MyProtocol {
}
```

The way you tell this class to conform to the protocol is the same way you tell the class to inherit from another class: You just use the colon followed by the name of the protocol you want implemented. The protocol definition goes inside the curly brackets.

Now you can create an implementation of this protocol. This protocol does not create any requirements, so the class implementation will be just as sparse as the protocol:

```
protocol MyProtocol {

}

class MyClass:MyProtocol {

}
```

If you run this in the playground, you will notice that there are no errors. However, if you add the requirement of a property to the protocol, like this, then the class will need to implement it as well:

```
protocol MyProtocol {
    var someProp:String { get set }
}

class MyClass:MyProtocol {

}
```

Now you'll get an error:

```
type 'MyClass' does not conform to protocol 'MyProtocol'
class MyClass:MyProtocol {
^
:3:9: note: protocol requires property 'someProp' with type 'String'
var someProp:String { get set }
^
```

What happened? Now you are saying that the protocol has a requirement: A property called someProp must be a getter and a setter. You can fix this error by giving the class the property that the protocol requires. Here's how you do it:

```
protocol MyProtocol {
    var someProp:String { get set }
}

class MyClass:MyProtocol {
    var someProp:String = ""
}
```

When this code runs, the error goes away. You are now strictly adhering to the requirements of the protocol. That is, you are now *conforming* to the protocol.

> **Note**
>
> Notice the words `get` and `set`. In this case, you are saying that `someProp` can be read (that's `get`) and written to (that's `set`).

Properties

This is a good time to talk briefly about getters and setters in Swift. In Swift, you can have a property of a class that is a getter or a setter or both. To see how this works, you'll create a class called `Human`, and then you'll see what it means to get and set properties of that class:

```swift
class Human {
    var eyeColor = "#00FF00"
    var heightInInches = 68
    var hairLengthInCM = 2.54
    var name = "Skip"
}
```

This class has four properties. You may or may not want all of these properties to be able to be rewritten. For example, after the eye color is set, you might want that to only be able to be read and not written to. There are also other details you can get from these properties being set. For example, you could say that this person's height in a string would be `"medium"`. You can use *computed properties* for this.

The types of variables you have been writing up to this point are called *stored properties*. You can either have a *variable stored property* or a *constant stored property*. You know from Chapter 1, "Getting Your Feet Wet: Variables, Constants, and Loops," that you use the keyword `var` to signify a variable stored property and the keyword `let` to signify a constant stored property. You can define a default value of a stored property when you declare it in a class, a struct, or an enum. You did this in the `Human` class with all the properties. You can also change the default value at initialization.

In addition to stored properties, there are, as mentioned earlier, *computed properties*. Computed properties are not stored values; they provide instructions to Swift on how to compute the value of a property. They are used to set and get other stored properties indirectly. You can provide a getter and optionally a setter, as shown here:

```swift
class Human {
    var eyeColor = "#00FF00"
    var heightInInches = 68
    var hairLengthInCM = 2.54
    var heightDescription:String {
        get {
            if heightInInches >= 92 {
                return "tall"
            } else if heightInInches <= 30 {
                return "short"
            } else {
```

```
                return "medium"
            }
        }
    }
}
```

```
var human = Human()
print(human.heightDescription) // medium
```

Here you create a height description, which describes the height of a human, in inches. You are basing this height on the `heightInInches` property of the `Human`. You can create a setter as well if you want to set the height of the person by using a description. Ideally, you would create an enum to describe the different heights available, but for this example you can just use `Strings`, like this:

```
class Human {
    var eyeColor = "#00FF00"
    var heightInInches = 68
    var hairLengthInCM = 2.54
    var heightDescription:String {
        get {
            if heightInInches >= 92 {
                return "tall"
            } else if heightInInches <= 50 {
                return "short"
            } else {
                return "medium"
            }
        }
        set (newHeightDescription) {
            if newHeightDescription == "short" {
                heightInInches = 50
            } else if newHeightDescription == "tall" {
                heightInInches = 92
            } else if newHeightDescription == "medium" {
                heightInInches = 60
            }
        }
    }
}
```

```
var human = Human()
print(human.heightDescription)
human.heightDescription = "short"
print(human.heightInInches)
```

Now you can set the height of the person in inches by using a `String`. You can now use the equal sign on that computed property. You can see this with `heightDescription`, where you use the equal sign to set the height description as a `String`, which in turn sets the height of the human, in inches. Although it isn't the most accurate way of setting a person, it might be helpful in a game in which you are creating people on the fly and you want to create 100 tall people. Instead of hard-coding their heights, you can just set them to be `"tall"`.

In the next example, you set the height from the parameter that was passed in: `newHeightDescription`. This is optional because you could rewrite this example and just use the default parameter `newValue`. Here you rewrite just the setter portion of the preceding example to use a parameter named `newValue` instead of providing a named parameter yourself:

```
set {
    if newValue == "short" {
        heightInInches = 50
    } else if newValue == "tall" {
        heightInInches = 92
    } else if newValue == "medium" {
        heightInInches = 60
    }
}
```

Notice that you don't have to declare a variable here. Instead, you use a variable, called `newValue`, that is available to you in all setters. Many languages with getters and setters use the same variable name of `newValue` or `value` or something similar for setters.

Notice that you cannot create read-only stored properties directly. Here's a little trick for creating read-only stored properties: Create a private stored property and a read-only computed property, and you have yourself a read-only stored property. Here is an example of a read-only stored property:

```
class Human {
    private var _name = "Skip"
    var name:String {
        get {
            return _name
        }
    }
}
var human = Human()
print(human.name)
human.name = "Jack"
```

Now you have a property that is being stored, and you have made it read-only. You use the underscore to denote a private variable, but this is only aesthetic so that you can use the variable name `name` twice. This tells the reader that these are the same variable.

The `lazy` Variable

The last topic in our little properties discussion is the `lazy` variable. Actually, `lazy` is pretty handy. You use it to create a variable that is not evaluated until it is actually used. You can declare this variable with the keyword `lazy`. This type of variable is useful when you won't have the initial value of this property until after initialization. Rather than throw an error, you can just tell Swift that you will have the value when you need it, but you just don't have it right now. Here is an example of using the `lazy` keyword, which you don't have at initialization but will have ready when it is needed (it runs once when it's first accessed):

```
class Namer {
    var name:String {
        get {
            //url request for name
            return "Jack"
        }
    }
}

class Human {
    lazy var namer:Namer = Namer()
}
var human = Human() // Namer hasn't been initialized yet
print(human.namer.name) // Now namer has been initialized
```

In this example, it is possible that the `Namer` class's `name` property won't be ready on initialization. Swift is okay with this, as long as you use the `lazy` keyword to inform Swift that it shouldn't try to grab the value from the `name` class yet.

And now back to your regularly scheduled program on protocols.

`Animizable` **and** `Humanizable`

In this section, you will make a protocol for the creation of any animal, and call it `Animizable`. This protocol will make sure that anytime someone creates an animal, it will have the proper properties and methods. A lot of times, the names of protocols have `able` at the end. These are some of the Swift standard protocols you will commonly come across:

- **`Equatable`:** You must overload the `==` operator. This allows you to test your type for equality.

- **`Comparable`:** You must overload the `<`, `>`, `<=`, and `>=` operators, which will allow you to compare your custom type.

- **`Printable`:** You must declare a property of type `String` called `description`, which will provide a `String`-based representation of the type.

Methods

You can use a protocol to declare a method requirement. In this case, the adopting implementation must use the methods listed in the protocol in order to conform to it. Here is an example of this situation with your new `Animizable` protocol:

```
enum Food:String {
    case Meat = "meat"
    case Veggies = "veggies"
    case Other = "something else"
}

protocol Animizable {
    var type:String { get }
    func eat(quantityInPounds:Double, what:Food)
}

class Animal:Animizable {
    var type = ""
    func eat(quantityInPounds:Double, what:Food){
        print("I am \(type) and I am eating
\(quantityInPounds) pounds of \(what.rawValue).")
    }
}

var human = Animal()
human.type = "human"
human.eat(2,what: .Meat)
```

Here you are creating an `Animizable` protocol, which requires that you add a property type and a method called `eat`. The implementation of the method must have the same parameters as the protocol's definition of the method. If you want `Animizable` to have a type method, you need to write that in the protocol. You could update the `Animizable` protocol to require a type method called `lbsToKg` as a convenience method to convert pounds to kilograms. You can update your code as follows:

```
protocol Animizable {
    var type:String { get }
    static func lbsToKg(lbs:Double) -> Double
    func eat(quantityInPounds:Double, what:Food)
}

class Animal:Animizable {
    var type = ""
    static func lbsToKg(lbs:Double) -> Double {
        return lbs * 0.453592
    }
    func eat(quantityInPounds:Double, what:Food){
```

```
        print("I am \(type) and I am eating
\(quantityInPounds) pounds of \(what.rawValue).")
    }
}
```

Now the protocol requires a type method. You must implement this method when creating your `Animal` class.

This also goes for mutating methods: If you want a function to be mutating, you must declare it in the protocol. The implementation of that protocol must then create a mutating method. Mutating is used only for enums and structs. If you implement a protocol that requires a mutating method using a class, you do not need to write the `mutating` keyword.

Delegation

Delegation is one of the most powerful features of protocols. Delegation is not special to Swift or Objective-C. It is a design pattern, a reusable solution to a common problem within a certain context. A friend of mine described delegation best without even knowing it. He said, "Doesn't a protocol allow you to send messages to anyone who implements that protocol?" Sort of. If you create a new iOS project, the first thing you will most likely see is the `AppDelegate`, which notifies you when certain things happen. For example, in `AppDelegate` there is a method called `applicationWillTerminate`. This method gets called when the application is about to be shut down. It can be called because it adopts `UIApplicationDelegate`. Let's look at how the delegate design pattern works.

Say that you create a protocol called `Humanizable`, where things will happen to `Human` (which adopts `Humanizable`), and you want to notify others of those things:

```
protocol Humanizable {
    var name:String { get set }
    func eat(quantity:Int)
    func play(game:String)
    func sleep()
}
```

You now have a protocol that can be adopted by any `Human`. You then create a `HumanizableDelegate` protocol that can be adopted in order to be updated with changes to the `Human`. Each function will get an instance of the `Human` that is doing the updating:

```
protocol HumanizableDelegate {
    func didStartEating(human:Humanizable)
    func didFinishEating(human:Humanizable)
    func didStartPlaying(human:Humanizable)
    func didFinishPlaying(human:Humanizable)
    func didStartSleeping(human:Humanizable)
    func didFinishSleeping(human:Humanizable)
}
```

You can now keep track of changes to the Human. You next create a class that conforms to the Humanizable protocol and will have a delegate to do the informing:

```
class Human:Humanizable {
    var name:String
    init(name:String) {
        self.name = name
    }

    var delegate:HumanizableDelegate?

    func eat(quantity:Int) {
        delegate?.didStartEating(self)
        print("Eating \(quantity) pounds of food, yum yum yum")
        delegate?.didFinishEating(self)
    }

    func play(game:String) {
        delegate?.didStartPlaying(self)
        print("I am playing \(game)! So much fun.")
        delegate?.didFinishPlaying(self)
    }

    func sleep() {
        delegate?.didStartSleeping(self)
        print("I am sleeping now. Shhhh.")
        delegate?.didFinishSleeping(self)
    }
}
```

You are now conforming to the Human class. Our Human class implements the actual functionality of the eat, play, and sleep methods of Humanizable. When the instance of the human sleeps, we tell our delegate when we have started sleeping and when we have stopped. Now all we have to do is make a human watcher to keep track of all the stuff happening with our human. This class will conform to HumanizableDelegate and truly get informed of changes.

```
class HumanWatcher:HumanizableDelegate {
    func didStartEating(human:Humanizable){
        print("We just were informed that \(human.name) started eating")
    }
    func didFinishEating(human:Humanizable){
        print("We just were informed that \(human.name) finished eating")
    }
    func didStartPlaying(human:Humanizable){
        print("We just were informed that \(human.name) started playing")
    }
```

```
    func didFinishPlaying(human:Humanizable){
        print("We just were informed that \(human.name) finished playing")
    }
    func didStartSleeping(human:Humanizable){
        print("We just were informed that \(human.name) started sleeping")
    }
    func didFinishSleeping(human:Humanizable){
        print("We just were informed that \(human.name) finished sleeping")
    }
}
```

Now you can be completely informed of the Human's activity and do something about it. Even if watching the Human means printing out lines to the console, that's what you'll do. The last thing you need to do is to create the actual instances of the Humans and their Human watchers. The fact that you are using protocols means you can guarantee that the Human will have certain methods. You do not have to worry about those methods not being implemented. Let's create the protocol design pattern using our new human, "Jeff":

```
let humanWatcher = HumanWatcher()
let human = Human(name:"Jeff")
human.delegate = humanWatcher
human.play("marbles")
human.sleep()
human.eat(5)
```

```
We just were informed that Jeff started playing
I am playing marbles! So much fun.
We just were informed that Jeff finished playing
We just were informed that Jeff started sleeping
I am sleeping now. Shhhh.
We just were informed that Jeff finished sleeping
We just were informed that Jeff started eating
Eating 5 pounds of food, yum yum yum
We just were informed that Jeff finished eating
```

With the delegate pattern, the delegate of an instance can notify you of things happening in that instance of a class.

Protocols as Types

You know that protocols don't implement any functionality themselves, but that doesn't stop you from using them as parameters or return types in methods. This is where protocols can become extremely powerful. You can use them as a type for a variable or constant or for arrays and dictionaries.

Here is a protocol that can work for anything that you would like to make walkable:

```
protocol Walkable {
    var name:String { get set }
    func walk(numOfSteps numOfSteps:Int)
}
```

Humans can walk and animals can walk, among other actions. Here's how you can make a human that can walk:

```
class Human:Walkable {
    var name = "John"
    func walk(numOfSteps numOfSteps:Int) {
        print("Human is walking \(numOfSteps) steps")
    }
}
func runWalker(walker:Walkable) {
    walker.walk(numOfSteps:10)
}
var somethingThatWalks = Human()
runWalker(somethingThatWalks)
```

In this example you create a `Human` class that takes anything that can walk. This works because it adopts the `Walkable` protocol. You create a top-level function that will walk any `Walkable`. Notice that the parameter that the `runWalker` function takes is `Walkable`. This means anything that adopts the protocol `Walkable` can be passed in. This gives you a lot of flexibility because now you just call walk on whatever is passed in. You know that what is passed in will have that function available because it adopts `Walkable`.

Protocols in Collections

Protocols can be used as types, so it shouldn't be a surprise that a protocol can also be used as the type of a collection. Think about the case of the `Walkable` class from the preceding section. Say that you want to create something else that can walk, such as a dog. Here's what you do:

```
class Dog:Walkable {
    var name = "Penny"
    func walk(numOfSteps numOfSteps:Int) {
        print("The dog is walking \(numOfSteps) steps")
    }
}

let dog = Dog()
let human = Human()
var walkers = [Walkable]()
walkers.append(dog)
walkers.append(human)
```

```
for walker in walkers {
    walker.walk(numOfSteps:10)
}
```

Here you have a Dog and a Human, and they are both Walkable. You also have an array that is strictly typed for anything that is Walkable. Because the array takes anything that adopts Walkable, you can append the Dog and the Human to the array, and it works just fine. You can imagine that if you took an even more generic protocol, such as BooleanType, you could make a very wide-ranging collection.

Protocol Inheritance

You can very easily make protocols inherit other protocols, which will add the requirements on top of one another. To see how this works, in this section, you'll create two other protocols: Runnable and Doggable. Runnable will add one more function requirement: run(). Doggable will inherit Walkable and Runnable. Doggable will have the requirement of a bark function. Because it will implement Walkable and Runnable, it will also need to implement walk and run functions. Here's how you create these protocols:

```
protocol Walkable {
    func walk(numOfSteps numOfSteps:Int)
}

protocol Runnable {
    func run(howFarInMiles howFarInMiles:Float)
}

protocol Doggable: Walkable, Runnable {
    func bark()
}

class Dog: Doggable {
    func walk(numOfSteps numOfSteps:Int) {
        print("Dog will walk \(numOfSteps) steps")
    }

    func run(howFarInMiles howFarInMiles:Float) {
        print("Dog will run \(howFarInMiles) miles")
    }

    func bark() {
        print("Woof")
    }
}

class FrenchDog:Dog {
    override func bark() {
```

```
        print("Le woof")
    }
}

var dog = Dog()
var leDog = FrenchDog()
dog.bark() // Woof
leDog.bark() // Le woof
```

Here the new `Doggable` class inherits both the `Runnable` and `Walkable` protocols. If you were to not include `walk` or `run` or both in the `Dog` class, Swift would throw an error. The way to have a protocol inherit from other protocols is the same way you use in classes: You create a comma-separated list following the semicolon. You can make a protocol inherit from as many other protocols as you want.

We just talked about how to inherit multiple protocols from other protocols, but how do you adopt multiple protocols at once from a class, a struct, or an enum? We'll look at that next.

Protocol Composition

Protocol composition is a fancy term for making a type adopt multiple protocols at once. If you need to make a type adopt multiple protocols, you use this syntax:

```
protocol<Protocol1, Protocol2>
```

Inside the angled brackets, you place the multiple protocols that you want the type to inherit. When you do this, you are creating a temporary local protocol that has the combined requirements of all the protocols you've listed.

Let's make a sort of powered speaker that uses protocol composition:

```
import UIKit
protocol Powered {
    var on:Bool { get set }
    func turnOn()
    func turnOff()
}
protocol Audible {
    var volume:Float { get set }
    func volumeUp()
    func volumeDown()
}
class Speaker:NSObject, Powered,Audible {
    var on:Bool = false
    var volume:Float = 0.0
    var maxVolume:Float = 10.0
```

```
        func desc() -> String {
            return "Speaker: volume \(self.volume)"
        }

        func turnOn() {
            if on {
                print("already on")
            }
            on = true
            print("Powered on")
        }
        func turnOff() {
            if !on {
                print("already off")
            }
            on = false
            volume = 0.0
            print("Powered off")
        }
        func volumeUp() {
            if volume < maxVolume {
                volume += 0.5
            }
            print("Volume turned up to \(volume)")
        }
        func volumeDown() {
            if volume > 0 {
                volume -= 0.5
            }
            print("Volume turned down to \(volume)")
        }
}
var speakers:[protocol<Powered,Audible>] = []
for n in 1...10 {
    speakers.append(Speaker())
}
func turnUpAllSpeakers() {
    for speaker in speakers {
        turnUpSpeaker(speaker)
    }
}
func turnDownAllSpeakers() {
    for speaker in speakers {
        turnDownSpeaker(speaker)
    }
}
func turnUpSpeaker(speaker:protocol<Powered,Audible>) {
```

```
    if !speaker.on {
        speaker.turnOn()
    }
    speaker.volumeUp()
    print(speaker)
}
func turnDownSpeaker(speaker:protocol<Powered,Audible>) {
    if !speaker.on {
        speaker.turnOn()
    }
    speaker.volumeDown()
    print(speaker)
}
turnUpAllSpeakers()
```

Before I explain anything else, I want to point out some really interesting information. There is a protocol called `Printable`, which allows you to output the textual representation of your type. To adopt `Printable`, you must add a description getter to your class. This does not make your class textual output go out to `print()`. There is also a protocol called `DebugPrintable`, which does the same sort of stuff as `Printable` but is made strictly for debugging purposes. This protocol also *does not* print to the `print()` output. The only way (as far as I know) to override the output of the `print()` representation of the class is to inherit from `NSObject` and create a description method that returns a `String`. You output the description to that function, and `print()` prints your custom output. Remember, though, that there is no base class in Swift, as there is in JavaScript, Java, and tons of other programming languages. You are not inheriting a description from a grand base class; it just happens to be associated with that class. Also, to use `NSObject` make sure you import UIKit or something similar.

The class `Speaker` adopts two protocols: `Powered` and `Audible`. The protocol composition happens in two places. You declare an array that takes only types that adopt those two protocols. You also create a `turnUpSpeaker` method, which takes the temporary protocol, which is made up of the two protocols. Luckily, the `Speaker` class fits the requirements just right, and you can pass in a `Speaker`. You provide `Speaker` with a way to turn on and off and a way to turn the volume up and down. You provide a max volume so you don't exceed that volume, and you check to make sure the speaker is on before you turn it on. You create ten speakers in a loop, using the `range` operator.

Why would you use protocol composition? Sometimes you have types that must match multiple protocols, and you can create a temporary protocol to meet the requirement.

Protocol Conformity

Sometimes it is necessary to check whether a type is of a protocols type. For example, if you create a `Human` class, which is `Humanizable`, you want to check an array of objects to see whether one of those elements conforms to the protocol. You use the `is` and `as` keywords to downcast the type to check its conformance to the protocol.

Using the keyword is returns true if the instance conforms to the protocol, and it is a good method to use if you do not need any downcast instance passed along to the inner scope of the if statement. If you do need a reference to the downcast instance, you can use the optional as? keyword. Here is an example of using both keywords. Notice that there is a little an extra detail you have to add in order to make this possible:

```
import Foundation
@objc protocol Animizable {
    var name:String { get set }
}

@objc protocol Humanizable:Animizable {
    var language:String { get set }
}

@objc protocol Bearable:Animizable {
    func growl()
}

class Human:Humanizable {
    @objc var name:String = "Frank"
    @objc var language:String = "English"
}

class Bear:Bearable {
    @objc var name = "Black Bear"
    @objc func growl() {
        print("Growllll!!!")
    }
}

class Other:Animizable {
    @objc var name = "Other"
}

var lifeCollection:[AnyObject] = [Human(),Bear(),Other()]

for life in lifeCollection {
    print(life)
    if life is Humanizable {
        print("is human")
    }
    if let humanizable = life as? Humanizable {
        print(humanizable.language)
    }
}
```

You have to add the @objc attribute in order to make this work. You use this attribute when you want your Swift code to be available to Objective-C code. However, you are not using it for that purpose here. If you want to check protocol conformance, you must mark the protocol with that attribute even if you aren't interacting with Objective-C code.

You can see that when you use the `as?` optional, you are able to call the `language` attribute of the `Human`, which would otherwise be just `AnyObject`. If you tried to get the `language` property of the `Human` from the `is` downcast, you would get an error: `error: 'AnyObject' does not have a member named 'language'`. This is because you never actually downcast the `AnyObject` to a `Humanizable`. This is very powerful because you have protocols that inherit other protocols. You would get a wider range if you checked for the conformance of `Animizable`.

> **Note**
>
> The `@objc` attribute can be adopted only by classes, and not by structures or enums.

When you are looping through the array, you check for the conformance of the protocol with both `is` and `as?`. In the case of `as?`, if there is a match and the element does conform to the protocol, the optional is unwrapped and assigned to the `let`, using optional binding. At that point, the element of the array is no longer `AnyObject` but is known as type `Humanizable`. The object itself is not changed but merely temporarily downcast when it is stored in the constant.

Optional Protocol Prerequisites

If you peruse the Swift pseudo-code by Command+clicking protocols, you will see that a lot of them have optional requirements. For example, when you start a new project of any type, you can inspect `UIApplicationDelegate`, and you should see something like what Figure 8.1 shows.

```
protocol UIApplicationDelegate : NSObjectProtocol {

    optional func applicationDidFinishLaunching(applicatio
    @availability(iOS, introduced=6.0)
    optional func application(application: UIApplication,
        AnyObject]?) -> Bool
    @availability(iOS, introduced=3.0)
    optional func application(application: UIApplication,
        AnyObject]?) -> Bool

    optional func applicationDidBecomeActive(application:
    optional func applicationWillResignActive(application:
    optional func application(application: UIApplication,
        point, please replace with application:openURL:sou
    @availability(iOS, introduced=4.2)
    optional func application(application: UIApplication,
        AnyObject?) -> Bool // no equiv. notification. ret

    optional func applicationDidReceiveMemoryWarning(appli
        possible. next step is to terminate app
    optional func applicationWillTerminate(application: UI
    optional func applicationSignificantTimeChange(applica
        savings time change

    optional func application(application: UIApplication,
        UIInterfaceOrientation, duration: NSTimeInterval)
    optional func application(application: UIApplication,
        UIInterfaceOrientation)

    optional func application(application: UIApplication,
        coordinates
    optional func application(application: UIApplication,
```

Figure 8.1   The `UIApplicationDelegate` protocol

You can see that most of the methods of this protocol are optional and therefore do not need to be implemented. You can mark any method as optional so that the compiler will not throw an error if a method is not implemented. Even though you can't see it in Figure 8.1, you need to mark a protocol with the @objc attribute if you plan on creating an optional method. This is true even if you are not planning on making your code available to Objective-C.

Let's look at a quick example. Apparently, bears cough when they are scared. So in this example, you create an optional cough method of the Bearable protocol:

```
import Foundation
@objc protocol Animizable {
    var name:String { get set }
}

@objc protocol Humanizable:Animizable {
    var language:String { get set }
}

@objc protocol Bearable:Animizable {
    func growl()
    optional func cough() //Apparently bears cough when they are scared.
}

class Human:Humanizable {
    @objc var name:String = "Frank"
    @objc var language:String = "English"
}

class Bear:Bearable {
    @objc var name = "Black Bear"
    @objc func growl() {
        print("Growllll!!!")
    }
    //Bear does not implement the cough method. He never gets scared.
}
```

Notice that you do not implement the cough method for the Bear class. You do not need to implement it because the protocol is marked optional for that method.

There is a possibility that you will try to call a method that does not exist at this point because it may not be implemented. In this case you would use optional chaining, discussed next.

Optional Chaining

When you have optional methods that may or may not exist, you need to be able to call them without the possibility of crashing your program. Did you think that the optional methods in protocols are just optional, meaning that you can include them or not include them? If you did, you were wrong. They are directly tied to optionals and can be checked via value binding.

Using optional chaining is another possibility instead of forcing the unwrapping of optionals. The big difference between optional chaining and forced unwrapping is that whereas forced unwrapping gives you an error and crashes your program if the thing you are looking for does not exist, optional chaining does not.

When you have an optional method that may or may not exist, you can use optional chaining to test for the existence of the method. To see how this works, you can expand your Bear example, like this:

```
class Bear {
    var name = "Black Bear"
    var paws:Paws?
    func growl() {
        print("Growllll!!!")
    }
    //Bear does not implement the cough method. He never gets scared.
}
class Paws {
    var count = 4
}
var bear:Bear = Bear()
bear.paws = Paws()
print(bear.paws?.count) // Optional(4)
```

What is super-interesting about this example is that the count of the paws returns an optional when it clearly was not set as an optional. That's what optional chaining does for you: It allows you to safely write code with optionals in the middle. Let me explain a little further. The bear has optional paws. (Obviously, in a real-life bear paws are never optional, but in this situation they might be optional.) When you create a new Bear, you do not know whether the paws will exist. So you mark the paws as optional, like this:

```
bear.paws?
```

Now this is going to return either an instance of the paws as an optional or nil. The program cannot crash at this point because you will get either optional paws or nil. Optional chaining then marks everything within the optional paws as optional as well, even if it isn't optional. So the count within the paws will become an optional Int. This is because the paws may not exist, so everything within the paws may not exist as well—and you don't want the program to crash because of that. When you grab the count, like this, it is now an optional or nil, depending on whether the paws exist:

```
bear.paws?.count
```

This returns an optional, so now you can perform optional binding to get the unwrapped optional out:

```
if let count = bear.paws?.count {
    print("The count was \(count)")
} else {
    print("There were no paws")
}
```

Now you can test for the existence of the paws and get the `count` out of the optional that it was placed in.

> **Note**
>
> The biggest takeaway here is this: The paws may or may not have existed, and therefore everything within the paws had to be made an optional in order to not crash the program. This technique is called *optional chaining*. If one link of the chain is broken, the whole thing crashes.

Back to Optional Protocol Requisites

With optional chaining tools in hand, you can now test to see whether your methods exist:

```
import Foundation
@objc protocol Bearable {
    @objc func growl()
    optional func cough() -> String //Apparently bears cough when they are scared.
}

class Bear:Bearable {
    @objc var name = "Black Bear"
    @objc func growl() {
        print("Growllll!!!")
    }
}

class Forest {
    @objc var bear:Bearable?
    @objc func scareBears() {
        if let cough = bear?.cough?() {
            print(cough)
        } else {
            print("bear was scared")
        }
    }
}
var forest = Forest()
forest.scareBears()
```

You check whether the `Bearable` implementation exists with optional chaining. You assign the return of the method with optional binding, and if it is not `nil`, you print the output of the method; otherwise, you just print `"the bear was scared"`.

Multiple chaining is going on in this situation. First, you check the optional `bear`, which could be `nil`. Then you check the optional `cough` method, which could also be `nil` and not implemented.

Useful Built-in Swift Protocols

Swift has a solid group of protocols you can implement in your classes to make stuff happen. The following sections describe them.

The `Equatable` Protocol

You use `Equatable` when you want one class to be comparable to another class, using the `==` operator. For example, if you have two `Car` classes that you want to compare for equality, you could adopt the `Equatable` protocol. You have to implement the `==` function (which can be written only on a global level), as shown here:

```
class Bear:Equatable {
    var name = "Black Bear"
    func growl() {
        print("Growllll!!!")
    }
}
func == (lhs:Bear, rhs:Bear) -> Bool {
    return lhs.name == rhs.name
}
var bear1 = Bear()
bear1.name = "Black Bear"
var bear2 = Bear()
bear2.name = "Black Bear"
print(bear1 == bear2) //true
```

Here you are comparing two bears. You would not normally be able to do this because Swift would not know how to compare two bears. Thankfully, you can let Swift know how to compare them. In this case, you have Swift compare the bears by name. If the names are the same, the bears are considered equal.

The `Comparable` Protocol

The `Comparable` protocol allows you to compare two objects by using at least the `<` operator. You can also override the other operators: `>`, `>=`, and `<=`. Consider that the less-than operator is required by law and Apple, and it must be implemented on the global scope. Here's how you can update the `Bear` class to make bears comparable by weight:

```
class Bear:Equatable,Comparable {
    var name = "Black Bear"
    var weight = 0
    func growl() {
        print("Growllll!!!")
    }
}
```

```
func == (lhs:Bear, rhs:Bear) -> Bool {
    return lhs.name == rhs.name
}

func < (lhs:Bear, rhs:Bear) -> Bool {
    return lhs.weight < rhs.weight
}

var bear1 = Bear()
bear1.name = "Black Bear"
bear1.weight = 275
var bear2 = Bear()
bear2.name = "Black Bear"
bear2.weight = 220

print(bear1 == bear2)
print(bear1 < bear2) // false
```

Here you are implementing the `Comparable` protocol to give Swift a way to compare the bears by using at least the less-than operator. You then write the global less-than function and give it two parameters of type `Bear`. You can make as many of those global functions as you need, as long as the parameters that it accepts are different.

The `CustomStringConvertible` Protocol

The `Printable` protocol allows you to provide a textual representation of a class, a struct, or an enum. It is supposed to be able to be used by `print`, but that does not work as you would expect. It does make your life a whole lot simpler when creating text, though. Instead of having to write something like `"my bear is \(bear1.name)"`, you can just write `"my bear is \(bear1)"`. `Printable` works in an app but not in the playground or in the REPL (the command-line Swift compiler, which can be run in Terminal using `xcrun swift`). You can add this protocol to be adopted by the `Bear` class like so:

```
class Bear:Equatable,Comparable, CustomStringConvertible{
    var name = "Black Bear"
    var weight = 0
    var description:String {
        return self.name
    }
    func growl() {
        print("Growlllll!!!")
    }
}

func == (lhs:Bear, rhs:Bear) -> Bool {
    return lhs.name == rhs.name
}
```

```
func < (lhs:Bear, rhs:Bear) -> Bool {
    return lhs.weight < rhs.weight
}

var bear1 = Bear()
bear1.name = "Black Bear"
bear1.weight = 275
print("Our bear is \(bear1)")
var bear2 = Bear()
bear2.name = "Black Bear"
bear2.weight = 220
print("Our bear is \(bear2)")

print(bear1 == bear2)
print(bear1 < bear2)
```

The DebugPrintable Protocol

DebugPrintable is the same as CustomStringConvertible but is used for debugging purposes. For its implementation, you use debugDescription instead of description. This protocol also does not work in the playground or the Swift REPL.

Summary

In this chapter you have learned how to create protocols of many varieties. You've learned how to check for optional protocol methods and properties. There are many more protocols available to you in the Swift library. The ones described in this chapter are the most important ones to remember and will come in handy.

This chapter describes how to create a protocol and all the different ins and outs of protocols, but in the end, it is up to you to know the right time for a protocol. After practicing with them for a while, I began to find myself using them more often and in really neat ways. For example, I created a text-based game in which anything that was able to be picked up fell into a protocol I created called PickableUpable. I then passed around PickableUpables instead of looping through each different thing that could be picked up. Then, using optional downcasting, I checked whether each item was the PickableUpable that I wanted. Sure, I could have called it PickUpable, but what fun would that be?

When you combine protocols with generics, you'll have a lot of power. You already have some great tools for abstracting code and making it reusable. With generics, you will be able to apply your protocols to generics to make methods work with any type of object that meets certain criteria.

9

Becoming Flexible with Generics

Generics are an awesome feature of Swift that allow you to accept more generic types when creating methods, parameters, properties of classes, and so on. Generics allow you to abstract away functionality that would have been repetitious to write. Sometimes you want to write a function that takes not just Ints, but Ints as well as Strings and anything Printable. Without generics, you would have had to write a method multiple times for each type. With generics, you can now write one method for all acceptable types. They're called *generics* because you are creating generic versions of a method. The exact type that you accept has not been decided yet. When you write generics, you are removing duplication while showing your intentions. When you examine the Swift pseudo-source code, you'll notice (when you read this chapter) that a good deal of Swift is written using generics. Take, for example, arrays, which can act as collections for *any* type. You can put Strings, Ints, or any other type inside an array. The same goes for dictionaries and many other things in Swift. By using generics, Apple didn't have to write an array for String, then an array for Ints, and so on. Apple wrote one array implementation and told Swift to accept a generic type. You might take it for granted that you can use any type with an array, but you should know that it is possible because of generics.

The Problem That Generics Solve

Let's talk about the problem that generics solve. Consider this function, which swaps two integers:

```
func swapTwoInts(inout a: Int, inout b: Int) {
    let temporaryA = a
    a = b
    b = temporaryA
}
var a = 10
var b = 1
swapTwoInts(&a,b: &b)
print(a) // 1
print(b) // 10
```

This works just as expected. You are able to swap the two Ints by passing them as inout parameters to the function. The *problem* is that this function works only with Ints. If you try setting the variable to 10.5 (a double) or "Hello there" (a string), it will not work because 10.5 is a Double and "Hello there" is a String. This function takes only Ints. The function's implementation itself (the code inside the function) is generic enough to take any of the other types, but the problem is the parameter's type. If you want to use this function for Doubles and Strings, you have to rewrite it for Doubles and then again for Strings. If you do that, you get a lot of repetition.

This is where generics come in. By creating a generic form of the function, you allow the function to accept any type. This will fix the problem of repeating yourself. Generics add even more power because you can limit the types it accepts by using protocols. That way you won't get errors when you're trying to run a function with parameters it isn't meant for. For example, you may use a generic that accepts only types that adopt Equatable, and then anything that is not Equatable will not be allowed. It's better to throw errors before the user compiles the code rather than crashing the program. Here's how you could reimplement your swap to use generics:

```
func swapValues<T>(inout a:T, inout b:T) {
    let temporaryA = a
    a = b
    b = temporaryA
}

var a = "hi"
var b = "bye"

swapValues(&a, b: &b)
print(a) // "bye"
print(b) // "hi"
```

This function looks almost exactly the same as the previous one. The difference is that special T in angle brackets. You haven't seen this yet. After adding the T, you can use this function with Strings. You can also now use this function with Ints, or Doubles, or any other data type. The T declares a type. However, this code does not describe what that type is. T is a placeholder for the type that will be sent via the parameters. That placeholder is used to act as the same type for your parameters. What type T is will be determined when the function is run. It all depends on what type you send the function.

By putting that T in angle brackets, you are saying to Swift "Do not look for a specific type now; I will tell you the type when the function is run." Then, as long as both parameters are the same type (because you used T for both; if you had used T and U or something else, T and U would represent different types), the function will work. This is true even though the T is not any specific type. This means that you can't pass two different types, like an Int and a String; you must pass the same type. The angle brackets at the beginning of the function tell Swift it is dealing with a generic type.

> **Note**
>
> You don't have to use T here, though; you can use anything you want. And, in fact, you can use multiple names. It is customary to use a single capital letter for generic types, but you can do whatever you want. It is also customary to use capital camel case when naming generic types. Using the same letter represents the same type, meaning that whatever type you decide to send in must match other types with the same name.

Other Uses for Generics

In addition to creating functions with generic types, you can provide your own custom types, using classes, structs, and enums. The array type is a good example of this. Notice that when you create an array, you are setting the type at creation time:

```
var a:[Int] = [1,2,3]
```

Notice that the preceding example tells the array to use Ints. Here's another way to do this:

```
var a:Array<Int> = [1,2,3]
```

This syntax is the generic syntax for an array. It tells you that what appears after the equal sign is an array made of Ints. Inside those angle brackets you declare that the array uses Ints. An array is just a list or sequence. You can create your own arraylike structure that has a similar implementation to the array but with your own added functionality. Let's call this custom arraylike structure a List, and this List will use a method named add instead of append.

Here's how you can make a List type that accepts and works with any type:

```
class List<T> {
    var items = [T]();
    func add(item:T){
        items.append(item)
    }
    var count:Int {
        return items.count
    }
    subscript(i: Int) -> T {
        return items[i]
    }
}

var l = List<Int>()
l.add(1)
l.add(2)
l.add(3)
print(l.count)
```

In this new List class, when you set the type during initialization, you can also add Ints to List. This List is a generic type, which means it is a type that can work with multiple *types*.

It will work with those types in the same way that arrays and dictionaries work with any type. When you define T as <T>, you are declaring that this *generic* type will be used throughout the rest of your code and represent one type. When you're using the generic type, if you instantiate T as an Int, then anywhere you use T in the class, it will be considered an Int.

Within the code, you create an array of Ts (whatever T will be, after the class is instantiated). You allow the user to access the array of Ts through the use of a subscript. This means you can get items from the list like so:

```
print(1[2])
```

Now you have created your own arraylike structure. Notice that if you try to loop through the list, you will get an error. That is because you didn't implement iterating for your custom type. The point is that you have a custom type called List, which has its own append-like method but does not have any of the other array methods. It is a light array, or diet array. Whatever type you assign when creating the List is the type that the List will use. List uses T as a generic type that will be defined at the time of creation. Also note that T could be a struct, an enum, a class, or a protocol—as long as it falls under the category of type.

Let's improve the list to make it more useful:

```
class List<T:Equatable> {
    var items = [T]();
    func add(allItems:T...){
        items += allItems
    }

    func deDup() {
        var uniques = [T]()
        for t in items {
            if uniques.indexOf(t) == nil {
                uniques.append(t)
            }
        }
        items = uniques
    }

    func indexOf(item:T) -> Int {
        for (index,t) in items.enumerate() {
            if t == item {
                return index
            }
        }
        return -1
    }

    var count:Int {
        return items.count
    }
}
```

```
        subscript(i: Int) -> T {
            return items[i]
        }
}

var l = List<Int>()
l.add(1,2,3,4,5,4,4,4,5,6,7,7)
l.deDup()
print(l.indexOf(10))
print(l.count)
```

There are a bunch of changes in this version of List. First, you declare the type of this List as T:Equatable. This means that any type you use must adopt the protocol Equatable. You need to use only types that implement Equatable in order to implement a JavaScript-style indexOf function because it needs to match types. Even though Swift now has an indexOf method, ours returns -1 when the item is not found instead of nil. This example is just for fun. To find a match, you need to use a ==. Only types adopting Equatable can use ==.

You implemented indexOf by using Swift's enumerate function to loop through an array while also grabbing the index. The code will compare the item you are looking for with the current item in the array. If it cannot find that item, it returns -1. If a match is found, it returns the index at which it was found. This is possible only because you can compare the equality of two objects. For this to work, those two objects must be Equatable. That is why this List must use a generic type that is Equatable. This concludes the implementation of your JavaScript-like indexOf function. Nice job!

You have also created a deDup function, which removes all duplicates of the array. deDup works by creating a new array and pushing all the unique items into that array by first checking whether they exist, using Swift's find function.

You also added some new functionality to the add method. The add method now takes any number of arguments and adds them into the list—overall a major improvement.

Generics for Protocols

Protocols can create/define generic types called *associated types*. You may sometimes want to create a protocol that uses some type that will be decided when you create the object. Earlier in the chapter, you created a List that has a couple of nifty methods and properties. Now you will create a protocol to describe some of the functionality. So here you'll create a Bucket protocol to describe adding functionality to the List so that you can add as many elements as you want—and remove them. You'll also make a Uniquable protocol, which describes the deDup functionality. Here are the two protocols and their implementation declaration in the List:

```
protocol Bucket {
    typealias SomeItem
    var count:Int { get }
    var items:[SomeItem] { get set }
```

```
    func add(allItems:SomeItem...)
    func indexOf(item:SomeItem) -> Int
    subscript(i:Int) -> SomeItem { get }
}

protocol Uniquable {
    func deDup()
}

class List<T:Equatable>:Bucket, Uniquable {
```

List is now fitted with two protocols it claims to adopt: Bucket and Uniquable. For the Bucket protocol, notice that you declare a typealias for SomeItem. You don't know the type of SomeItem right now, but when the List gets created, SomeItem will be the same type as T. You declare the add method to take a type of SomeItem. You also declare indexOf to take a type of SomeItem. Notice that you do not need to declare SomeItem for the Uniquable protocol because the deDup functionality does not need it in its method signature in order to operate. The List class already implements both of these protocols. When creating protocols, you can use that typealias of SomeItem (and you can name it whatever you want) anywhere you would need to declare the generic type that is used in the class, struct, or enum in which you are declaring the generic type.

To conform to the Bucket protocol, you need to implement the following:

- A property count

- An add method that takes a variadic parameter named allItems of type SomeItem so that you can add as many items as you like

- An indexOf method that takes a parameter named item of type SomeItem and returns an Int (this way you can see, using indexOf, whether a specific item exists in the List)

- A subscript so you can directly access the members of the List and that returns a type of SomeItem

To conform to the Uniquable protocol, you need to implement only one method, deDup, which takes no parameters and returns nothing. Because this method does not use the generic type in its signature, you do not need to declare the typealias of SomeItem for it.

The List class already provides an implementation for these requirements, so you are good to go there as well.

The where Clause

If you want to provide an extra utility knife for the List collection, you can write a couple of functions that do some useful stuff to the List. You will have very strict criteria for the parameters of the function, even stricter than a protocol. Enter the where clause! You can specify that parameters must meet certain criteria before being passed in. This of it like a bouncer at a club. Let's say you are comparing two Lists. You want to make sure that both Lists being passed in meet the criteria of a List. You can make a function that will combine all Lists passed in and deDup them all at once, leaving you with one list with all unique values:

```
protocol Bucket {
    typealias SomeItem
    var count:Int { get }
    var items:[SomeItem] { get set }
    func add(allItems:SomeItem...)
    func add(allItems:[SomeItem])
    func indexOf(item:SomeItem) -> Int
    subscript(i:Int) -> SomeItem { get }
}
```

There is a functionality that Swift arrays currently do not have but I really wish they did. The functionality—passing an array to a variadic parameter—is otherwise known as the splat operator in other languages. You can implement this functionality yourself. The implementation looks like this:

```
class List<T:Equatable>:Bucket, Uniquable {
    var items = [T]();
    func add(allItems:T...){
        items += allItems
    }
    func add(allItems:[T]) {
        items += allItems
    }
...
```

Now you are ready to create the new combineUnique function. This function will combine two arrays and then remove the duplicates. It is important to carefully watch what *types* are passed into this function. That is why you need to implement the where clause here. Here's what you need:

```
func combineUnique<L1:Bucket,L2:Bucket
    where L1.SomeItem == L2.SomeItem, L1:Uniquable>(list1:L1,list2:L2) -> L1 {
    list1.add(list2.items)
    list1.deDup()
    return list1
}
```

Take a look at this supermeaty where clause. Here's what's going on:

- First are the angle brackets with the two generic types declared:

  ```
  <L1:Bucket, L2:Bucket
  ```

  This says that you will use two different generic types in this function, and both must adopt the Bucket protocol.

- The where clause compares the typealias of L1 and L2:

```
where L1.SomeItem == L2.SomeItem
```

This means that the items in L1 and L2 must be the same. They can be whatever you want, but they must be of the same type. They can both be Ints, or both be Strings, or whatever you want, as long as they are the same type.

- A comma says that one more condition must be met. You want to make sure that L1 adopts the protocol Uniquable:

```
L1:Uniquable
```

You need to do this because you will need to deDup the first list after you add list2's items to it.

So the where clause must meet the following criteria: The types of list1 and list2 must adopt the Bucket protocol, *and* the items contained within list1 and list2 must be of the same type, *and* list1 must adopt the protocol Uniquable.

Providing such a strict where clause means that the actual code (the implementation) that makes this happen is very short. You abstracted away some of the dirty work and gave it to the implementation of the Bucket protocol. You don't need to write the code that combines arrays or the code that removes the duplicates. All you need to do is write the two lines of code that do the removal of duplicate elements, and you are done. You know that this method will work because of the strict where clause. You gave this method strict guidelines to abide by, and by doing so the developer who uses this code will be greeted with errors before he compiles the code. Classes must meet certain criteria to even be considered for this function.

You might be wondering, as I did, why you need all these complicated where clauses in a function. Why can't you just use one type: L1:Bucket, Uniquable? Because you need to combine the lists, and in order to do that, the contents of the lists must be the same type. You can't combine a list of Ints and Strings because that would not work. You need to make sure the junk in list1 is the same type as the junk in list2. If you left it as L1:Bucket, Uniquable, then you could make two different lists with different types and pass them in.

This way of using where clauses also frees you up to spend time doing error checking. You know that anything that got into this function meets the requirements of this function. You don't need to do any downcasting or type checking because the where clause does that for you.

Now it would be really nice if you could see the contents of this array that you've deDuped and combined. To do that, you need to implement a generator so that it can loop through the contents of the array. You could implement your own generator, but you can also take a shortcut to implement it. Because the items of your List form an array, and arrays have the implementation of looping already built in, you can use an array, like this:

```
protocol Bucket {
    typealias SomeItem
    var count:Int { get }
    var items:[SomeItem] { get set }
    func add(allItems:SomeItem...)
    func add(allItems:[SomeItem])
```

```
        func indexOf(item:SomeItem) -> Int
        subscript(i:Int) -> SomeItem { get }
}

protocol Uniquable {
    func deDup()
}

class List<T:Equatable>:Bucket, Uniquable, SequenceType {
    var items = [T]();
    func add(allItems:T...){
        items += allItems
    }

    func add(allItems:[T]) {
        items += allItems
    }

    func deDup() {
        var uniques = [T]()
        for t in items {
            if uniques.indexOf(t) == nil {
                uniques.append(t)
            }
        }
        items = uniques
    }

    func generate() -> IndexingGenerator<Array<T>> {
        return items.generate()
    }

    func indexOf(item:T) -> Int {
        for (index,t) in items.enumerate() {
            if t == item {
                return index
            }
        }
        return -1
    }

    var count:Int {
        return items.count
    }
    subscript(i: Int) -> T {
        return items[i]
    }
}
```

```
func combineUnique<L1:Bucket,L2:Bucket
    where L1.SomeItem == L2.SomeItem, L1:Uniquable>(list1:L1,list2:L2) -> L1 {
        list1.add(list2.items)
        list1.deDup()
        return list1
}

var l = List<Int>()
l.add(1,2,3,4,5,4,4,4,5,6,7,7)
var l2 = List<Int>()
l2.add(1,2,3,4,5,4,4,4,5,6,7,7,8,9,10)
print(combineUnique(l,list2: l2).count)
for n in l {
    print(n) // 1,2,3,4,5,6,7,8,9,10
}
```

The main idea behind making your class loopable is to make your class/struct adopt the SequenceType protocol. The SequenceType protocol wants you to create a function called generate that returns some sort of generator. You could write one yourself by subclassing one of the many generators. Instead, here you took a shortcut and used the items generator that is already built into the array. Of course, you could always start with a blank slate and implement the whole thing, but you didn't need to.

Summary

Generics provide a great way to abstract your code so that when you create a new fancy List type, it will work the same for a list of Strings, Ints, or even NSDates. Generics give you a great way to write code that is type-safe so that instead of writing code to check types, you can rest assured that types are coming in as you expect them to.

10

Games with SpriteKit

In Chapter 5, "SpriteKit," you learned how to program a game with SpriteKit. This chapter continues to build on those concepts, but it focuses more on animation. This chapter focuses on making a game, as well as how to build basic game concepts such as 2D animation, basic physics, and sound playback.

The Game

The game we will make is very basic in its appearance but will teach you the most important concepts of SpriteKit that you'll definitely use every time you make a game. In this simple game, your user will control the hero as he runs away from an enemy that's chasing him. The enemy watches your every move and stays within the bounds of the game while you try to collect the diamonds on the screen. The main point of this game is to show you how simple it is to make a basic game with SpriteKit for any device. Your game should be running at a solid 60 frames per second, which is impressive for all the collision detection that will be going on.

The Setup

Our first step in making our game is to create a project using Xcode. We have done this in other chapters, so you should already know how to do it.

Open up your version of XCode. You should have three options for creating a project. Click Create a New XCode Project.

This will bring you to a screen where you can choose from a number of predefined projects. You are going to use the setup for a game. Select Game and click Next.

At this point you can customize the name of your project, language, and supported devices. Give your game any name you want. I used Chase Game. Give yourself an organization name, and if you don't have one, make one up. I call my organization Bisonkick, just for fun. I own the domain bisonkick.com so I know that this project is going to use a unique organization name. I don't use the domain for anything; I just keep it around in case I want to use it later and so that I can claim the name Bisonkick. Therefore, my organization name is com.bisonkick, which makes my Bundle Identifier com.bisonkick.chase-game. Your bundle identifier will be set automatically.

For the language you can choose Swift, and for the Game Technology choose SpriteKit. For devices you can choose Universal. Click Next.

The next screen will ask you to save your game somewhere, so choose a location to save your game and click Create.

You now have your project all set up and ready to be coded.

Tour the Code

You are now ready to write the code for your game. Let's take a quick tour of the generated code. In your project navigator, where all the files sit you will see a bunch of files that make up the default game that comes with SpriteKit. If you haven't already done so, run your game once to see the default game that SpriteKit comes with.

You should see a spaceship rotating on the screen. When you tap the screen, you will see more spaceships appear. At the bottom of the screen, you will see a count of how many nodes are on the screen. Each time you tap the screen, you'll notice that a node is added to the node count. Notice it starts with three nodes and increments every time you add a spaceship to the screen.

The first step is to remove this default code so we can write some of our own. Your code starts in the `AppDelegate.swift` file, which is responsible for everything related to application setup and shutdown and everything that happens in between. We won't need to do anything with this file this time around. Next, our code will go to the Storyboard, which is in `Main.storyboard`. In this file you can see one controller on the screen. Its background is completely black. Your game will be played inside of this view. This view is an `SKView` being controlled by a `UIViewController` named `GameViewController`. We covered all of this in Chapter 5, so we don't need to repeat everything here. `GameViewController` code is in the file `GameViewController.swift`. If you open up `GameViewController.swift`, you will see the setup of your initial scene that will run your game. The most important thing to notice here is the `scaleMode` and how it's set. You'll recall that we talked about the scale mode in Chapter 5 as well; so if you need a refresher on `scaleMode`, refer to Chapter 5. Finally, at around line 29, the `GameViewController` presents our scene and we are directed to `GameScene.swift` for the first scene of our game.

The Game

There are two files that pertain to our `GameScene` class: `GameScene.sks` and `GameScene.swift`. `GameScene.swift` is the actual code that represents our `GameScene` class. `GameScene.sks` is the file that also represents our `GameScene` class in a visual GUI. When a game is being made, each object that is put on the screen (an enemy, a hero, a plant, a zombie, a background, fire, smoke, or anything else) is going to be an `SKNode`. It may be an `SKSpriteNode`, for attaching an image/sprite to something happening onscreen; or an SKLabelNode, for text that you can manipulate onscreen; or an SKEmitterNode, for adding smoke or other effects to your game. Adding a node to the game programmatically takes a few lines of code and takes some organization on your part to keep track of that node and everything that it will represent. Apple tries to make this easier on you by allowing you to add all of your nodes in the sks file. The sks file is a SpriteKit scene editor. It allows you to set various properties of your scene visually, as well as add nodes to your scene that you can then control programmatically. The SpriteKit editor is a new feature of Xcode and has frankly been a bit of a hassle, so we won't use it right now except to check out the size of our scene. The Spritekit editor does what you can do in code, except with a graphical user interface.

Step 1: Create the World

Our first step in creating our game is to create our world with the assets we have. We are going to create each level from our info.plist, and that way we can load as many levels as we want. By storing level data in our info.plist, we won't have to change any code to create new levels for the game. The info.plist is really just a giant dictionary that you can edit without having to change any code. It can be accessed from your code by using NSBundle.

Create the Levels

Open up your info.plist by clicking on it. The plist editor appears and you can add new rows for your levels by right-clicking in the whitespace below the list and clicking Add Row (see Figure 10.1).

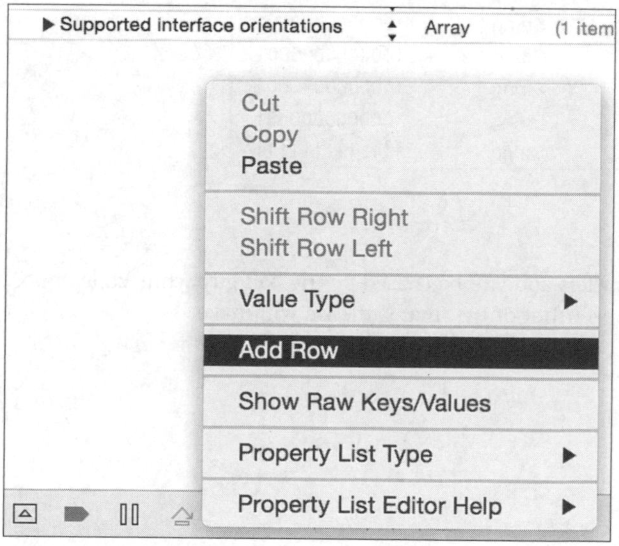

Figure 10.1   Add a row

You can name your new row Levels and set the Type to be Array. At this point your array of levels will have 0 items in it. Each level will be an element of the array, so add a new level to your Levels. The easiest way to do this is to expand the Levels by clicking the arrow to the left of it and clicking the plus button, which will add a new element to the array (see Figure 10.2).

▼ Levels	↕ ⊕ ⊖ Array	(1 item)
Item 0	⊕ ⊖ String ↕	

Figure 10.2   Add a new level to your Levels row

This Item 0 should then be set to an array as well since it will contain main rows for the level. You can add about ten rows to your level. Each will be a string. We will use a different character to represent different blocks for the game. We will use "d" for diamond, "1" for a regular boundary block, "0" for empty space, "b" for the bad guy, and "h" for the hero. You should only have 1 "h" in each level. You can see how I made my level look in Figure 10.3.

▼ Levels	↕	Array	(1 item)
▼ Item 0	⊕ ⊖	Array	↕ (10 items)
Item 0		String	111111111111
Item 1		String	100d00000d001
Item 2		String	100000000001
Item 3		String	1000000b00001
Item 4		String	100000000001
Item 5		String	100d000000001
Item 6		String	100000000001
Item 7		String	1000000000d01
Item 8		String	1000000000h01
Item 9		String	111111111111

Figure 10.3   Level with ten rows

This way, the hero will stop at the borders and will be chased by the bad guy while collecting the diamonds. Figure 10.4 shows a screenshot of the final game we will make.

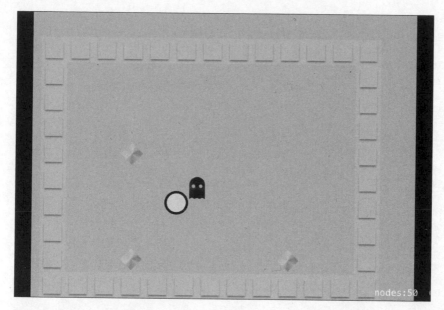

Figure 10.4   The final game

This game will contain 50 nodes and will still run at a smooth 60 frames per second.

Every time a new level is needed, it can be added directly to the array of levels in the info.plist. How easy is that?

Creating the World in Code

For our game we will want to organize our code a little better than just sticking all the code in GameScene.swift. We want our files to do some of the heavy lifting for us, so we've put together a few files to help us out. Create the following files:

- Tile.swift

- GameManager.swift

- GameHelpers.swift

- Hero.swift

- Ghost.swift

- Diamond.swift

With all of these files ready to be written to, we can start writing some code.

Our GameManager will keep track of all of our characters and blocks, with some help from the GameHelper. The GameHelper class will contain some methods that help us do some otherwise tricky stuff, like check who collided with whom. For example, if the bad guy collides with the hero, it's game over. However, if the hero collides with the diamond, we collect it and get a point. The bad guy should not collide with the diamond, but shouldn't be able to run off the level. Let's start by writing our GameManager class.

The first thing we need to do is create a skeleton class for our GameManager class:

```
import Foundation
import SpriteKit
public class GameManager {

        var currentLevel = 0
        var maxLevel = 0
        var levels = [[String]]()
        var tiles = [SKSpriteNode]()
        var main:SKScene!

    init(main:SKScene) {
            self.main = main
            loadLevelData()
    }

        private func loadLevelData() {
                levels =
NSBundle.mainBundle().objectForInfoDictionaryKey("Levels") as!
[[String]]
                maxLevel = levels.count
                load(levelNumber: 0)
        }
}
```

This code provides our GameManager with some basic functionality, but it is not complete yet. Let's go over what it does.

The first thing our GameManager class does is to define some important variables. currentLevel will keep track of what level the user is currently on. maxLevel will keep track of how many total levels there are in our info.plist. This is so that we don't advance the user to a level that does not exist. Also, when the user beats the last level, she has beaten the game completely.

In levels we store the array of level data in its entirety. If your level data is extremely large, you might want to load only one level at a time into the game's memory. In the info.plist the Levels is an array of arrays of strings, so we set the levels variable to be the same type: [[String]], meaning an array of arrays of strings.

We create an initialization method, which takes one parameter, the scene that we will add our characters to. By keeping a reference to the main game scene, we can add things to the scene from this class. We then make a call to a method called loadLevelData.

In `loadLevelData`, we grab the data from the `info.plist` and load it into our levels variable so that we can then parse our level data into our game. In this way we can change the `info.plist` anytime and change the whole game.

We call the load method and tell it which level to load. We haven't written this method yet, so let's write it. In your `GameManager.swift` in the `GameManager` class, add the following code to load the requested level.

For your global variables add the following global variables to the top of your `GameManager` class:

```
var tileSize = CGSize(width: 70, height: 70)
var tileAtlas = SKTextureAtlas(named: "tiles")
var ghosts = [Ghost]()
var diamonds = [Diamond]()
var hero:Hero!
```

We don't have all of these classes defined yet so let's define a skeleton class for each.

Let's first create the code for `Tile.swift`. Open up `Tile.swift` and add the following skeleton code:

```
import Foundation
import SpriteKit


class Tile:SKSpriteNode {
}
```

We will add more code to this class later. The `Tile` class will be used for any regular blocks that sit around the screen. I wish it were this easy to tile a room in my home!

Next let's create our characters and objects, starting with our hero: `Hero.swift`. Open up the `Hero.swift` file and add the following code:

```
import Foundation
import SpriteKit


class Hero:SKSpriteNode {
}
```

We'll use this class to hold our `Hero`. We'll need more code for our `Hero` class in a little bit, but this will get us started.

Next let's add some code for our `Ghost` class. Open up `Ghost.swift` and add the following code:

```
import Foundation
import SpriteKit


class Ghost:SKSpriteNode {
}
```

This will handle the movement of our bad guys on an individual level.

Finally, let's add some code for a diamond class. Open up `Diamond.swift` and add the following code:

```
import Foundation
import SpriteKit

class Diamond:SKSpriteNode {
}
```

The diamond, ghost, hero, and tile classes all inherit from the `SKSpriteNode`. With this set up, we can attach an image to the node. In other words, we want to have a ghost node that has an actual picture of a ghost on the node. We can then animate our nodes.

We will use atlases to store our images because this will significantly improve the performance of our application. You can use texture atlases for storing images to use later and animating them easily as well. We don't need to animate any of our images right now, so we'll just store them to be used in our sprites.

We have four images in our texture atlas. We have our regular block, ghost, diamond, and hero (see Figure 10.5). You can find files for all the images here:

http://imgur.com/a/SfT18

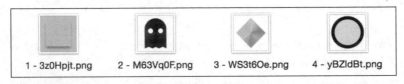

Figure 10.5   A regular block, a ghost, a diamond, and a hero

These have these default names if you got the files from Imgur. To add these sprites as a texture atlas, open up your `Assets.xcassets`. Right-click just below where it says "AppIcon" and "Spaceship." Click New Sprite Atlas (see Figure 10.6).

Figure 10.6   New Sprite Atlas

Rename the new folder from Sprites to tiles. And rename each tile so we can easily identify it later. I renamed the plain gray tile to tile_1. I renamed the ghost to tile_b for bad guy, or you could do tile_g for ghost. I renamed the diamond to tile_d for diamond, and the hero to tile_h for hero.

Finally, we can add the code for our load method, which will load the tiles on the screen based on the level data:

```
private func load(levelNumber level:Int) {
    // remove all the tiles first
    main.removeAllChildren()

    var reuseTile:SKSpriteNode!
    var start = CGPoint(x: 0, y: 0)
    start.x = ((CGFloat(String(levels[level][0]).characters.count) *
tileSize.width) / 2.0) * -1.0
    start.y = ((CGFloat(levels[level].count) * tileSize.height) / 2.0) * -1.0
    for (rowIndex, row) in levels[level].enumerate() {
        for (columnIndex, tile) in Array(row.characters).enumerate() {
            let thisTile = String(tile)
            let texture = tileAtlas.textureNamed("tile_\(thisTile)")
            switch thisTile {
                case "0":
                continue
```

```
                case "h":
                reuseTile = Hero(texture: texture, color:
SKColor.clearColor(), size: texture.size())
                hero = reuseTile as! Hero
                case "b":
                reuseTile = Ghost(texture: texture, color:
SKColor.clearColor(), size: texture.size())
                ghosts.append(reuseTile as! Ghost)
                case "d":
                reuseTile = Diamond(texture: texture, color:
SKColor.clearColor(), size: texture.size())
                diamonds.append(reuseTile as! Diamond)
                default:
                reuseTile = Tile(texture: texture, color:
SKColor.clearColor(), size: texture.size())
                tiles.append(reuseTile)
            }
            if thisTile == "0" {
                continue
            }

            reuseTile.position = CGPoint(
                x: start.x + CGFloat(columnIndex) * tileSize.width,
                y: start.y + CGFloat(rowIndex) * tileSize.height
            )
            reuseTile.name = thisTile
            tiles.append(reuseTile)
            main.addChild(reuseTile)
        }
    }
}
```

I know there is a lot of code here, but what this method does is fairly straightforward. Most of the code is taken up in a giant `switch` statement, which decides which tile to put down. Let's break this code apart and figure out what it does.

The first thing this method needs to do (since it will be called multiple times per game, every time the user advances to a new level) is to remove any existing tiles from the screen. We have a reference to the main scene from our initialization method, so we can just call `main.removeAllChildren()`, and it will remove all the tiles from the screen.

The next step is to create a tile that will be reused so we can save some memory. We create the `reuseTile` to be used over and over when populating the screen with multiple tiles. Next, we set some starting points by doing some math on the number of tiles there are. `CGPoint` is used to store an x and y position together in one variable. You'll notice that SpriteKit uses a lot of `CG` classes to store data. `CGPoint` takes two `CGFloats`. These `CG` classes are all compatible with Swift's number classes. We store `start.x` and `start.y` as the starting points of our tiles. You'll notice that we have to do a lot of converting when working with Swift, which makes this code look a little more complicated. The main idea behind the start values is that we need to know how many characters are used for each row. We assume that each row has the same number of characters. Let's assume that the first row is made up of the following:

```
1111111111111
```

In our case each row will be made up of 13 characters. Taking the number of tiles in each row and multiplying it by the tile size will tell us how much width our game will take up. For `start.x` and `start.y` we are setting an initial position for our game.

In our first `for` loop, we loop through the array of rows in level data. We use the `enumerate` method of the array to get the index of the loop at the same time.

On the inner `for` loop, we loop through each character of the string of characters in the current row. For example, if the row contained the string `"100d00000d001"`, we would loop through each of the 13 characters of that string, one at a time. We would first get `"1"`, then `"0"`, then `"0"`, then `"d"`, and so on. The way in which you loop through each character in a string has changed in Swift 2. Now you run `enumerate` on the `characters` property of a string. This makes the string iterative by character.

We then get the current character and retype it as a string. We need it to be a string so we can mix/concatenate it with another string later to generate the name of the texture atlas. We will write that on the next line.

Next, we grab the texture atlas from the `xcassets` library by grabbing the texture by name:

```
let texture = tileAtlas.textureNamed("tile_\(thisTile)")
```

This takes the name of the tile, which will be something like "1" or "b" or "h" and combines it with the word "tile" to create "tile_h" or "tile_1" and so on. This method of using texture atlases to load images is the fastest way to process images in SpriteKit, and it should be used when many images will be used instead of using the plain old `xcassets` library.

Next we run a `switch` statement to load the right tile and add it to the screen.

If the tile is "0", we skip it and move along.

If the tile is "h", we want to add the hero to the screen. We use our `Hero` class to generate a new `Hero`. We are really just initializing an `SKSpriteNode`, from which the `Hero` inherits. We then set the global `hero` variable for the `GameManager`.

If the tile is a "b", we add the bad guy, aka the ghost, to the screen. We want to convert our `reuseTile` from an `SKSpriteNode` to a `Ghost`, so we use `as!` to convert from `SKSpriteNode` to `Ghost` explicitly. We know that the conversion will work since we inherited from `SKSpriteNode`.

If the tile is a "d", we add the `Diamond` to the screen. We want to do the same thing we did for the `Hero` and `Ghost` by converting the reuse tile from an `SKSpriteNode` to a `Diamond` type.

The default (which would be a "1" tile) is to add a regular tile texture to the screen.

Setting Up the GameScene

Now that we have the basic level loader ready, we can set up our `GameScene` class to use the `GameManager`. Open up your `GameScene.swift` and remove all the default code that comes with the project. Your `GameScene` class should now look like this:

```swift
import SpriteKit

class GameScene: SKScene {
    override func didMoveToView(view: SKView) {
    }

    override func touchesBegan(touches: Set<UITouch>, withEvent event: UIEvent?) {
    }

    override func update(currentTime: CFTimeInterval) {
    }
}
```

Now we add in the use of our `GameManager` class to get the ball rolling. If we initialize our `GameManager` and reset the `anchorPoint` to be the middle of the screen, we should be good to go. Your `GameScene` class can be rewritten to look like this:

```swift
import SpriteKit

class GameScene: SKScene {
    var gameManager:GameManager!

    override func didMoveToView(view: SKView) {
        anchorPoint = CGPoint(x: 0.5, y: 0.5)
        gameManager = GameManager(main: self)
    }

    override func touchesBegan(touches: Set<UITouch>, withEvent event: UIEvent?) {
    }

    override func update(currentTime: CFTimeInterval) {
    }
}
```

The second-to-last thing we want to do before we run this code is change the project to be in landscape orientation and not in portrait. Click on your main project, which brings up all the project settings. In the project settings in the General tab, you should see a section called Deployment Info. Uncheck the Portrait option, and make sure that Landscape Left and Landscape Right are checked (as in Figure 10.7).

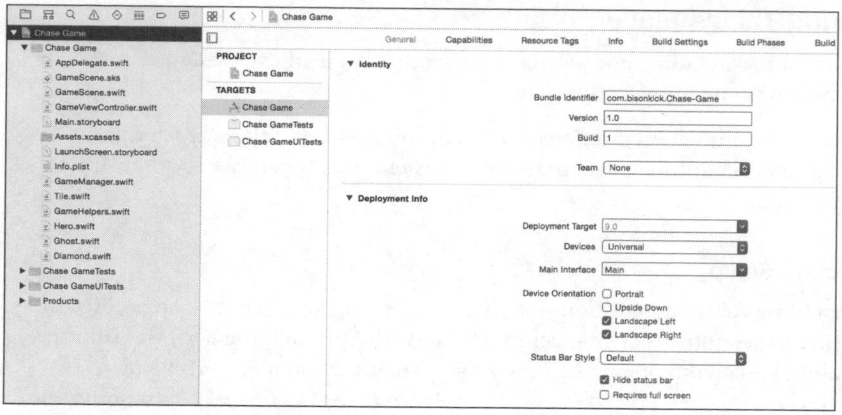

Figure 10.7   Changing the project to landscape

One last thing we want to change is to set this game's scaleMode to .AspectFit. Open up GameViewController.swift, and where the scaleMode is set to .AspectFill, change it to be .AspectFit.

When you run the game, you get all the tiles on the screen, and everything should look great except that no one is moving. You'll also notice that the game is running at 60 frames per second on every device except iPhone 6 Plus and iPhone 6s Plus (see Figure 10.8).

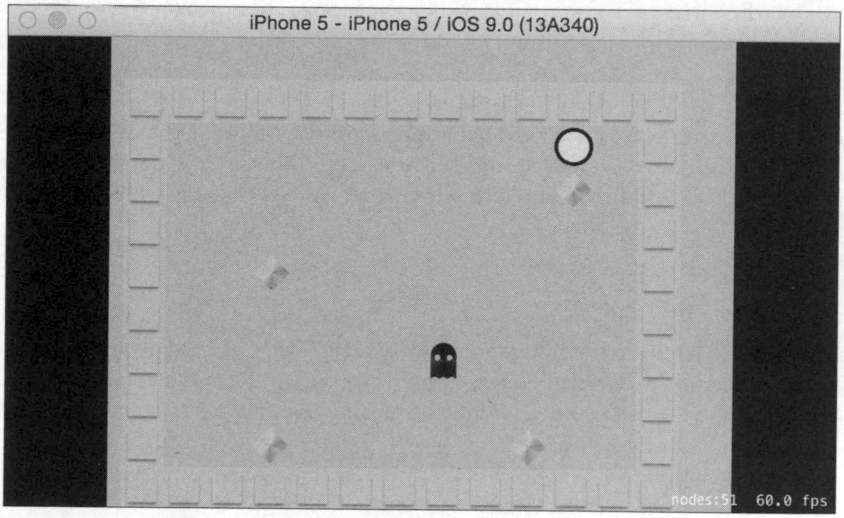

Figure 10.8   Game running at 60 fps

The next step is to get our hero moving and collecting diamonds and to have the bad guy chase him.

Step 2: Making Things Move

In our second step of making our game, we have the world set up and we've added our characters, and now it's time to make things move.

We need to detect collisions between different items in the game, and the way we will do this is by using SpriteKit's built-in collision detection system. It is super-easy to add collision detection to any game.

Collision Detection Setup

The first step in adding collision detection to a game is to set up your scene to be notified of collisions. The way to get notified of changes in iOS is usually through the delegate pattern. The most common delegate that you use all the time, perhaps without even realizing it, is `ApplicationDelegate`. `ApplicationDelegate` is used in `AppDelegate.swift` to notify the app when the phone wakes up and goes into the background.

We will use the special `SKPhysicsContactDelegate` to be notified of collisions that happen in our app. The setup for `SKPhysicsContactDelegate` is simple and is similar to other types of delegate setup. In your `GameScene.swift` modify the class declaration:

```
class GameScene: SKScene, SKPhysicsContactDelegate {
```

The `SKPhysicsContactDelegate` will call `didBeginContact` when a collision happens that you asked SpriteKit to test for. Not all collisions will show up, only the ones you ask for. We will see how we can ask to test for certain collisions.

The next step is to tell the `GameScene` class that it will be the receiver of messages regarding physics contacts:

```
physicsWorld.contactDelegate = self
```

Now that our class will get notified of collisions that happen, we need to write the method that gets called when the collisions happen. `SKPhysicsContactDelegate` has a method called `didBeginContact`. If we add that method to our class, it will get called when collisions happen. Add this method to your `GameScene` class:

```
func didBeginContact(contact: SKPhysicsContact) {
}
```

The parameter `contact` will tell us many things about the collision that just happened. Most important, it has two properties, `bodyA` and `bodyB`. Those will contain the two bodies that made contact with each other. If, for example, you had a ghost and a hero contact, `bodyA` or `bodyB` would contain the ghost physics body and `bodyA` or `bodyB` would contain the hero. The only issue is that you won't know which contains which. `bodyA` or `bodyB` may contain what you want, so you have to check both. Within `bodyA` and `bodyB` you have more information, including the `categoryBitMask` and sprite node itself as `node`. The `categoryBitMask` will tell us which category of objects this body belongs to, which we will talk about in just a second. This is where our `GameHelpers` class comes in handy. We will write some methods that will help us detect collisions much more easily. Let's put that class together. Open up your GameHelpers.swift class and let's add the categories for the objects that will collide:

```
class GameHelpers {
    enum Character:UInt32{
        case Hero =        0b001
        case Ghost =       0b010
        case Diamond =     0b011
        case Wall =        0b100
    }
}
```

Here we are using binary to set a flag for each type of character. Just remember that the flag cannot be 0. Hero is 1, Ghost is 2, Diamond is 3, and Wall is 4. Here we are just counting in binary, and the way that you write binary in Swift is to prefix the number with 0b.

Let's write another helper method for our class to check whether one object collided with another. This takes care of the issue with checking bodyA and bodyB for the right object. With this method you can just say "Did ghost collide with hero?" Add this method to your GameHelpers class.

```
class func didCollideWith(contact
contact:SKPhysicsContact,collideA:UInt32, collideB:UInt32) ->Bool {
    let bitMaskA = contact.bodyA.categoryBitMask
    let bitMaskB = contact.bodyB.categoryBitMask
    let b = bitMaskA & collideA != 0
    let c = bitMaskB & collideB != 0
    let a = bitMaskB & collideA != 0
    let d = bitMaskA & collideB != 0
    return (b && c) || (a && d)
}
```

Now we can pass in the contact object and the binary category of the object, and this function will tell you whether one collided with the other, by doing some binary operations on the categoryBitMasks. We would add this method in our didBeginContact method because that method has access to the contact that just happened. We can say something like this:

```
func didBeginContact(contact: SKPhysicsContact) {
    if GameHelpers.didCollideWith(contact: contact,
        collideA: GameHelpers.Character.Ghost.rawValue,
        collideB: GameHelpers.Character.Hero.rawValue) {
            print("ghost and hero collided")
    }
}
```

Notice we use the rawValue of the enum in the GameHelper to get the integer back from the enum. Although the method is a large amount of code to write, it is terse in its implementation.

Now we have a tool to see whether two nodes collided. We could use one more helper method to quickly return the node from a contact that has a specific name value. For example, if we know that two nodes collided and we want to grab the one node named `hero` back from the collision quickly, we can do so with this method. Add this method to your `GameHelper` class:

```
class func getNodewith
(contact contact:SKPhysicsContact, nodeName:String) -> SKNode? {
    if contact.bodyA.node != nil &&
        contact.bodyA.node!.name != nil &&
        contact.bodyA.node!.name! == nodeName {
            return contact.bodyA.node!
    } else if contact.bodyB.node != nil &&
        contact.bodyB.node!.name != nil &&
        contact.bodyB.node!.name! == nodeName {
            return contact.bodyB.node!
    } else {
        return nil
    }
}
```

This method is simple in that it just has to check whether the node is in `bodyA` or `bodyB` and, if it is, return it. It has to return an optional because we don't know that any node exists with that name in the contact. For example, if the collision was between a hero and ghost and we are looking for a node named `diamond`, we probably won't find it.

With these small helpers in hand, we can make our `Hero`, `Ghost`, `Diamond`, and `Tile` classes more detailed so they know with whom they will collide.

Let's first update our `Hero` class and talk about how we can tell SpriteKit who we want the node to collide with.

Add the following initializer to your `Hero` class in `Hero.swift`:

```
override init(texture: SKTexture?, color: UIColor, size: CGSize) {
    super.init(texture: texture, color: color, size: size)
    physicsBody = SKPhysicsBody(circleOfRadius: size.width/2.0)
    physicsBody?.affectedByGravity = false
    physicsBody?.categoryBitMask = GameHelpers.Character.Hero.rawValue
    physicsBody?.collisionBitMask =
        GameHelpers.Character.Wall.rawValue |
        GameHelpers.Character.Diamond.rawValue |
        GameHelpers.Character.Ghost.rawValue
    physicsBody?.contactTestBitMask =
        GameHelpers.Character.Diamond.rawValue |
        GameHelpers.Character.Ghost.rawValue
}
```

Here we are adding an initializer so that when the `Hero` gets initialized we also add a bunch of defaults to set the physics properties. Most important, we initialize the physics collision detection by initializing the SKPhysicsBody. As soon as you initialize a new SKPhysicsBody on your sprite's physicBody, the physics gets turned on for that sprite. We initialize it with a collision area as big as the size of the sprite. We use a circle for the collision area of the Sprite. Circles are very efficient to use in SpriteKit. In fact, circles and rectangles are the most efficient shapes you can use in collision detection.

We also turn off the gravity for the hero. You can use the built-in physics to simulate physics or you can just use its collision detection. If we turn off gravity, the objects will collide but they will not fall. Since we are creating a top-down view, it makes more sense not to have the objects fall.

We set the categoryBitMask to be the binary value of the hero from the character enum. We are telling Swift what kind of physics object this is by assigning it a binary value. When we set this value on the walls, the ghosts, and the diamonds, we will be able to say what collides with what, and Swift will compare by their CategoryBitMask. In this case we are saying that this is a Hero. We will set this categoryBitMask for the diamond, as GameHelpers.Character.Diamond.rawValue. When this is combined with the collisionBitMask and the contactTestBitMask, we can detect who is colliding with whom.

We set the collisionBitMask to say what things will collide with the hero. These things will surely collide, but they might not register with didBeginContact unless we set the contactTestBitMask. We use the binary OR operator to combine the binary values together. What we are saying here is that the hero can collide with a wall, a diamond, or (hopefully not) a ghost.

We set the contactTestBitMask to tell Swift when the didBeginContact method should be called. We are saying what type of collision we want to test for.

We have a hero that will collide with walls, diamonds, and ghosts, and we will test that collision for diamonds and ghosts.

Also, remember that when you write the Ghost class, if you are already testing for hero colliding with ghost, you shouldn't need to write to test for ghost colliding with hero. One case can handle both directions.

Let's update the Ghost class to update how the ghost should collide. Add the following code to the Ghost class:

```
override init(texture: SKTexture?, color: UIColor, size: CGSize) {
    super.init(texture: texture, color: color, size: size)
    physicsBody = SKPhysicsBody(circleOfRadius: size.width/2.0)
    physicsBody?.affectedByGravity = false
    physicsBody?.categoryBitMask = GameHelpers.Character.Ghost.rawValue
    physicsBody?.collisionBitMask =
        GameHelpers.Character.Wall.rawValue
}
```

We are doing roughly the same thing we did for the hero. We don't need as much code because the hero covers a lot of the details we need. We don't need to say that the ghost will collide with the hero if we already said the hero will collide with the ghost.

Let's update our `Diamond` class initializer. Update the code in `Diamond.swift` as follows:

```
override init(texture: SKTexture?, color: UIColor, size: CGSize) {
    super.init(texture: texture, color: color, size: size)
    physicsBody = SKPhysicsBody(circleOfRadius: size.width/2.0)
    physicsBody?.affectedByGravity = false
    physicsBody?.categoryBitMask = GameHelpers.Character.Diamond.rawValue
    physicsBody?.contactTestBitMask = GameHelpers.Character.Hero.rawValue
}
```

Here we are doing the same thing we did with the hero and the ghost. We made the collision area of the diamond a circle since it will give the user more area to hit to collect the diamond. Creating an actual custom shape to collide with in this case is unnecessary, but it is possible. Just remember that it is extremely expensive computationally so we want to do it only on a limited basis. This situation is certainly not the situation to do custom shape collision detection.

Let's update the `Tile.swift` `Tile` class. Add the following code to your `Tile.swift` class:

```
override init(texture: SKTexture?, color: UIColor, size: CGSize) {
    super.init(texture: texture, color: color, size: size)
    physicsBody = SKPhysicsBody(circleOfRadius: size.width/2.0)
    physicsBody?.dynamic = false
    physicsBody?.categoryBitMask = GameHelpers.Character.Wall.rawValue
}
```

There is one tiny detail to pay attention to here. That is that we are setting the `dynamic` property of the physics body to `false`. Dynamic bodies can move and be moved, whereas static bodies (setting the `dynamic` property to `false`) cannot be moved. That is why we set the tile to be `dynamic false`. Therefore, the tiles will be unmovable objects.

Making Things Move with `SKActions`

At this point not much has changed visually in the game except that we now have collision detection working. It would be nice if we could see the collision detection in action. Let's make our hero move.

The way to make things move in SpriteKit is to use `SKActions`. You don't have to manually change the position properties of the node itself. Instead, SpriteKit politely takes care of all the movement.

Let's add two methods to our `Hero` class to make the hero move when we tap the screen. We will need a `moveTo` method to make the hero move to a location. We also need a `cancelMove` method so that the hero can be stopped from performing a move. Add the following code to the hero class:

```
public func moveTo(location location:CGPoint) {
    removeAllActions()
    let path = CGPathCreateMutable()
    CGPathMoveToPoint(path, nil, position.x, position.y)
```

```
    CGPathAddLineToPoint(path, nil, location.x, location.y)
    runAction(SKAction.followPath(path, asOffset: false, orientToPath:
false, speed: 500))
}

public func cancelMove() {
    removeAllActions()
}
```

Our `moveTo` method takes a location to move the hero to. We move the hero along a path. There are many ways to move a sprite, and in this case we use `followPath`. Let's take a look at some other ways to move a sprite:

- `moveTo`: For moving the sprite directly to a location instead of moving by a certain amount. Works for X and Y.

- `moveBy`: For moving the sprite by a certain amount (using a delta). Works for X and Y.

- `moveByX`: The same as `moveTo`, but for moving the sprite along the X coordinate.

- `fadeInWithDuration`: For fading in a sprite, in seconds.

- `fadeOutWithDuration`: For fading out a sprite in seconds.

- `resizeToWidth`: For resizing the sprite to a certain width by changing the size property.

There are many more `SKActions` available in the documentation, and most are very straightforward to implement. Make sure you check out the documentation. When we run `runAction`, we don't need to orient to the path because our hero is a circle. We set the speed to be 500 so that our hero will move at a consistent speed instead of using a duration to move the hero. If we had used a duration, the hero would move at different speeds. A farther distance but the same time would mean the hero would have to move faster to get to his point. This way the hero always moves at a constant speed.

We also have the special method `removeAllActions()`, which will (as you can probably guess) remove all actions from the list of actions currently running on the hero. This is good when we want to stop the hero from moving.

We can't move the hero yet because we haven't implemented the tap for our program yet.

Tap the Screen to Move the Hero

Now we can implement the tapping of the screen to move the hero. In your `GameManager` class we can implement a method `touchDownAt` to move the hero when the screen is touched. Add the following code to your `GameManager` class:

```
public func touchDownAt(location location:CGPoint) {
    hero.moveTo(location: location)
}
```

All that this method does is call the hero's move method. You can imagine that if you needed more things to respond to a tap, you could implement them here.

What is going to call the GameManager's method? The GameScene is listening for the user to tap the screen. Add the following code to your GameScene to listen for the user to tap the screen and send that tap off to the GameManager:

```
override func touchesBegan(touches: Set<UITouch>, withEvent event: UIEvent?) {
    if let touch = touches.first {
        gameManager.touchDownAt(location: touch.locationInNode(self))
    }
}
```

With this method we listen for only the first touch. You can grab all the fingers that are touching the screen, but since we need only the first touch on the screen, we grab that first touch and send its location to the game manager. We use locationInNode(self) to say, in effect, "We want the location of touch that happened in this scene," with self referring to the GameScene itself. We need a location coordinate that refers to the scene as a whole.

At this point you can run the game. You will notice that when you click the screen the hero runs to your finger. If he hits any diamonds or ghosts along the way, he will collide with them and probably move the diamonds out of the way.

We should make it so that when the hero collides with the diamonds they disappear off the screen.

Eat the Diamonds!

Now that our hero is moving, we can make him collect the diamonds. This is a fairly straightforward task, since we are already looking for collisions.

How do we get started? We need to add a method to our GameManager that gets called when a collision between the hero and a diamond happens. When that happens, we want to stop the hero from moving (we already wrote that method). We then want to remove the diamond from the screen. We could write a method in the diamond class to remove it from the screen. We would normally do that if this game got any more complicated. However, we are currently just removing the diamond from the screen, so we'll do that directly from the GameManager. Add the following code to your GameManager class:

```
public func heroHitDiamond(diamond:Diamond) {
    hero.cancelMove()
    diamond.removeFromParent()
    diamonds.removeAtIndex(diamonds.indexOf(diamond)!)
    if diamonds.count == 0 {
        print("win level")
    }
}
```

We will call this method from our GameScene, which is detecting any collisions that happen between the hero and the diamond. We stop the hero from moving. This is optional and depends on how you want your game to play. You may decide that the hero should continue moving when he collects diamonds. The choice is yours. We then remove the diamond from the screen by calling `removeFromParent()`. This method will remove the item itself from the screen by removing it from its parent. This is very straightforward and different and easier than in other game frameworks where you have to know the parent to remove the child. For example, if your view hierarchy is much more complicated, you may not know who owns this sprite, so it's great that Apple has `removeFromParent()`. This makes it supersimple to remove a sprite node from the screen.

We have a list of the diamonds on the screen. When we remove the diamond from the screen, we also need to remove the diamond from the array of diamonds so that we can keep track of how many diamonds are left on the screen. We use `removeAtIndex` to remove the diamond at a specific index, while simultaneously getting the index using the new `indexOf` method of the array class. This will remove the diamond from the array of diamonds at the specified index.

So far we can run this game and start collecting the diamonds. Play around with the code and make it fit your style of game. If you think the hero should not stop when collecting diamonds, take that line out. If you think the hero moves too slowly, speed him up.

We now have a game that works, but it isn't very hard since there aren't any enemies to stop us from collecting the diamonds. It would be great if that ghost would chase us instead of sitting around like a lazy bum.

Making the Ghost Chase the Hero

To make the ghost chase the hero, we can just put him on a timer. Every so often he will attempt to move to where the hero is. How often he attempts to chase the hero can be changed based on how far the user has progressed in the game.

Let's first write a method to make the ghost move toward the hero, and then we'll move the ghost on a timer. We can move the ghost to the hero in two lines of code. The first line of code is to remove all existing actions the ghost is currently performing. The second line of code will move the ghost to the position of the hero. Add this code to your `Ghost` class:

```
private func moveGhostToHero(heroPosition:CGPoint) {
    removeAllActions()
    runAction(SKAction.moveTo(heroPosition, duration: 1.5))
}
```

We make the ghost run at a duration because I think it's neat to have the ghost run at various speeds. When the ghost movement is set to a duration, the ghost will move at different speeds depending on how far away he is from the hero.

The next step is to move the ghost at a specific time interval. He should run for you every n seconds. Let's add two global variables to our `Ghost` class:

```
var lastUpdate = CFTimeInterval()
var moveInterval = 0.5
```

The `lastUpdate` will be the last time that the ghost ran for the hero. The `moveInterval` will be how often the ghost runs for the hero. The higher the number, the less often the ghost will run at the hero. Next, we want to write a method that gets run every frame of the game and

decides when it's the right time to go into attack mode. Add the following code to your
Ghost class:

```
public func update(currentTime:CFTimeInterval, heroPosition:CGPoint) {
    let now = NSDate.timeIntervalSinceReferenceDate()
    let sinceLastUpdate = now - lastUpdate
    if sinceLastUpdate > moveInterval {
        lastUpdate = now
        moveGhostToHero(heroPosition)
    }
}
```

We take the current time stamp by using `timeIntervalSinceReferenceDate()`. That method
gets the number of seconds that have passed since 12:00 a.m. on January 1, 2001. That specific
date does not really matter; all that matters is that x number of seconds have passed since
that date and you need that date to be constant. By subtracting now from the lastUpdate,
we return how much time has passed since the lastUpdate. If that time is greater than our
threshold for our moveInterval, we will set the lastUpdate to be now and we will move the
ghost using the move ghost method we just wrote.

We are almost ready to have a moving ghost. We just need to make sure that this update
method gets called on every frame. How do we do that? Let's create an update method in our
GameManager to update the ghosts. Add this code to your GameManager:

```
public func update(currentTime: CFTimeInterval) {
    updateGhosts(currentTime)
}
```

The update method of our GameManager can obviously take much more code if you decide to
add functionality to this game, but for now all it will do is call a method to update all of our
ghosts (although there is only one for now). Let's write that method updateGhosts(). Add the
following code to your GameManager:

```
private func updateGhosts(currentTime:CFTimeInterval) {
    for ghost in ghosts {
        ghost.update(currentTime, heroPosition: hero.position)
    }
}
```

This code simply calls the ghost update method on every ghost that exists. Not much going on
here except a loop through every single ghost.

How is our GameManager going to get updated? We need to call update on the GameManager
from the GameScene. In your GameScene, there is a built-in update method that gets called on
its own without any work from you. Let's update that update method in GameScene. Add the
following code to your GameScene:

```
override func update(currentTime: CFTimeInterval) {
    gameManager.update(currentTime)
}
```

All that this method does is update our `GameManager` class every frame. If you run this code, you will see your ghost running after the hero. Game on!

At this point our game works. The hero can collect the diamonds, and the ghost chases the hero. We can detect collisions between any two objects in the game. The rest of the work to make this a full-fledged game for the App Store is up to you. Make a scoreboard so that when the user collects the diamonds, the score increases. Make it so that when the user collects all the diamonds and doesn't get hit, the user moves to the next user-defined level. Make multiple ghosts chasing the hero. All the code I am suggesting as an exercise will be fairly simple to implement, thanks to everything you've learned from this chapter.

Summary

In this chapter you learned how to make a basic SpriteKit game. You learned the best way to move the sprites on the screen. You learned how to use texture atlases to make a smooth running game with nice assets. You learned the best ways to detect collisions in your game even if you aren't simulating physics in any other way. And you wrote some useful helper functions, which you will no doubt use in your own games to make your life simpler.

11

Making Games with Physics

SpriteKit makes it easier than ever to make physics-based games. In this chapter we will create our own physics-based game, without any extra math needed. SpriteKit will do all the physics-based animations and take care of everything needed to make a fully functional game in Swift. We are going to make a game similar to Peggle. You drop a ball and it hits other balls, and each ball it hits gets removed at the end of the ball's journey to the bottom. This game will be the basis for any other ball-dropping game you want to make. In the process of making this simple game, you will understand how you can take this game further and make your own game. We will cover collision detection again, but this time we will go deeper. We will cover the physics engine and how you apply basic physics properties to sprites to make them do whatever you want. Let's get started.

In this chapter we will cover a lot of material, and we will move at a little faster pace so we don't repeat stuff we learned in other chapters. If you haven't read the first two chapters on SpriteKit (Chapters 5 and 10), you might want to do that first.

Making a Physics-Based Game

Making a physics-based game in SpriteKit is the same process as making a non–physics-based game. In fact, the games we have been making in SpriteKit have been physics-based games already because we have used the built-in collision detection. The only thing we haven't taken advantage of is gravity (and, in turn, many other physics properties). To get started, let's take a look at the game we will make (see Figure 11.1).

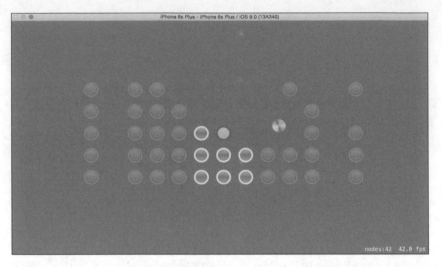

Figure 11.1   Our physics-based game

In this game the ball falls from the top and hits other balls. When the ball gets to the bottom, the game removes all the balls you hit. If for some reason the ball gets stuck, the game removes the balls you've hit and moves on. Let's get started.

Creating the Project

To create this project, open up Xcode and select File, New, Project. Select the Game template and click Next. Give the project a name; I chose Bouncy Balls. Make sure the language is set to Swift, the Game Technology is set to SpriteKit, and the Devices option is set to Universal, and click Next.

Xcode will ask you to save your game somewhere. Choose a location and click Create. You are presented with the same SpriteKit files as before. The first thing you'll want to do is make this game a landscape game. By default, you should be on the project page, on the General tab, and you should see Deployment Info. If not, select the project name in the file explorer and choose the General tab and look under Deployment Info.

Under Deployment Info, unselect Portrait and make sure that Landscape Left and Landscape Right are selected.

The next step is to erase all the default game code. Open up GameScene.swift and then erase all the code and make it look like this:

```
class GameScene: SKScene {
    override func didMoveToView(view: SKView) {
    }
    override func touchesBegan(touches: Set<UITouch>, withEvent event: UIEvent?) {
    }
```

```
override func update(currentTime: CFTimeInterval) {
    }
}
```

Congrats—you now have a beautiful blank game. Change that background to white and put this app directly on the app store and label it "Flashlight." I'm kidding—don't do that, that's shameful, and we can do so much better.

Adding the Assets

This game will have exactly four beautifully painted and hand-signed .pngs. Let's just grab those assets and plop them in the asset library. You can grab the assets at http://imgur.com/a/14XCS.

Add those assets to the asset library as you've done in previous chapters. You can remove the spaceship from the xcassets library.

Your asset library should look like mine (see Figure 11.2).

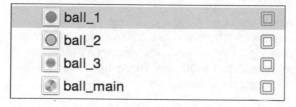

Figure 11.2   The asset library

Name each ball. Red ball is ball_1, yellow ball is ball_2, blue ball is ball_3, and silver ball is ball_main.

We will use the ball_main as our game ball, the ball that interacts with all the other balls.

Let's set up our levels. We will use the info.plist for this.

Adding the Levels

The next step is to add our levels to the game. When the player hits all the balls on the screen and there are no balls left, we will load the next level. Our first step is to open up the info.plist and add a new row called Levels. You'll want to make the data type for levels an array. I made our levels look like what you see in Figure 11.3.

▼ Levels	⬍ ➕ ➖	Array	⬍ (2 items)
▼ Item 0		Array	(5 items)
Item 0		String	0,1,0,1,1,1,2,2,2,1,1,1,0,1,0
Item 1		String	0,1,0,1,1,1,2,2,2,1,1,1,0,1,0
Item 2	➕ ➖	String	0,1,0,1,1,1,2,3,2,1,1,1,0,1,0
Item 3		String	0,1,0,1,1,1,2,2,2,1,1,1,0,1,0
Item 4		String	0,1,0,1,1,1,2,2,2,1,1,1,0,1,0
▼ Item 1		Array	(2 items)
Item 0		String	0,0,0,1,1,2,2,2,2,2,1,1,0,0,0
Item 1		String	0,0,0,1,1,2,2,2,2,2,1,1,0,0,0

Figure 11.3   Adding the levels

Again, if you haven't checked out the first two chapters on SpriteKit, you may be wondering how to edit an `info.plist`, and in that case I encourage you to review those chapters.

After you have your levels added, feel free to add as much data for your levels as you want. Right now we have two levels total. You can easily add a third level. The game will automatically advance to the next level on its own.

For our level layout, the numbers refer directly to the assets in the asset library. In the asset library we have `ball_1`, `ball_2`, and `ball_3`, in which a 1 in the level data refers to `ball_1`, 2 refers to `ball_2`, and so on. The 0 in the level data refers to an empty space. It's sometimes nice to add empty spaces on either end in case you want to add a ball on its own. You should have the same number of items in each row. Our game is expecting the same number of items in each row.

Generating the Levels

You will find that this game involves very little code. You would think that making a game like this would be more complicated, but it's not, thanks to SpriteKit's built-in physics library. We will use three extra classes (aside from `GameScene`), which will hold logic for a single ball, the different types of colliders, and a `BallManager` class.

Add to your project three files:

- `BallManager.swift`
- `Ball.swift`
- `Collider.swift`

Colliders for `BitMasks`

Open up `Collider.swift` and let's create `categoryBitMasks` for the different types of items that will collide:

```
struct Collider {
    static let HERO:UInt32 = 0x1 << 1
```

```
    static let BALL:UInt32 = 0x1 << 2
    static let CAGE:UInt32 = 0x1 << 3
}
```

If you remember from the last SpriteKit chapter (Chapter 10, "Games with SpriteKit"), we made multiple categories using binary numbers. This time we are using bit shifting to create the numbers, but the result is exactly the same. We want to make sure that our hero ball collides only with the things we want it to collide with, and the same for the other categories.

This class is pretty straightforward and shouldn't be complicated if you remember category bit masks from the other chapter. We covered how we use category bit masks to define the different objects on the screen to make sure that certain objects interact only with other objects that we expect them to interact with.

The Balls

The next step is to create our `Ball` class. This will define a basic `SKSpriteNode` with a built-in physics body so that we can have a basic ball that can switch between different textures.

The initializer for this class will choose between different ball types and add the right texture to them accordingly. Here is the code for our `Ball` class:

```
import SpriteKit

public class Ball: SKSpriteNode {
    public var type:Int = 0
    public var hit = false
    init(type:Int) {
        self.type = type
        let texture = SKTexture(imageNamed: "ball_\(type)")
        super.init(texture: texture,
        color: SKColor.clearColor(), size: texture.size())
        physicsBody = SKPhysicsBody(circleOfRadius: texture.size().width/2)
        physicsBody?.dynamic = false
        physicsBody?.categoryBitMask = Collider.BALL
        physicsBody?.collisionBitMask = Collider.HERO
        physicsBody?.contactTestBitMask = Collider.HERO
    }

    public required init?(coder aDecoder: NSCoder) {
        fatalError("init(coder:) has not been implemented")
    }
}
```

Here we are defining a `Ball` class, which inherits from an `SKSpriteNode`, so you know we are going to add a texture to our sprite.

We allow the users to initialize the ball by type. All they have to add to the initializer is a 1, 2, or 3. In other words, they could initialize the ball like so:

```
let ball = Ball(type: 2)
```

This will initialize an `SKSpriteNode` with a texture of `ball_2`.

We set a variable `hit`, so we know whether the ball has been hit. We don't want to count for a ball being hit twice. We will also have a variable to save the type of the ball if we need later.

Finally, we initialize this sprite using the super class. We pass in the texture we generated from the `xcassets`, we set the color to be clear (a `.png` is clear), and the size of the sprite is the same size as the texture so we can just use `texture.size()`. Interestingly enough, `SKSpriteNode` uses `.size` and textures use `.size()`.

The next four lines define the physics body of the sprite. We have to initialize a physics body for our sprite, and we'll do it with the initializer `circleOfRadius`. Since radius is half the width (or diameter) of a circle, we can just grab the `size().width` of the textures and divide by 2. This will obviously give us the radius. Since the balls will be stationary while the main ball bounces around, we will set `dynamic` to `false`. A nondynamic physics body is called a *static body*. It cannot be moved and things will bounce off of it.

We set the category bit mask to be `BALL` in order to say "This is a ball."

We set the collision bit mask to be `HERO` to say "This ball should collide with objects assigned to the category bit mask of `HERO`."

We set the contact bit mask to be `HERO` to say "This ball should be tested for collision with objects assigned to the category bit mask of `HERO`."

When creating something that subclasses an `SKSpriteNode`, we must use a `required init` in the class; otherwise, we'll get an error. Xcode will automatically generate that `required init` for you.

That's all for this small bit of code. The next step is to write the level generation for the `BallManager`.

The `BallManager` Level Generator

Open up your `BallManager.swift` with your `BallManager` class in there. Make sure that you import SpriteKit in each of these files. It usually is not necessary to import `Foundation`, but it isn't going to hurt anything to have that import statement in there. At this point this is what your `BallManager` class should look like:

```
import SpriteKit

class BallManager {
}
```

The first step for your `BallManager` class is to load the level data. Let's create some global variables that we'll need in order to store things like the level data and the current level.

```
public var balls = [Ball]()
private var levels = [[String]]()
private var mainBall:SKSpriteNode!
public var currentLevel = 0
```

Here we define an array to hold all the balls. The array holds things of type `Ball`. We define an array to hold the level data. This is an array that holds an array that holds strings. We hold a reference to the main ball that gets dropped from the top. We hold a reference to the current level. Since we are going to be moving to the next level after all the balls disappear, we need to keep track of the current level. Before we create the method for creating the level, let's write an initializer to load our level data from our `info.plist` file. Add this to your `BallManager` class:

```
init() {
    levels = NSBundle
        .mainBundle()
        .objectForInfoDictionaryKey("Levels") as! [[String]]
}
```

This method simply initializes our `BallManager` class and grabs the level data from the `info.plist` and assigns it to the `levels` variable.

Let's write the whole method for creating the level, which is a good 31 lines of code. We'll go through it one line at a time.

```
public func loadLevel(scene:SKScene) {
    if levels.count == currentLevel {
        print("You win the game")
    }
    let spaceBetween:CGFloat = 1.5

    //next lines are to get the ball in the center X
    let ballsPerRow = levels[0][0].characters.split{$0 == ","}.map(String.init).count
    let tempBall = Ball(type: 1)
    let ballsWidth = CGFloat(ballsPerRow) * (tempBall.size.width * spaceBetween)
    let toCenterPaddingX =
        ((scene.size.width - ballsWidth) / 2) + tempBall.size.width

    let ballsHeight = CGFloat
        (levels[currentLevel].count)
        * (tempBall.size.height * spaceBetween)
    let toCenterPaddingY =
        ((scene.size.height - ballsHeight) / 2)
        + tempBall.size.height


    for (i, row) in levels[currentLevel].enumerate() {
        let ballList = row.characters.split{$0 == ","}.map(String.init)
        for (j, ball) in ballList.enumerate(){
```

```
                let ballSprite = Ball(type: 1)
                if ball == "0" {
                    continue
                }
                if ball != "1" {
ballSprite.runAction(SKAction.setTexture(SKTexture(imageNamed:
"ball_\(ball)")))
                }
                ballSprite.position =
            CGPoint(x: toCenterPaddingX
            + (CGFloat(j) * ballSprite.size.width * spaceBetween),
             y: toCenterPaddingY
            + (CGFloat(i) * ballSprite.size.height * spaceBetween))
                balls.append(ballSprite)
            }
        }
}
```

The first thing this level loader does is grab one parameter. That one parameter is the scene that we should add all the balls to.

We write an `if` statement which says that if the number of levels we have stored in the `info.plist` is the same as the current level we are on, you win the game.

In the next line we define a variable, `spaceBetween`, which will be a `CGFloat` since most numbers defined in SpriteKit are `CGFloat`. This variable defines the space between each ball. Feel free to play around with this number.

The next line is more of a magical incantation:

```
let ballsPerRow = levels[0][0].characters.split{$0 == ","}.map(String.init).count
```

We want to get how many balls we will use per row. `levels[0][0]` is the first item in the levels array. We are getting the first row of the first level. What we want to do next is split that row of strings by the comma (`","`). To do that, we need an array of the characters. We can get that array by using `characters`. That property is not an array, but it is an array-like structure. We then use the split method to split this list of characters in some way. We pass a closure to this method. This closure matches commas. It will return `true` when the character is a comma. When we use map with that and pass `String.init`, we will get an array of characters that were separated by commas. So if the row was

```
0,0,0,1,1,2,2,2,2,1,1,0,0,0
```

then this method will return an array of those characters:

```
[0,0,0,1,1,2,2,2,2,1,1,0,0,0]
 // a real array, not just a textual representation of one.
```

Finally, at the end we have the `count` of that array.

So what does that magical line of code do? It counts the number of characters in the first row of the first level so that we know how many balls to loop through.

The next line stores a temp ball so that we can reuse that variable when we loop through our level. It's good to store a ball we can reuse later.

The next line gets `ballWidth` by taking the number of balls per row and multiplying it by the width of one ball and multiplying that by the space between each ball.

When we loop through each ball, we need to add an initial padding to the balls to make the whole level centered. To get the center X padding, we can get the width of the whole scene and subtract the total width of all the balls. We then divide that by 2 (see Figure 11.4).

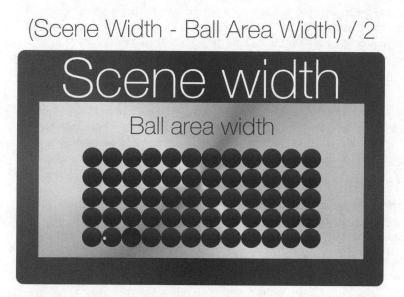

Figure 11.4   Getting the center X padding

For the ball area height and the padding Y, we do a very similar calculation, except for height and the Y axis.

Now it's time to loop. To get our rows and columns, we need to do a loop within a loop. Our first loop will loop through each row in the list of rows for this level. We use the `enumerate` method of the array because it enables us to get back the index of the current item as well as the current item at the same time.

On the next line we grab a list of the balls in the same way we described previously, except this time we don't need the count of the array, we need the array itself. This will return the array of balls, something like this:

```
[0,0,0,1,1,2,2,2,2,2,1,1,0,0,0]
```

We can then loop through each ball for the current row:

```
for (j, ball) in ballList.enumerate(){
```

For each ball in the list of balls, we want the ball itself (`ball`) and the index of the ball (`j`).

The next step is to create a ball to which we will add the texture of the `ball_1` by default. If we need to, we can change the texture.

If that current ball is `0`, we want to just move along because `0` is a blank space.

Now we have a ball that has the `1` texture. We test it and if this ball is not equal to `1`, we need to change the texture of the ball.

To change the texture of a sprite, we need to use an `SKAction`. Specifically, we can use `SKAction.setTexture` and pass in a texture. Now we have a ball with the proper texture; the only thing left to do is to properly position the ball on the screen. We know exactly where this ball should go because we have padding for X and padding for Y so that the group of balls will be perfectly centered on the screen.

To position the ball in the right place, remember that the `i` index is for the Y position and the `j` is for the X position. We first add the `toCenterPaddingX` to place the ball in the center of the screen in relation to the group of balls. To get the total space occupied by each ball, we have to take the `ballSprite.size.width` and the `spaceBetween` into consideration. We do this calculation for both X and Y and we should have a ball perfectly positioned on the screen.

The last thing to do is to add the ball to this list of balls (the `balls` array).

Now, the interesting thing about this method is that all it really does is add a bunch of balls into an array. It spends most of its time positioning elements and figuring out widths of things. It does not actually add anything to the scene. Let's make sure each method does one thing.

To add the balls to the scene, we should create a separate method, so let's create that now. Add this method to your `BallManager` class:

```
public func addLevelTo(scene scene:SKNode) {
    for ball in balls {
        scene.addChild(ball)
    }
}
```

As you can see, this method is straight and to the point. It goes through the arrays of balls that we just created and adds them to the scene that you pass to this method.

Now we are ready to see the results. We need to call these two methods from our `GameScene` class, so open up `GameScene.swift`. Update your `GameScene` class in `GameScene.swift` to add the `BallManager` class and initialize it with the current level. While we're at it, we'll add a nice gray background as well:

```
let ballManager = BallManager()

override func didMoveToView(view: SKView) {
```

```
    backgroundColor = SKColor.grayColor()
    ballManager.loadLevel(self)
    ballManager.addLevelTo(scene: self)
}
```

Now our ball manager is initialized and the balls should be added to this scene. We created a global variable `ballManager` just in case we need to call any other functions for our ball manager. When you run the game, you should see your level laid out perfectly and ready to be played (see Figure 11.5). The only problem is that we don't have the main ball programmed yet, so we can't play the game. Let's do that next.

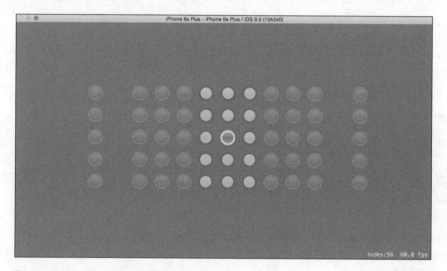

Figure 11.5   The game laid out

Making a Playable Game

To make this game fun to play, we need a ball to play with. For this we can use our `ball_main` from our `xcassets` library. In our `BallManager` we already have a reference to a `mainBall` but we haven't assigned it to a sprite yet. Let's create a method that will drop a main ball on the scene at a specific coordinate. Add this to your `BallManager` class:

```
public func dropMainBall(onScene scene:SKScene, atLocation:CGPoint) {
    if mainBall != nil {
        return
    }
    mainBall = SKSpriteNode(imageNamed: "ball_main")
    mainBall.physicsBody = SKPhysicsBody(circleOfRadius:
mainBall.size.width/2)
    mainBall.position = atLocation
    mainBall.physicsBody?.restitution = 1
```

```
    mainBall.physicsBody?.angularVelocity = 0.1
    mainBall.physicsBody?.categoryBitMask = Collider.HERO
    mainBall.physicsBody?.collisionBitMask = Collider.BALL |
Collider.CAGE
    mainBall.physicsBody?.contactTestBitMask = Collider.BALL |
Collider.CAGE
    scene.addChild(mainBall)
}
```

What is happening here is very straightforward, and you've seen it before. If the main ball is not nil, we return (abort the method) because we want to drop only one main ball at a time.

If the main ball is nil, we don't have a main ball currently dropping. We create a main ball and give it the texture of main_ball. We give it a physics body using a circle of radius, which will be half the size of the width of the texture (since radius is half the width). We position the main ball at the location passed in to the method. We add a restitution of 1. Restitution is essentially the bounciness of the ball. The number will be from 0 to 1, and 1 makes for a very bouncy ball. I have noticed that for games like this, the bouncier the ball, the better. We also add a small angular velocity, which gives the ball a little spin.Now things are getting interesting!

We do the normal business of adding a category bit mask to be the HERO since this ball is considered different from the other balls. This is the playing ball. We set the collision bit mask to say that this hero ball should collide with regular balls and the container (also known as the cage), which we haven't created yet. We also want to test whether the hero ball hits the regular balls or the cage. Finally, we add the ball to the scene.

We can test this out, but first let's add some code to our GameScene class so that when the user taps the screen we will drop the ball. Open up your GameScene class and update your touchesBegan method:

```
override func touchesBegan(touches: Set<UITouch>, withEvent event: UIEvent?) {
    if let touch = touches.first {
        ballManager.dropMainBall
        (onScene: self, atLocation:
        CGPoint(x: touch.locationInNode(self).x,
        y: CGRectGetMaxY(frame) - 100))
    }
}
```

For touchesBegan, we test when the user taps the screen. When the user does tap the screen, we make sure there is a touch to test for, and if there is, we call ballManager.dropMainBall. For that method we pass in the location of the x position of the user's finger and a y position above the top of the screen. That way the y position is always the same and the x position is where the user tapped. At this point you can run the game, but you will notice that although you can drop the ball, you can drop it only once time and it's gone forever. Although that does make for a very interesting game, it isn't very fun. What we need to do is catch the ball when it falls and remove it from the screen and set it to nil so that we can drop another ball.

Creating the Cage

What we need to do to make sure the ball does not exit the screen and fly out of our control. To do this, we will build a cage around the size of the scene. Doing so is simple. All we need to do is know the size of the scene and we are in business. Let's write a method called `addCage()` that will add a boundary around the screen to trap the ball when it falls. Add the following code to your `GameScene` class:

```
func addCage() {
    let physicsBody = SKPhysicsBody (edgeLoopFromRect: self.frame)
    self.physicsBody = physicsBody
    self.physicsBody?.categoryBitMask = Collider.CAGE
}
```

To implement this method, we can call it from the `didMoveToView` method of our `GameScene` class. Update your `didMoveToView` method in your `GameScene` class to add a call to this method:

```
override func didMoveToView(view: SKView) {
    physicsWorld.contactDelegate = self
    backgroundColor = SKColor.grayColor()
    addCage()
    ballManager.loadLevel(self)
    ballManager.addLevelTo(scene: self)
}
```

Now our ball won't fly into the cosmos; it will be kept within the boundaries of this world. If you run this code, you will see that the ball hits the bottom of the screen and bounces. The ball is trapped by the boundaries of the game, which is great but doesn't provide us with a full solution. Wouldn't it be great if the ball hit the cage and just disappeared, and that way when we tap the screen again it will be ready to fall from the sky again? Let's give that a try. To make the ball disappear when it hits the cage, we have to detect the collision of the main ball to the cage. We have to set up collision detection. We've done this before, so now you are a pro. The first step to setting up collision detection is to make your `GameScene` adopt the `SKPhysicsContactDelegate` protocol. Update your class declaration in your `GameScene.swift` to include the delegate:

```
class GameScene: SKScene, SKPhysicsContactDelegate {
```

Now our game is almost ready to be collision detected. The only other step is to tell our physics world that we want to be the ones to get notified when a collision happens. To get notified, we need to assign our `GameScene` class to be the delegate of the `SKPhysicsContactDelegate`. Let's give that a try. Update the `didMoveToView` method of your `GameScene`:

```
override func didMoveToView(view: SKView) {
    physicsWorld.contactDelegate = self
    backgroundColor = SKColor.grayColor()
    ...
```

Now our class is ready to receive notifications when things collide. When objects (physics bodies) do collide, the delegate will call a couple of methods. First it will call `didBeginContact`, so we need to add that to our `GameScene` class:

```
func didBeginContact(contact: SKPhysicsContact) {
    // hit the bottom
    if contact.bodyA.categoryBitMask == Collider.CAGE ||
        contact.bodyB.categoryBitMask == Collider.CAGE {
        ballManager.removeHitBalls()
        if ballManager.isGameOver() {
            ballManager.currentLevel++
            ballManager.loadLevel(self)
            ballManager.addLevelTo(scene: self)
        }
    }
}
```

In this method we are detecting whether the main ball hit the cage. Since the only dynamic body in the game is the main ball, we don't have to check for it. This will work great, but we are missing a couple of methods. We need to write a method in the ball manager for removing the hit balls and a method in the ball manager to check whether we can advance to the next level (`isGameOver()`).

Notice that if all the balls are gone and `isGameOver` returns `true`, we automatically load the next level. The next level will automatically appear on the screen.

The only issue is that we are not detecting whether the main ball hits one of the game balls. Before we do anything else we need to check whether the main ball hits one of the regular balls. Let's update our `didBeginContact` method to include a check for the regular balls getting hit by the main ball:

```
func didBeginContact(contact: SKPhysicsContact) {
    if contact.bodyA.categoryBitMask == Collider.BALL {
        ballManager.ballHit(contact.bodyA.node as! Ball)
    } else if contact.bodyB.categoryBitMask == Collider.BALL {
        ballManager.ballHit(contact.bodyB.node as! Ball)
    }

    // hit the bottom
    if contact.bodyA.categoryBitMask == Collider.CAGE ||
...
```

Now if the player's main ball hits the regular static balls or the cage, we will get notified. We have to write a method to do something when the main ball hits the regular static balls. You can see in the code that we call a method we haven't written yet: `ballManager.ballHit`. Let's write that method. You can see that this method takes a `Ball` as the parameter, and to type/convert the parameter as a `Ball` we use `as!`. The node from the `contact` is an `SKNode`, and we really need it to be a `Ball`. The `Ball` is a descendant of the `SKNode` by way of the

SKSpriteNode, so this should work well. Ball inherits from SKSpriteNode, which inherits from SKNode.

Let's open up the BallManager.swift and write the method ballHit:

```
public func ballHit(ball:Ball) {
    if ball.hit {
        return
    }
    ball.hit = true
    ball.runAction(SKAction.fadeAlphaTo(0.1, duration: 0.3))
}
```

Remember that the Ball class has a hit property. When the ball gets hit, we want to make sure that it isn't already hit. We don't want weird stuff to happen, so if the ball is already hit we aren't interested in anything this method has to offer and we return. To mark the ball as hit, we dim it down by lowering the alpha (the opacity). We use an SKAction to lower the alpha value over a period of 0.3 seconds. We also mark the ball as hit so that we can remove it after the ball goes to the bottom of the screen, and we won't mess with this ball again until it needs to be removed.

This method will work well for marking the balls as ready to be removed. We can now write the method to remove the balls after the main ball hits the bottom of the cage.

Let's open up the ball manager and write the method for removing the hit balls. A little magic has to take place here in order to remove the balls properly without causing a big fat error to appear. When you remove items from an array while looping through the array, you have to be careful not to mess up the index of the array. Usually this is achieved by looping through the array backward.

```
public func removeHitBalls(removeMainBall:Bool = true) {
    for (i,ball) in balls.enumerate().reverse() {
        if ball.hit {
            ball.hit = false
            ball.removeFromParent()
            balls.removeAtIndex(i)
        }
    }
    if mainBall != nil && removeMainBall{
        mainBall.removeFromParent()
        mainBall = nil
    }
}
```

This method is simple in that all it does is remove balls that have been hit from the scene and remove them from the balls array. Since enumerate() allows us to get the index and the element while looping, we can remove the item at the specific index perfectly fine. However, if we were to remove the item at an index while looping, that would mess up the entire index, so we need to loop backward. We can use reverse() for this. reverse() reverses an array, and since enumerate returns a sequence type we can reverse it, too. From here we can remove the ball from the scene and remove it from the array using its index. This is safe because we are looping backward.

The second half of the method where it removes the mainBall will remove the main ball from the screen because it hit the bottom of the cage. It also marks the mainBall as nil so that we can launch a new ball when the user taps the screen again.

After these two methods are in place, if we head back over to the GameScene class, we notice we still have one error because we are missing the method isGameOver(). Let's head back over to our BallManager class and write that method. It's super-easy to tell whether we can advance to the next level in this game because there just have to be 0 balls left in the balls array and we are golden. Add the following code to your BallManager class:

```
public func isGameOver() -> Bool {
    if balls.count == 0 {
        return true
    }
    return false
}
```

This code is fairly simple once again. If 0 balls are left in the balls array, we return true, and otherwise we return false.

What did we do in this section?

We added collision detection testing. We looked for hit balls and made them appear faint to mark them as hit. We made a cage around the scene to protect from losing balls. When the main ball hit the bottom of the screen, we had it removed for the next turn.

At this point you should be able to run your code and the game is almost complete. When you drop the ball, it hits other balls and they are marked for removal; when the main ball hits the bottom or the sides of the cage, the main ball is removed and you can take another turn. There is one little snafu you may have run into. Let me illustrate it with a picture (see Figure 11.6).

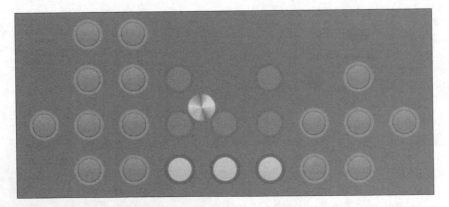

Figure 11.6   One little snafu

If you haven't noticed yet, the ball can get stuck in between the balls. The easy solution is to make the gap bigger. To be honest, this can happen when users play your game harder than you expected and find some little bug where the ball can get stuck. It's best to plan ahead for this rare but possible bug. To fix this bug the easiest way I know how, we want to test whether the main ball has stopped moving. The physics body has a property called `resting` that will tell you whether the ball is currently in motion. The property is more complicated than that, but you can think of it as a ball that is done moving and interacting for now. Resting in physics simulation saves computation from unnecessarily being calculated when it isn't needed. Anyhow, if the main ball is resting, we can remove all the balls it has hit so far and move on. To do this, we have to constantly check whether the main ball is resting. We can use the `update` method for this. Let's write an `update` method in our `BallManager`:

```
public func update() {
    if mainBall != nil {
        if mainBall.physicsBody!.resting {
            removeHitBalls(false)
        }
    }
}
```

This method is again easy as pie. Our main ball may be `nil` because it may have been taken off the scene or it may have never existed yet, so we want to check whether the main ball is `nil`. If it is not `nil`, we can check whether that main ball is resting. If it is resting and hasn't been removed by the bottom cage, we can safely assume that the ball is stuck; we can remove the balls that have been hit so far and this will unstick the main ball. To call this method, we will need to update our `GameScene` class. Update the `update` method of your `GameScene` class to be as follows:

```
override func update(currentTime: CFTimeInterval) {
    ballManager.update()
}
```

Now if our main ball gets stuck, we can unstick it by checking whether it is resting. If it is resting, we will clear the balls we've hit so far. This effect is really neat to watch happen; it has a little delay so it looks as though we are really thinking about whether we want to help you with your problem.

At this point we have a fully functioning game. The best part is that we already wrote in the next-level generation. Test the game out and try and beat the level. With some additional properties thrown in and some time, you can probably design a much better level than I did. After you remove all the balls from the scene by hitting them, the next level will appear. It will continue to generate new levels as long as you have them available in your `info.plist`.

Summary

In this chapter you learned how to write a SpriteKit physics game using the available physics library built directly into SpriteKit. Thankfully, this library is a piece of cake to use and will allow you to make some truly remarkable games.

You learned about game management and making games that have multiple levels to play. You learned about solving bugs that you may encounter when your users play your game harder than you had imagined.

Take this game and modify it as much as you can. Here are some things you can try to spice it up:

- Make the balls disappear when they are hit.
- Make the balls fall when hit, instead of disappearing.
- Make hitting different color balls do different things. Maybe the yellow one reverses gravity.
- Go have fun and make a high-score board and release this app to the app store.
- Make a limited number of balls available and show those numbers on the screen with an SKLabelNode.

12

Making Apps with UIKit

Apple has two major kits available in its library: UIKit and AppKit. AppKit is for desktop applications, and UIKit is for iOS applications. In this chapter you are going to explore UIKit and take a look at how to build a common application.

Thanks to the Storyboard, size classes, and constraints, automatically laying out your application is super-easy.

Application Types

Each app gets a Storyboard, which is named `main.storyboard`. This file is a graphical (not code) way of writing the user interface for your application. In this chapter you'll learn how to implement common user interface designs using Swift. Let's get started by creating a new project. Select File, New, Project. At this point you should be presented with a screen that looks like the one shown in Figure 12.1. The following sections describe the application types shown in this figure.

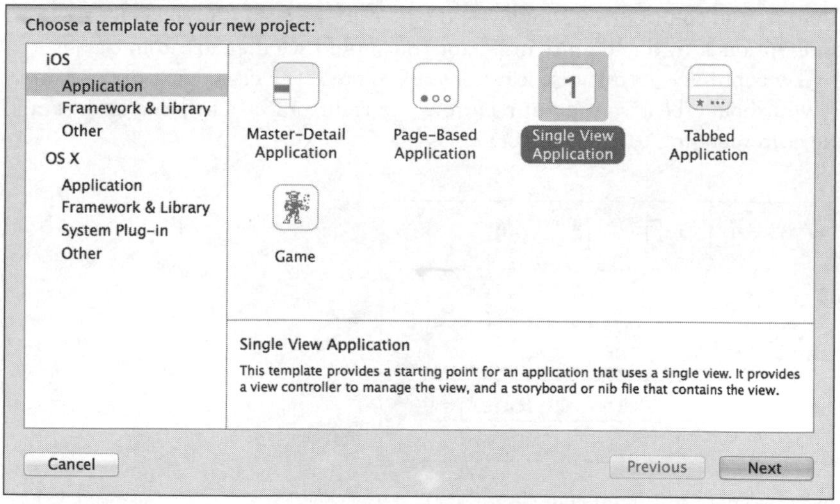

Figure 12.1   Choosing your application starting point

Single-View Applications

Choose a single-view application to get started with our timer app. We will build a timer app that tracks your study sessions. You should probably study for at least 5 minutes at a time. When that time is up, we log that study session and you can start another one. We'll also keep track of things on your Apple Watch using WatchKit.

Give this project a name and make sure that the language is set to Swift and the device is set to universal. We'll call this app StudySessions. Click Next. Xcode will ask you to save your project somewhere, so choose wisely and click Create.

The first thing you want to do is make sure that this app runs only in portrait mode.

We now are presented with the default project setup for a Single View Application. You have your Storyboard for graphically laying out your project. You have your view controller for controlling the code in your Storyboard, and you have a bunch of other files that aren't important at the moment. For now we'll focus on the Storyboard and the ViewController.swift. How are they connected? Let's find out.

Open up the Storyboard by clicking it one time. You'll see a view controller with an arrow pointing toward it. That right-pointing arrow means that this view is the view the user will see when starting your app. If you click in the middle of the view, you should see three symbols appear at the top of that view. You will see a yellow circle with a white square in the middle and two orange symbols. Let's concern ourselves only with the yellow circle with the white square. This white square represents a view in your app. You have one view, hence the name Single View Application. There has to be some sort of code that will control this view, some code that makes sure that when you click on stuff, things happen. That code is called the view controller, and just like it sounds, it controls the view. To see the view controller that is controlling this view, click on that yellow circle with the white square in the middle. When you hover over it, you see the words "View Controller" in the third column (the utilities column). If you can't see the third column, press Command-Option-0, which toggles its visibility. In that utilities column, you should see the identity inspector; if you can't see it, press Command-Option-3. In the identity inspector you should see that a custom class is assigned to your view controller. In this case it is the ViewController class. Next to the word "ViewController" you should see a right-pointing arrow (see Figure 12.2). Click that arrow and it takes you to the corresponding ViewController class.

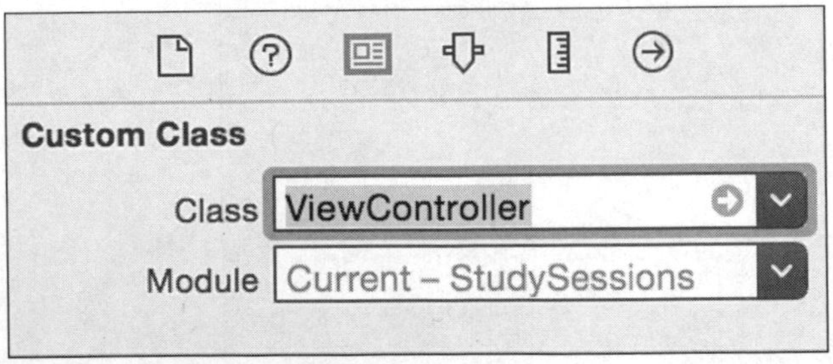

Figure 12.2   The ViewController custom class

That is the relationship from the view to the view controller. The view is controlled by code, and you can connect the two with the view controller. Control the view with the view controller. Control any view with a view controller. Biff, bam, boom.

For our app we want to make a study app so that people can break their study sessions into blocks of time.

In the end when your study session is over, it will be logged in the bottom portion, which is a table of study sessions. Notice we also have that nice perfectly round border for the button. When the study session is going, the button turns red and changes the text to "Paused" (see Figure 12.3). When the study session is paused or hasn't started yet, the button turns green and reads "Start" (see Figure 12.4). This app combines a nice little collection of different app components to make a simple app, with knowledge you can carry to other app-building ventures. Let's make it happen.

Figure 12.3   Study session going

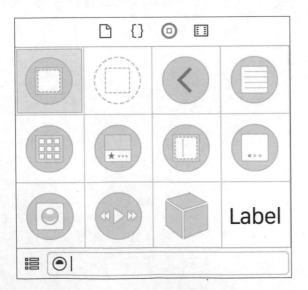

Figure 12.4   Study session not going

Creating the User Interface

The first step is to head into our Storyboard and build out our user interface. You first need to add the timer label to the screen. You can find the label in the Object library, which has a text box at the bottom where you can type "Label." After you find the label in the object library (see Figure 12.5), you can drag it onto the Storyboard. Try to drag it toward the top of the view.

Figure 12.5   The label in the object library

At this point, with the label selected, you want to open up the attributes inspector (see Figure 12.6). It is part of the third column on the right, the utilities column. If you don't have it open, you can either click the fourth icon in the utilities or press Command-Option-4.

Figure 12.6   The attributes inspector

Here you can change the font to Custom, and then you can change the font to Helvetica Neue, the style to UltraLight, and the size to 109. Drag the label to be the full width of the view, and it should snap into place. Double-click the label and write in the text 0:00.

Now find a button in the Object Library (the same place you found the label), and drag that onto the middle of the screen. You should get some crosshairs confirming that you are in fact dropping it in the middle. Don't worry, we'll add styles and constraints in just a minute to make sure it stays there. Double-click the button and label it Start. Also resize the button to be the same width and height. I resized it to 100 height and 100 width.

Now find Table View in the Object library, but be careful not to accidentally grab Table View Controller because we are specifically looking for a table view. Drag that table view onto the bottom of the screen. It should lock into the bottom of the screen and make it about the bottom 15% in height; just eye it when you drag its size around, but do make it exactly the full width of the screen.

Find a table view cell in the Object library, and drag it into the table you just created. Now be careful when selecting things on the view because you might be selecting the table itself or the cell within the table. Be sure to make that distinction by checking what you selected in the attributes inspector; it should indicate the thing you selected at the top. Make sure you have the table view itself selected and the attributes inspector selected; then set the Table View Content to be Dynamic Prototypes and set the Style to be Grouped.

Now select the single row itself within the table view. Your attributes inspector should read, at the top, "Table View Cell." Change the Style to be Custom. Set the Identifier to be studySessionCell. Selection is nice when it's set to Blue. If you scroll down a little in the attributes inspector, I also like to set the Background to be White Color.

You should be good to go as far as setting up your initial view. We need to add some constraints so that your view stays in place nicely when we have different devices.

Adding Constraints

By adding constraints, we will make sure that our devices can all view a neatly formatted version of our app even if the screens are different sizes. We have to specify at least the X and Y of a constraint for it to be legit, but I like to add a width and a height too to be complete. When you add constraints, they will start out red in color, which means that you haven't added enough constraints or information for Xcode to figure out how you want your objects laid out.

To add a constraint, you simply click and drag from the item you want to add a constraint to while holding down Control on the keyboard. The direction in which you drag and how far you drag will determine what type of constraint gets added. We want to first add a width and a height constraint. We are constraining this component to itself, so this will be a constraint added directly to the label from the label. Click and drag from the label to the left while pressing Control on the keyboard, and don't drag outside the label but stay within its bounds. When you let go of the mouse, you should see a drop-down appear for adding a constraint for width. Click that constraint and now we can add a height constraint. Click and drag while holding Control, and this time drag upward. You should see a constraint option pop up for a height. Click that constraint and you are good to go for the width and height of the label. We should now add constraints for the X and Y position of the label. We want it to be horizontally centered in the view and positioned based on the top layout guide.

By the way, your label should still have red constraint marks around it because we have not fulfilled the constraint yet for at least the X and Y. To add the top layout guide constraint, drag (while holding down Control) up and out of the label. When you get to the top, the view should highlight (turn blue, instead of just the label). Let go and you should have two options, one to center vertically and the other labeled Vertical Spacing to Top Layout Guide—that's the one you want.

You now have three constraints for this timer label. To add the center-horizontally constraint, just click and drag outside and to the left and down (normally to the left only, but because there isn't any room over there, we drag to the left and down), while holding Control, and you should get a choice of constraint for Center Horizontally in Container. After you have those four constraints, our label is constrained and good to go. The constraint lines should now all be blue with no red lines visible, so we know that Xcode agrees that we are good to go, too.

The next step is to add constraints to the button. We just want to center it horizontally and vertically in the container. So just click and drag while holding down Control to the left outside of the button, and choose Center Vertically in Container. Click and drag while pressing Control downward outside of the button, and select Center Horizontally in Container.

We also want to add constraints to our table. Since we can't easily add a bottom constraint for our table, the easiest way to achieve this is to use the document outline. If the document outline isn't showing, you can go to Editor, Show Document Outline, which will make the document outline appear. When you have the document outline visible, you can click and drag while holding down Option, in the same way you did from the Storyboard, so click and drag from the table view to the view and select Vertical Spacing to Bottom Layout Guide (see Figure 12.7). Now that you are a pro at adding constraints, also add width and height, and center horizontally for the table.

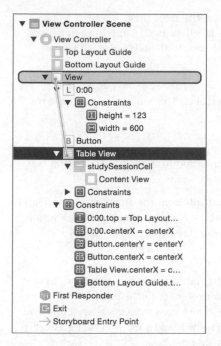

Figure 12.7   Adding constraints in the document outline

After you have all those constraints for the table, we are all set with constraints. The next step is to hook up the UI elements to our code.

Hooking Up the UI to Code

Now we need to be able to control these UI elements in our code so that we can do things like change the label from `0:00` to `2:34`. To do this, we want to have the Storyboard and the code open at the same time. It helps to first hide the document outline (Editor, Hide Document Outline). It also helps to hide the utilities (Command-Option-0). We want to show the assistant editor by clicking the Assistant Editor button (see Figure 12.8) or pressing Command-Shift-Return.

Figure 12.8   The Assistant Editor button

You should now have the code and the Storyboard open at the same time. We need a few things to happen here. We need a reference to the timer label, we need something to happen when we click the Start/Pause button, and we need a reference to the table view so we can populate it. First, the label.

Click and drag from the label into the class right above `override func viewDidLoad()`. Choose the Connection as Outlet and the Name as TimerLabel. This will make a variable we can reference when setting things on the timer label.

```
@IBOutlet var timerLabel: UILabel!
```

Now we need a reference to the Start/Stop button and a method to run when the button is clicked.

Click and drag over to the code (while holding down Control) from the Start/Stop button, and do the same thing. Choose the Connection as Outlet and the Name as timerStartPauseButton, and click Connect. This will add the following code to your `ViewController` class:

```
@IBOutlet var timerStartPauseButton: UIButton!
```

Now we also need to be notified when someone clicks that button, and run a method. Click and drag from the button again (while holding down Control) over to the bottom area of the code (below the `didRecieveMemoryWarning` method). Choose the Connection as Action and the Name as timerStartStopTapped, and click Connect. This will add a method that gets called every time that button is tapped. This nets you the following method:

```
@IBAction func timerStartStopTapped(sender: AnyObject) {
}
```

At this point we need only one more reference and that is to our table. Click and drag the table (while holding down Control) over to the top area of the code, and choose the Connection as Outlet and the Name as studySessionTable. Click Connect and we are good as gold. Now it's time to write the code to make this app work.

Writing the Code

At this point we have hooked up a serious number of UI elements to our code, and we are ready to write code that will change the UI components. You can switch out of the split-screen view (the assistant editor) and move over to the standard editor, where we can see one view at a time, and then click on the `ViewController.swift` so that we can start editing our code.

First things first: Let's make some global variables so that we can control our timer and time left and other little things. Add the following code to your `ViewController`:

```
var timer:NSTimer!
var paused = false
var timeLeft = 0
var defaultTimeLeft = 180
```

Here we are just setting some global variables by creating a timer that we can use to do the actual countdown with. We also want to know whether the timer is paused. We obviously have to know how much time is left, since the NSTimer does not count down but only counts. We want to make sure that we are counting down using the amount of time we agreed would be left. This time is in seconds, and we start this off with 180 seconds, which is 3 minutes. For debugging code, however, I would change this number to 5 or 3 so that you don't have to wait 3 minutes for the timer to be done every time you test this; then, when you are ready for production, you can set this to 180 for 3 minutes, or even make it customizable.

The next step is to update our viewDidLoad method, which gets called when this view is loaded. Let's add some code to our viewDidLoad to initialize the variables:

```
override func viewDidLoad() {
    super.viewDidLoad()
    studySessionTable.delegate = self
    studySessionTable.dataSource = self
    changeStartButton()
    timeLeft = defaultTimeLeft
}
```

We are jumping ahead of ourselves a little bit here. To control that table and make changes on it and get informed of changes that happen, we need to make our class a special table class. Specifically, we need to make our class adopt two protocols, UITableViewDelegate and UITableViewDataSource. These two protocols have different meanings and functionality. The UITableViewDelegate is for controlling a table and controlling such things as number of rows and sections. The UITableViewDataSource is for controlling the data inside of that table. We need to be able to properly populate that table, and that's why we need both protocols. To adopt these protocols, we need to update the class signature:

```
class ViewController: UIViewController, UITableViewDelegate, UITableViewDataSource {
```

Now the two lines of code in our viewDidLoad will make more sense. We want to know what class should be notified when changes take place on our table, and the answer is this class right here:

```
studySessionTable.delegate = self
studySessionTable.dataSource = self
```

In our initializer we also set the default time left to be whatever we decided it should be.

The next step is to fill in the missing method that we are calling changeStartButton(). Add this method to your ViewController class:

```
func changeStartButton() {
    if paused {
        timerStartPauseButton.setTitle("Paused", forState: .Normal)
        timerStartPauseButton.setTitleColor(UIColor.redColor(), forState: .Normal)
        timerStartPauseButton.clipsToBounds = true
        timerStartPauseButton.layer.cornerRadius =
        timerStartPauseButton.frame.size.width/2
        timerStartPauseButton.layer.borderWidth = 1
        timerStartPauseButton.layer.borderColor = UIColor.redColor().CGColor
    } else {
```

```
        timerStartPauseButton.setTitle("Start", forState: .Normal)
        timerStartPauseButton.setTitleColor(UIColor.greenColor(), forState: .Normal)
        timerStartPauseButton.clipsToBounds = true
        timerStartPauseButton.layer.cornerRadius =
        timerStartPauseButton.frame.size.width/2
        timerStartPauseButton.layer.borderWidth = 1
        timerStartPauseButton.layer.borderColor = UIColor.greenColor().CGColor
    }
    paused = !paused
}
```

This method has a lot of code, but what it does is simple. If the timer is paused, we set the button text to be "Paused," we set the button to be red, we set the button to be circular, and we set a border to be red as well. We do the same thing if it is not paused, except the button text is "Start" and the button and its border are green. We are duplicating the look of the iPhone timer button and its perfectly circular appearance. It also changes from red to green when paused and not paused. Adding `clipsToBounds` helps make a nice-looking button and keeps the contents of this view in its own bounds. Play around with these numbers and settings to get your own desired effect.

The next step is to update our Start/Pause button when it gets tapped. We already have a method that gets called when it gets tapped, so let's take a look at that method and write the code needed to start the timer. We may still have an error in our code about not adopting a protocol for the data source, which we will fix in a few lines from now. Update your `timerStartStopTapped` method as follows:

```
@IBAction func startStopTapped(sender: AnyObject) {
    if paused {
        timer = NSTimer
        .scheduledTimerWithTimeInterval
        (1,
        target: self,
        selector: Selector("timerTick:"),
        userInfo: nil,
        repeats: true)
    } else {
        timer.invalidate()
    }
    changeStartButton()
}
```

Here we are checking, when the user taps the Start/Stop button, whether the study session is paused. If it is currently paused, we will unpause it by creating a new timer that ticks every 1 second. When that timer ticks, it will call the method `timerTick`. We obviously have not written the method `timerTick` yet, but it's coming. If the timer is not paused, we want to pause the timer, which can be done by calling `timer.invalidate()`. In a way we are not pausing the timer but killing the timer completely and remaking it from scratch each time. To quote the documentation for `invalidate`:

- "Stops the receiver from ever firing again and requests its removal from its run loop."

It is clear that we must make a new timer to unpause the timer. After this method is complete, we call the `changeStartButton` method to update the appearance of the Start button based on whether the session is paused. That method also takes care of setting the paused variable to be toggled.

We have not yet written the method that gets fired when the timer ticks, so we should write that method next. Let's add the following code to our `ViewController` class. The `timerTick` method will do two things: format the time properly for display on the `timerLabel`, and, if the timer has no time left on it, invalidate the timer once again and add a new record to the list of study sessions. We will use a special custom study session class, which hasn't been created yet, which we will create after this method.

```swift
func timerTick(timer:NSTimer) {
    if --timeLeft > 0 {
        let seconds = Int(timeLeft % 60)
        let minutes = Int((timeLeft / 60) % 60)
        let strMinutes = minutes > 9 ? String(minutes) : "0" +
String(minutes)
        let strSeconds = seconds > 9 ? String(seconds) : "0" +
String(seconds) ·
        timerLabel.text = "\(strMinutes):\(strSeconds)"
    } else {
        timeLeft = defaultTimeLeft
        timerLabel.text = "00:00"
        timer.invalidate()
        changeStartButton()
        StudySessionManager.sharedInstance.sessions.insert(
            StudySession(
                createdAt:NSDate().timeIntervalSince1970,
                finishedAt:NSDate().timeIntervalSince1970
            )
            , atIndex: 0)
        studySessionTable.reloadData()
    }
}
```

Holy wall of text, Batman! It's a lot of code, but let's break it down. We spend most of the code formatting the time and saving sessions. Let's review it. First we have to check how much time is left. We might as well decrement the time left while we are checking whether it is less than 0. It's important to decrement before we check. We don't want –1 to show up on our timer.

We take the next four lines to format the time for the timer. We use these variables to format the seconds left into minutes and seconds with appropriate leading 0s if necessary. We use some ternary operators for this task. We need to update the timer with our new nicely formatted timer text, so we do that next.

If the timer has gone below 0 and time is up, we need to reset the `timeLeft` variable to be back to the default time left (3 minutes or 5 seconds or whatever you set the default time to be). Just setting the variable won't change anything visually yet. We set the timer label to be "00:00" so that it appears that there is no time left. We kill the timer with `timer.invalidate()`. We change the appearance of the start button once again. We use our special Study Session Manager to insert a new study session. Finally, we reload the table data because we just made a new record for the table and we want it to show up.

Because we don't have our study session class, we should make that next. We'll use the singleton pattern here to keep a single instance of the Study Session Manager around. Create a new file, `StudySessionManager.swift`, and add the following code to it:

```
import Foundation
class StudySessionManager {
    static let sharedInstance = StudySessionManager()
    var sessions = [StudySession]()
}
struct StudySession {
    var createdAt:NSTimeInterval
    var finishedAt:NSTimeInterval = 0
}
```

Here we make a basic model for our study session. We create a sort of study session object that has `createdAt` and `finishedAt` variables just in case we need both. We make the Study Session Manager a singleton by using the `static let sharedInstance` be equal to a new instance of `StudySessionManager`. Static variables function in the same way as class functions in that they belong to the class and not the instance of the class. There aren't class member variables yet but you can use static, which functions in a similar way. The main difference between `static` and `class` is that `class` can be overridden in a subclass and `static` cannot.

Adding this class and struct to our code gets rid of the error in the `ViewController` from the missing `StudySessionManager`, which is good, but still doesn't get rid of our error with the protocol for the `UITableViewDataSource`. Let's work on that issue now.

The `TableView`

We have this table at the bottom of the screen, which holds data relating to our previous study sessions. To update that table, we must use some basic table delegate methods that come with the table. The easiest thing to do is to set the header. When we get more data, we want to show that in the header—something like "2 study sessions" to indicate the total study sessions.

Add the following method, which comes from the table view, because we are adopting its protocols:

```
func tableView(tableView: UITableView,
       titleForHeaderInSection section: Int) -> String? {
    let sessionCount = StudySessionManager.sharedInstance.sessions.count
    var sessionsPlural = "s"
    if sessionCount == 1 {
        sessionsPlural = ""
    }
    return "\(sessionCount) study session\(sessionsPlural)"
}
```

The method `tableView: titleForHeaderInSection: section` will act as a main header for the table since we will have only one section. We set the text of that header, with one caveat. We'd like to get the plural of the word "session." This method returns a string optional because you can return the text you want to appear in the header. Of course, because it's an optional, you could return `nil` if you wanted a blank header, or just return a blank string.

While we're on the subject of sections, we should set the number of sections in this table to be one section total:

```
func numberOfSectionsInTableView(tableView: UITableView) -> Int {
    return 1
}
```

We just use the table's method that is available to set the number of sections in the table. If this were a more complicated app, we could have sections in the table and set the number of sections here. Since that is not what we are trying to achieve, we won't do that.

We need to also know how many rows will be in each section, so we'll query our `StudySessionManager` for those answers. We of course must use the built-in method that answers this question for the table we are trying to render. The table will look to this method when it wants to know how many rows there will be:

```
func tableView(tableView: UITableView,
numberOfRowsInSection section: Int) -> Int {
    return StudySessionManager.sharedInstance.sessions.count
}
```

When telling the table how many rows there will be in each section, what we want to know in our case is how many rows there will be in total since we have only one section.

The final and most important method is the method that tells the table what cell to render at the current cell index:

```
func tableView
        (tableView: UITableView,
        cellForRowAtIndexPath indexPath: NSIndexPath)
        -> UITableViewCell {
    let cell = studySessionTable
        .dequeueReusableCellWithIdentifier("studySessionCell")!
```

```
        let dateDiff = NSDate()
            .timeIntervalSince1970 - StudySessionManager
            .sharedInstance.sessions[indexPath.row].createdAt
        var formattedTime = NSDateComponentsFormatter().stringFromTimeInterval(dateDiff)!
        if formattedTime.rangeOfString(":") == nil {
            formattedTime = "\(formattedTime) seconds ago"
        } else {
            formattedTime = "\(formattedTime) ago"
        }
        cell.textLabel?.text = formattedTime
        return cell
}
```

This method gets called when the table needs to know how to render the current cell, what text belongs in that cell, and other details. In our case we decided to format the time since this study session was created and show that time in a nice little format. If the number is in seconds only, we show only those seconds. If the time is in minutes too, we show the seconds and minutes and change the phrasing so it makes more sense. We do some date kung fu here by using the new NSDateComponentsFormatter, which makes it significantly easier to format a date. To get how much time has elapsed, we take the time stamp from 1970 (the number of seconds since 1970; see Unix Time), which we use as the current time, and subtract the time when that session was created. By subtracting those two numbers, we should get how much time has elapsed since that session was created.

The last thing to do is to properly format that time, which we do using stringFromTimeInterval. This method almost magically handles everything for us. As long as you pass this method the right data in the right format, it can almost magically return a nicely formatted string. At the end of this method, you must return the cell you created so that the library can put it into the table in which it belongs. The one thing to remember is that if you have hundreds or thousands of rows, Apple is not rendering all of those rows at once; instead it is rendering only the visible rows in order to keep things tidy and moving quickly. Notice also that after we add in this method, we have gotten rid of all of our errors.

At this point you can run your app, and you'll notice you have a fully functioning study timer. Feel free to use it for your own studying. Also make sure you play around with the different aspects and customize the app to your heart's content. It would be nice if you could add a custom time that the user can set on his own. Also if the user can set goals—for example, if he wanted to finish ten study sessions—congratulate him when he does.

Summary

In this chapter you learned how to make a basic app and in the process learned about table views and the different protocols. You learned how to style buttons to make them pretty by using code. You learned about constraints and how you can make sure that your app looks great no matter what device it is on. You also learned how to format time using some newer libraries.

Index

Symbols

A

D

N

O

P

REGISTER YOUR PRODUCT at informit.com/register

Access Additional Benefits and SAVE 35% on Your Next Purchase

- Download available product updates.

- Access bonus material when applicable.

- Receive exclusive offers on new editions and related products.
  (Just check the box to hear from us when setting up your account.)

- Get a coupon for 35% for your next purchase, valid for 30 days. Your code will
  be available in your InformIT cart. (You will also find it in the Manage Codes
  section of your account page.)

Registration benefits vary by product. Benefits will be listed on your account page
under Registered Products.

InformIT.com—The Trusted Technology Learning Source
InformIT is the online home of information technology brands at Pearson, the world's foremost
education company. At InformIT.com you can

- Shop our books, eBooks, software, and video training.
- Take advantage of our special offers and promotions (informit.com/promotions).
- Sign up for special offers and content newsletters (informit.com/newsletters).
- Read free articles and blogs by information technology experts.
- Access thousands of free chapters and video lessons.

Connect with InformIT—Visit informit.com/community
Learn about InformIT community events and programs.

the trusted technology learning source

Addison-Wesley · Cisco Press · IBM Press · Microsoft Press · Pearson IT Certification · Prentice Hall · Que · Sams · VMware Press

ALWAYS LEARNING